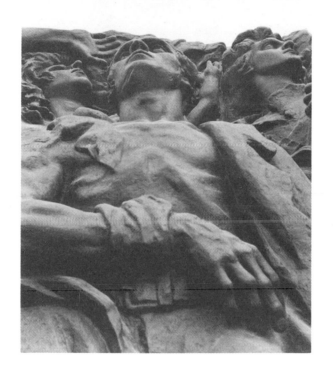

Fighters Among The Ruins

The Story of Jewish Heroism During World War II

Yisrael Gutman

Published by
The International Quiz on Jewish Heroism
During World War II
and

B'nai B'rith Books

Washington, D.C.

Jerusalem • London • Paris • Buenos Aires • East Sydney

Library of Congress Cataloging-in-Publication Data
Gutman, Israel (Yisrael).
Fighters among the ruins.
1. World war, 1939-1945—Underground movements, Jewish.
2. Holocaust, Jewish (1939-1945)
3. World War, 1939-1945—Participation, Jewish.
I. Title.
D810.J4G855 1988   940.53'15'03924   87-36654
ISBN 0-910250-14-6 (B'nai B'rith)

*Fighters Among the Ruins: The Story of Jewish Heroism During
World War II* has been selected to be a part of the B'nai B'rith Judaica
Library. The library is sponsored by the B'nai B'rith International
Commission on Continuing Jewish Education in an effort to promote
greater popular understanding of Judaism and the Jewish tradition.

Publication of this book is made possible
by generous grants from:
Eleanor and Mel Dubin
Rita and Irwin Hochberg
Hanni and Irving Rosenbaum

Contents

Chapter 1

The Jews of Europe: Trapped in Tragic Circumstances

On January 30, 1933, Adolf Hitler was appointed Chancellor of the German Republic. Few events in the history of mankind have heralded such profound change, destruction and tragedy as the ascent to power of Hitler and National Socialism. We Jews were the principal target of Nazi racism and paid the heaviest price in blood.

NAZI RACIAL THEORY AND THE STATUS OF THE JEWS DURING THE EARLY YEARS OF THE THIRD REICH

The racist theory which National Socialism propounded added a new dimension to anti-Semitism. Until then, the hatred of Jews had been characterized by a few dominant ideas: hostility rooted in Christian dogma, which held that the Jews were the Messiah's people who had denied the truth; general hatred, which accused the Jews of greed and worship of money and of being responsible for the spread of capitalism in Europe; and political hatred, including claims that the Jews were a radical, destabilizing element infecting other peoples with alien, revolutionary notions, preaching international class solidarity and thereby undermining domestic peace. Racist anti-Semitism, however, channelled the accusations and hatred in a new direction. The danger of the Jew lay neither in his religious beliefs, his

1

professional or business activity, nor in his political opinions. The danger was his Jewishness itself, his blood, his biological structure.

Hitler argued that the substance of Jewishness is not religious life, and that Jewish "religious" institutions were merely a means of organization and a tool for dominating the world. The Jews had aspired for generations to dominate the world so as to shape it according to their will, and they turned against any nation, society or organization standing in their way. Jewish domination of the world would not lead just to a harsh and oppressive stability, but to a Jewish dictatorship ending in total destruction and the extinction of mankind. In Hitler's words, "the Jews' victory will be a death blow to humanity, and the planet will once again become empty of people, just as it was ages and ages ago."

Why would Jewish domination mean the end of the world? Why would their domination leave no place for human life? Hitler provided an explanation. The Jew was the ultimate parasite, a creature living off other productive people and nations. The Jew had never had a country and he was unable to maintain a country of his own. The essence of human creativity, the link to land and working the land, were alien to the Jew.

There were many contradictions in this ideological morass: on one hand, the Jew was portrayed as the dominating and controlling force in the social and political order of countries; on the other, he was persecuted, downtrodden and unwanted, with no country prepared to give him refuge or a home. Anti-Semites have never bothered to explain the outright contradictions and paradoxes in these falsehoods.

Anti-Semites, when it suits them, accuse the Jews as a whole of persistent and unwavering loyalty to their religion. And when it suits them, the Jewish nation becomes a cult of nonbelievers, spreading atheism and leading people away from religion and faith. Jews are accused at certain times of being poor, penniless, incurable loafers, a burden on the national budget, and at other times as diligent, unified and crafty as misers amassing fortunes, and as members of the rich upper classes. Jews are identified as imperialists and capitalists by left-leaning anti-Semites and are called radicals, communists and revolutionaries by right-wing anti-Semites. To some anti-Semites they are staunch conservatives, impeding social change and progress, while to others they sow the seeds of dissent and unrest, ceaselessly fomenting rebellion and upsetting the social order.

The simple truth is that anyone whose senses have not been dulled by hate knows that Jews have varied opinions and come from different social backgrounds, and that Jews, as a nation, are just like other nations and ethnic groups, and that all nations have their workers and their idlers, their wealthy and their penniless, their conservatives and their advocates of change; and that Jews have unique characteristics and habits which are the result of centuries of development, varying and taking on different forms over the course of time.

One typical example is the common claim voiced by several generations in European countries that Jews are cowards and unfit for military service and the sacrifice required of soldiers in the field. Imperial Germany conducted a survey of its army during the First World War to examine where Jewish soldiers were serving. It was the result of anti-Semitic slander claiming that Jews were avoiding active service on the front and seeking out comfortable positions in offices and noncombative services. This claim, like others of its type, had no basis in reality.

Today, now that an independent Israel exists, there is no need to prove that Jews are capable of bravery and sacrifice, and know how to wage war. Today's anti-Semites, of course, claim that the Jews have militaristic tendencies. There is no such thing as a typical Jew, just as there is no such thing as a typical Frenchman, Australian or American. If the Jews managed until recently to maintain a cohesive and largely closed community administered according to uniform rules, then this unity was also to a large degree the result of persecution by, and forced isolation from, the surrounding society. Internal, unique Jewish frameworks did not persist in Europe after the French Revolution, when the principles of liberty, equality and emancipation were adopted. Since then, Jewish society has become more varied, and it has been characterized by differences in political ideology and serious social, educational, and cultural schisms. Jewish uniformity, the stereotype of rigid Jewish outlook and characteristics, and the uniformity of Jewish ideas and opinions, are figments of the imagination of anti-Semitism, and have no basis in reality.

But let us return to the Nazis. The Nazis had no need for proof based on reason. It was enough that Jews were depicted as dismal demonic beings, devising schemes and plotting against mankind. Just as the unrestrained hate of the individual leads to psychosis, in which people lose sight of reality and become prisoners of a monstrous, frightening world, Hitler's theory about the Jews led to the edge of an abyss in which only insane fantasies were visible. According to Hitler, after the Jews gain control of the world, the productive and creative body from which they sucked their vitality would cease to exist. Once the body on which the parasite lives ceases to be, the parasite itself is unable to survive. Accordingly, after the Jews carried out their plot and became masters of the world, everything would be destroyed, including the Jews themselves.

That this fantasy was created by a human being comes as no surprise. What is surprising and disturbing is the thought that the man who wrote such paranoid statements rose to the rank of leader and pseudo-saviour of a large European nation. It makes no difference whether the German masses believed Hitler's contradictory delusions and actually saw the Jews as demonic, apocalyptic beings, or whether they thought that Hitler suffered from a complex of delusions about the Jews, but thought and acted lucidly and rationally on all other matters, particularly in those areas which benefitted the German people. In either case, the Germans permitted or tolerated the persecution of a minority living in their midst.

Allan Bullock, author of a well-known biography of Hitler, *A Study in Tyranny*, writes:

> In all the pages which Hitler devotes to the Jews in *Mein Kampf*, he does not bring forward a single fact to support his wild assertions. This was entirely right, for Hitler's anti-Semitism bore no relation to fact. It was pure fantasy: to read these pages is to enter the world of the insane, a world peopled by hideous and distorted shadows. The Jew is no longer a human being; he has become a mythical figure, a grimacing, leering devil invested with internal powers, the incarnation of evil into which Hitler projects all that he hates, feels and desires. Like all obsessions, the Jews are not a partial but a total explanation. [Allan Bullock, *Hitler: A Study in Tyranny*, Bantam, New York, 1961]

Nazism did not stop at describing the Jews as destructive and as an organized community and a threat to the world. According to Nazi ideology, Judaism is a racially-based brotherhood with its racial nature rooted in human biological structure. Hitler always referred to "blood," saying that "a Jew can never be a German . . . no matter how much he may try, he can never become a German in his heart. There are several reasons for this: his blood; his character; his desire; and his activity." Race is not inherent in language, culture, way of life or work, but in blood.

National Socialism left Jews with no options. One can change one's religious beliefs or profession, but not one's blood. Those who maintain that blood can be evil, as did the Nazis, are liable to come to insane and radical conclusions like the "Final Solution"—the use of bloodshed and murder to eradicate the plague.

To its theory of biological racism, Nazism added the accusation that the Jews were plotting a secret international scheme to dominate the world. In order to "prove" this, they relied upon a collection of documents known as the *Protocols of the Elders of Zion*, a work of evil produced by the Secret Police of Czarist Russia, and which was proven to be a forgery. Hitler claimed that the Jews, who were engaged in a long-term struggle against the superior "Aryan" race for mastery of the world, had launched a decisive battle in the twentieth century, and that the Soviet Union was the first country which they had conquered. Other European nations could expect a similar fate, ending in total destruction. Hitler and Nazism were therefore duty-bound to raise the call to arms to fight the Jews, and to "save" mankind from the danger threatening it. One may thus conclude that the motivation for the war conceived and planned by Hitler was not only German nationalism and a desire for imperialistic expansion, but also destruction of the Jews.

Hitler and other Nazi leaders were especially vocal about the supposed existence of a Jewish strike force poised to attack Germany. The Jews' hatred of Germany was purported to be the result of the unique status of the Germans as a nation and race which had maintained its purity and sense of purpose. In Hitler's partly autobiographical book, *Mein Kampf*, he wrote:

> And so the Jew today is the great agitator for the complete destruction of Germany. Wherever in the world we read of attacks against Germany, Jews are their fabricators, just as in peacetime and during the War the press of the Jewish stock exchange and Marxists systematically stirred up hatred against Germany until state after state abandoned neutrality and, renouncing the true interests of the peoples, entered the service of the World War coalition. [Adolf Hitler, *Mein Kampf*, Boston 1971, p. 623]

The truth in this case, as with all the other hate propaganda, is the exact opposite of what Hitler claimed. The Jews of Germany were for the most part deeply in love with the country and its culture. They were patriotic and fiercely loyal. German Jewry had often acted coldly and reservedly in matters of international Jewish interest, because of the fear that their involvement with Jewish affairs might be interpreted as preference for Jewish solidarity over their duty to Germany. German Jewish leaders took care not to become involved in activities which might be interpreted as fraternizing with bodies and organizations which could be considered part of an "international Jewish front" and inconsistent with Germany's interests.

When the First World War broke out, Kaiser Wilhelm II announced that, in view of the difficult times facing Germany, he no longer recognized any barriers between the various Germans and that they were now united in the war effort. The Jews of Germany interpreted this declaration as an expression of the fact that they were a fundamental part of the nation in its struggle. On the 7th day of August, 1914, the *Judische Rundschau*, a German Zionist journal, published a declaration including the following words: "Jews of Germany! We call on you in the spirit of the age-old Jewish sense of duty to join, with all your heart and soul, and all your wealth, in the service of the fatherland." The statement was signed by the Union of German Zionists. Various Jewish writers of the period praised German arms and soldiers, and the first member of the Reichstag to be killed in the war was a Jewish volunteer, a member of the Social Democratic faction.

In actual fact, the patriotism of the Jews of Germany and their physical sacrifice were of little help. When the fortunes of war swung in favor of the Allies and Germany was forced to declare a cease-fire and negotiate terms of its surrender, an anti-Semitic campaign was launched in Germany. Radical nationalist elements attacked the Jews, blaming them for everything. It was they who had headed the revolutionary movement and had perpetrated the revolution in Germany toward the end of the war. (In truth Rosa Luxemburg, Kurt Eisner, and others who played leading roles in the revolutionary movement in Germany were of Jewish origin, but they had denied the Jews and renounced their Jewishness). It was the Jews who were responsible for the oppressive peace terms which were dictated to Germany, for the loss of its territories, for the anti-German sentiments prevailing in other countries and for the accusation that Germany was the aggressive and uncompromising party which had caused the war.

Anti-Semites further declared that the Weimar Republic was a

Jewish republic and that Jewish immigration from the East was flooding Germany in a torrent. Indeed, the Weimar Republic gave full rights to the Jews, thereby removing the restrictions which had been enforced during the days of the Second German Reich, such as the rule against Jews becoming officers in the German Army, joining the diplomatic corps or reaching senior positions in the academic world. However, close examination of the subject shows that the part played by Jews in the Weimar government and its bureaucracy was less significant than in neighboring France. Moreover, many of the refugees who "flooded Germany" were Jews from the Poznan and Upper Silesia districts, which had been annexed to Poland. They chose to move to Germany out of a sense of solidarity with and feeling of belonging to Germany. Furthermore, the Polish Endek Party condemned the Jews, and not just the Jews of Germany but all the Jews of the world, advertising themselves in their propaganda as supporters and saviors of Germany and as furthering the interests of the Germans in the international public and political arenas. Meanwhile in Italy, Mussolini denounced the Bolshevik Revolution as a plot hatched by the Jews in collaboration with the Germans.

In summary, according to Hitler and Nazi ideology, the world came to the brink of destruction and demise in the wake of the First World War as the result of the increasing domination of the world by the Jews. The Jews never campaigned openly, but attacked and weakened the nations of Europe by means of their clandestine infiltration of forces and movements, which eroded and weakened the Aryan race from the inside. Those same Jews were also the inventors and propagators of humanism, liberalism and other "isms," which served only to weaken the patriotic Aryan fabric, and were now fanning the flames of class hatred and pointing to imaginary discrimination.

The Jews were the leaders of all revolutions. They had wrested control of the Soviet Union, annihilated the Russian intelligentsia, and were now quickly succeeding in capturing controlling positions in Western European countries. Germany, as the country and racial core of the German people, was defending itself against Jewish aggression, but had nevertheless been tainted by the plague of class differences, and internal dissent had also taken its toll. The objective of National Socialism was to restore the glory of the German people and protect their status as the "master race" in the family of nations consisting of races of varying degrees of superiority. The capture of territories, expansion of the "Lebensraum" of the German nation, and the elimination of Jewish influence as a race engaged in a never-ending fight against Germany were the major tasks facing the German people in their struggle.

Italian fascism and other fascist movements also aspired to national greatness on the basis of past imperialistic power, molding the nation into a united, resolute force, undivided by class distinctions. They were prepared to use any means in order to achieve their ends, including domestic terror and war with other countries.

Soviet communism advocated lofty ideals of equality, universal brotherhood and redemption of the world. However, the advocates of these same ideals paradoxically adopted methods involving force, oppression and genocide in the name of a better future, and were plagued by power struggles. This resulted in an enormous discrepancy between words and actions. Instead of the promised government of the oppressed majority, there arose a government of a tyrannic minority. Instead of sounds of liberation prophesying change, might and fear were imposed, silencing everything and erecting barriers of terror and estrangement between people.

Nazism did not merely set itself ambitious nationalistic goals. It stated openly that it aspired to re-establish human society based on a racist hierarchy, with racial origin forming the key to granting individuals and societies rights to government, freedom, and wealth. The might of the Germans and the victories which followed were intended not only to satisfy their burning hunger for territories and control of other resources throughout Europe, but also to put Germany in its destined position among the family of nations. This theory considered the "Aryan" German to be the elite of mortal beings, who, when in power, would formulate and institute new ways of living and new cultures and establish a "thousand-year" government in which a new racial order would replace religion, democracy, and other such values.

Many historians point to the fact that Nazism came to power under the conditions of national frustration, political and social distress, economic crisis and mass unemployment which prevailed in the Weimar Republic after the First World War. The victorious powers imposed a restrictive, oppressive peace on Germany, blaming it for starting the war and forcing it to accept a republican form of government that it did not want. In this atmosphere of bitterness and resistance to terms which the Allies had dictated, the Nazis and other similar factions were nothing but marginal, vociferous elements. It was only after the stage had been set by this severe crisis, which eroded the very fabric of law and order, that the Germans succumbed to the temptations and promises bandied about by Hitler and his cronies.

Field Marshall Hindenburg shaking Reichschancellor Hitler's hand, March 21, 1933.

There seems to be a great deal of truth in this description of the course of events. However, one must not forget that the terms which were imposed on Germany, although severe, were no worse than those that Germany would have dictated had it been the victor. One practical example of this is the peace agreement imposed by Germany on Russian at Brest-Litovsk in early 1918. It must also be remembered that the Great Depression was not limited solely to Germany, but was an international phenomenon. Furthermore, the Nazi ascendance to power was no revolution. Hitler's appointment as Chancellor in 1933 was a democratic procedure; he was invited by President von Hindenburg to serve as head of government. The first government he assembled consisted of a coalition of right-wing forces, some of which deluded themselves that they would be able to guide and direct Hitler, who lacked political experience, as they wished. However, nobody in Germany can claim that Hitler's form of government and society came as an unexpected surprise. Hitler's opinions and plans were published openly and explicitly in his book *Mein Kampf* (My Struggle), a weird blend of autobiography and political and ideological manifesto. The Nazis did not hide the fact that to them democracy was nothing but a tool they would use to gain power, and which they had no intention of upholding once they had achieved their ends. The Nazi Party declared explicitly and publicly that it would unilaterally revoke the Treaty of Versailles, because it intended to reconstruct the German army and to regain control of those parts of the fatherland that had been lost in the War and even to expand its borders according to long-held nationalistic aspirations.

Nothing came as a surprise or was unexpected. On the contrary, Hitler's path to power was characterized by his consistent keeping of promises (although with concealment of true intentions in a calculated tactical maneuver) and persistent machinations for the implementation of objectives which he had made clear many years before becoming the Fuhrer. If there is anything surprising or confusing in Hitler's ascendancy to complete dictatorial power in the Third Reich, it is the lack of any substantial opposition to him, the enthusiasm and fanaticism at home, and the indifference or encouraging tolerance shown by other countries. Anyone studying the evolution of the Nazi ascendancy to power is astounded by the complete breakdown of the left-wing parties and the national and liberal center, which had millions of members and supporters; the almost total subservience of the Christian churches in the face of the Nazi pagan ideology and a set of values which violated the basic tenets of Christianity; its acceptance, if not outright enthusiasm, by the armed forces, the bourgeoisie and the aristocracy; and the nation's cohesiveness in rallying around the Fuhrer and his doctrine.

Some German historians stress that racism and anti-Semitism were not of great or overwhelming importance in the German people's admiration of Hitler and their eager identification with the Nazi regime and its deeds. Those who hold this opinion cite the success of Hitler and Nazism in eliminating unemployment, introducing law and order in government, restoring the nation to productive work, and giving Germany respected international status as the factors which reinforced their supporters and convinced the doubters. However, the proponents of this theory cannot deny that a significant proportion of the people, the hard, loyal core of Nazis, initiated and took active part in the campaign of persecution against the Jews. The over-whelming majority of Germans, with the exception of a few noted in-dividuals, did not raise their voices against the progressive stages of Nazi policy toward the Jews, from their removal from public service or cultural and scientific activity, to the adoption of the Nuremberg Laws, to the confiscation and theft of their property, to Kristallnacht and the burning of synagogues.

After World War II, there was disagreement among historians and thinkers in Germany and other countries over the role of Nazism and its attitude toward the values and political aspirations in the history of the German people. According to some historians, Nazism was not the result of a quirk or breach in the course of German history. They say that Nazi ideology should rather be seen as an orderly and logical development, as the continuation and radical maturation of ideologi-cal forces which were rife in German culture and society.

Some historians believe that these threatening phenomena had gained influence in the Second Reich under Prussian hegemony. German nationalism, which had come to life during the period of Na-poleonic occupation, urged the unification of the multitude of Ger-man states and principalities into a single, united country. Internal contradictions and different conceptions arose. The liberals wanted to implement social change while establishing a unified country based on the bourgeois-liberal classes. Others believed that unity should take the form of Hapsburgian hegemony. Yet others saw vi-brant, mighty Prussia and its king as the focal point for the unifica-tion and rule of all Germans.

One must remember that it was not the liberal-revolutionary movement (which saw itself as an offshoot of pan-European liberal nationalism) which led the national German movement for unity, but the military elite headed by Chancellor Bismarck, who planned to achieve his aims by means of "blood and iron." Otto von Bismarck, the personification of a strong Germany under the leadership of Prussian royalty, paved the way for Prussian hegemony. Prussian-German power appeared rather late in the European arena as a com-petitor among the great powers. This heightened appetite quickly became an aggressive force, upsetting the fragile European balance of power and causing local battles which inevitably led to world-wide war.

Some historians claim that the roots of the aggressiveness, cruelty and sense of superiority which allowed the Germans to violate the rights of nations and people who were not of the German race can be found farther afield. According to these historians, the roots of these tendencies and characteristics lie in the culture of the Teutonic tribes and are expressed in ancient myths, folklore, and popular habits. Even if these deep-rooted characteristics are not the only or the overwhelming themes in the course of development of the German people, they are nevertheless inherent, and break out ferociously from time to time, according to this theory, with particularly severe effect in times of hardship. Nazism and the regime it gave rise to are radical manifestations of this legacy.

The German historian Friedrich Meinecke, who attempted toward the end of his life, after World War II, to discover the causes of the "German catastrophe," argued that the Nazi period was a deviation from the normal course of German history. Hitler, as an Austrian, was a foreign element who gained control of Germany during a period of confusion and loss, when Germany was beset by political and economic crises.

It appears that those dealing with this chapter in history made two assumptions, the first of which was that all agreed that Nazism was an exception unparalleled in European culture and society, and second was that everyone, or almost everyone, agreed that many Germans embraced Nazi ideology, seeking in it solutions to personal difficulties and the national crisis.

Revisionist ideas apologizing for the German embrace of Nazism began to appear in Germany only after decades had passed. The sources of these ideas are varied. It may well be that the fact that West Germany is a normal democratic country, just like other European countries, reinforced the theory that the national character of Germany was free of any weaknesses or unusual defects, or it may be that the older generation of Germans were loath to admit and reveal the horrible truth to their children and grandchildren, and subconsciously and consciously avoided the truth and its consequences.

Theories arose that fascism and totalitarianism were common phenomena throughout Europe, of which Nazism was merely an offshoot or variation, no different from the others in substance. Without going into an analysis of these theories, it is important to state that they cannot be accepted and that the differences between Nazism and Fascism or other totalitarian ideologies are far greater than the similarities.

Theories attempting to depict Nazism as a regime which was part of the development of the twentieth century gloss over Nazi racism and ignore the enormous differences between it and other political movements. Revisionist historians cannot deny the unspeakable crimes committed, unprecedented in dimension and form, and the annihilation of the Jews of Europe. It is actually the comparison with Italian Fascism which most clearly demonstrates the difference. The Italians did not cooperate in the deportation of the Jews and adamantly refused to hand over Italian Jews to the Nazis when it became clear that they would be murdered.

The actual enactment of racist legislation in Italy encountered resistance from below, and Jews in hiding in Italy were usually able to rely on the protection and assistance of those around them. The very same ordinances regarding Jews which were in force in both Germany and Italy were implemented quite differently. The enthusiasm and thoroughness with which the Germans operated had an infectious, decisive effect in the implementation of evil in German-occupied areas.

The Italians acted differently. Some maintain that the Italians were lax in their implementation of orders to deport the Jews because of their lack of order or discipline, and that the laws regarding the Jews suffered the same neglect that all Italian affairs suffered. Any researcher delving into the debate among the Italians regarding the fulfillment of the German demand that the Jews be delivered to them or sent to the East, and the methods of evasion and refusal adopted by the Italians, must conclude that the Italians were not lax at all, but put much thought and effort into sabotaging their instructions, the foremost reason being elementary humanistic feeling.

An analogy with the Soviet Union should also be rejected. Communism, despite its distortions, gross lies and disregard for honor and human life, did not adopt racist theory, which denies the equality of all humankind. It did not systematically murder babies, and did not build gas chambers. The method of planned murder of an entire race, carried out with obsessive enthusiasm, and the diverting of vital military forces and trains so as to make genocide possible, are phenomena peculiar to Nazi thought and its German perpetrators during the Second World War.

This crime, which was given a quasi-ideological cover, has no equal in history, and will stand forever as a chilling , bloody indictment. The lesson of this crime to Germany and the Germans, as well as to other nations, requires honest and bold confrontation of the truth, cruel and harsh as it may be.

THE NAZI RISE TO POWER AND THE PATH TO WAR—1933-1939

The stabilization of the Nazi regime took place in two stages. First, the bureaucracy, institutions and social framework of Germany were dismantled and then reassembled to conform to a dictatorial form of government and the atmosphere of Nazi cultural and political life. Second, the armed forces were rebuilt. The obligations imposed on Germany in the Treaty of Versailles were annulled, and Germany embarked on a campaign of territorial expansion and domination. These changes were possible because of the weakness and surrender of democratic governments and their failure to understand the dangers presented by the Nazi threat and the inherent inevitability of war.

With literally stunning speed, Hitler and his followers succeeded in dismantling the institutions and parties on which democratic government was based in the days of the Weimar Republic, eliminating all political parties but his own, of which he was the leader, or "Fuhrer."

The first victims of the Nazis were the leftist parties—the Communists, the Social Democrats and the trade unions. Overnight, a whole range of organizations, whose members and supporters numbered in the millions and who controlled newspapers, published books, and supported youth and sports associations, ceased to exist.

Nazism's political opponents were the first to be destroyed. They were followed by the liberals and those close to or allied with the government. The forces which helped appoint Hitler as Chancellor assumed that they would be able to guide him according to their principles, but they were quickly deprived of power and lost their effectiveness in public and political life. Hitler even purged his own party. When the radical faction of the Nazi party, headed by SA commander Ernst Rohm, demanded the implementation of the social articles of the Nazi party manifesto and insisted on the conversion of the army into a trained force in the spirit of the party and the SA, Hitler carried out, on June 30, 1934, an operation called the "Night of the Long Knives."

The process of Nazi domination of all aspects of life did not leave

the Christian churches untouched. The churches were not dismantled or outlawed, but they were forced to accept the supremacy of the
government and to adhere to its line, which clearly and openly went
against the principles of Christianity. the Catholic Church signed an
anti-Christian agreement (*Concordate*) with the dictatorship, and a
church was established under the auspices of the Evangelist Church,
preaching Nazism under a religious guise.

Judges taking a vow of loyalty to the Führer.

The communications media and German cultural organs of expression were consolidated and hitched to the Nazi wagon. The free
press vanished, and with it objective information and public debate.
Writers and scientists who did not adopt the regime's spirit and obey
its dictates were deprived of their right to work or publish, and their
writing were banned. In May, 1933, there was a public book-burning
during which, along with the works of Jewish writers and thinkers,

books by gentiles such as Thomas and Heinrich Mann were thrown on the bonfires.

The works of Jews who had contributed to the development of culture and science in Germany were banned and destroyed. For example, the works of the noted Jewish poet Heinrich Heine were banned. His poem "Lorelei," which had become a folk ballad, could not be eradicated, so it was described by the Nazis as an "anonymous ballad." Academic freedom was abolished and the universities became institutions subordinated to the cultural authorities. Their administration was overseen by loyal Nazis. Many public figures, artists, writers and thinkers were forced to leave Germany. Among these émigrés were famous Jews such as Albert Einstein, Leon Feuchtwanger, Stefan Zweig, Max Reinhardt, Arnold Scheinberg, Sigmund Freud, and many others. The worlds of theater, music, cinema and the arts became propaganda tools for the party, and their creators were forced to bow to the dictates of Nazism as to the form and content of their works. All of the arts were subordinated to Nazi propaganda minister Josef Goebbels, a talented and fanatical demagogue and member of Hitler's inner circle.

Berlin students burn over 20,000 books, May 10, 1933.

There was no government in the ordinary sense in the Nazi state, nor was there any responsible parliamentary body. Almost nothing remained of the independent, autonomous government of the German states. The central government was headed by a small group of senior functionaries, loyal to the Fuhrer. A hierarchy of regional party heads, called *gauleiters*, developed alongside the central government. The pyramidal structure was headed by the Fuhrer, who distributed honors and decorations. This status of supreme arbiter gave Hitler an authority against which there was no appeal, but failed to prevent in-fighting and competition between the various power centers of the country and the party fighting for their share of power.

Nazi ideology took hold of Germany without encountering much resistance. Children, teenagers, women and other sectors of the population were organized into party divisions and units. Fanaticism and charismatic idolization of Hitler filled the souls of millions. Racism gave the Germans self-confidence, and a sense of supremacy, together with the belief in their right to mold everything according to their wishes, to oppress and disenfranchise those whom they considered to be racially inferior. Thus the indifference to the suffering and deprivation of their enemies, whether real or imagined.

In foreign affairs, Nazi policy adopted a line of national ambition and territorial expansion. Hitler devoted most of his efforts and energies to the political military area. The Nazis revoked the Treaty of Versailles, which had imposed territorial limitations and restrictions on Germany. The adopted an aggressive foreign policy, which was at the same time both crafty and cautious. For example, a short time after the Nazis ascended to power, Germany resigned from the League of Nations. Its resignation was not a demonstrative step of leaving the family of nations and a threat to peace. On the contrary, the Nazis claimed that Germany was resigning from the League of Nations because of the arguments and debates over disarmament, claiming that they were in favor of peace and general disarmament, but objected to disarmament applying only to Germany; this gave the impression that Nazi Germany aspired to peace and opposed the use of force.

The Nazis exploited the fact that many in the West, particularly in Great Britain and the United States, agreed that the Treaty of Versailles was unjust and unfair to Germany. They made calculated use of the reticence and fear of war in many countries in the wake of

the horrible consequences of the First World War. Politicians and lay-
men alike were prepared to make painful concessions in the hope of
guaranteeing peace. This led to the formation of the "appeasement"
school of thought, which had many followers in Great Britain. On the
other side of the Atlantic, the trend toward isolationism and non-
involvement in the affairs of argumentative Europe gathered force.

The Great Depression, the weakness of the governments and the
lack of respected leaders in Europe gave the impression that democracy was bankrupt and unable to deal properly with social and
economic problems. The answer appeared to lie in a form of government based on totalitarianism and strong leadership. This trend was
heightened by the fear of Communism. Hitler exploited this fear,
claiming that the only alternative to National-Socialism was
Communism.

In the thirties, in almost all European countries, parties and movements were established which were influenced by fascism and
National-Socialism and acted as loyal tools for Nazi propaganda and
the political exercises of the Third Reich.

In March, 1935, Hitler established compulsory military service
in Germany, which restored the army to its full size. This decision
was a gross, unilateral revocation of the Treaty of Versailles, according to which Germany was permitted to maintain an army of
only 100,000 men, with only 4,000 officers. The Western countries
reacted to this step only with verbal objections, which had little effect on the Nazis.

In March, 1936, Hitler went one step further in his campaign of
aggression and expansion. German soldiers entered the Rhine
provinces. To a certain extent, this was more significant than the
reintroduction of compulsory military service. According to the
Treaty of Versailles, the Rhine provinces were to have been demilitar-
ized, as a means of preventing any possible aggression by Germany
against France. While the expansion of the army was not directed
against any particular democratic country, the army's entry into the
Rhine provinces was a clear threat to France and its security. At that
time, the German army (Wehrmacht) was not yet a serious force. Had
France and its allies reacted with deeds, calling up their armies and
declaring that the Germans' actions would be countered with military opposition, they would have forced Hitler to retreat, and the retreat would likely have had fateful repercussions for the future of his
regime. The failure of the Western powers to demonstrate their oppo-

sition led Hitler to conclude that the democracies were unable to act in their own self-defense. The Germans, and their military leaders in particular, learned from that course of events that Hitler's judgment could be relied upon.

In 1936, the Spanish Civil War began, following the establishment of a republican regime and the victory of the left in the elections held there. In response to the leftist victory, units of the Spanish Army headed by General Francisco Franco began a rebellion which quickly became a prolonged civil war. The war did not remain an internal power struggle in divided Spain, as forces from the outside intervened. The fight in Spain divided public opinion in the international arena into two opposing camps: Italy and Germany assisted Franco almost openly by supplying arms and military forces, while leftists from various countries around the world travelled to Spain to join the International Brigades fighting alongside the Republicans. Franco and his allies had the upper hand in the conflict. This intervention in the European arena doubtless reinforced fascism and Nazism and added to their political stature. It is noteworthy that the Soviet Union supported the Republicans.

In 1937, Nazi Germany launched a four-year plan, piloted by Marshal Hermann Göring, the goal of which was to expand Germany's armaments capabilities and to strengthen its economic independence, particularly in the areas of natural resources and industrial output. In practice, the plan prepared the Germany economy for war.

In 1938, German political aggression reached a peak, taking the form of determined change by means of *faits accomplis* and threats. In March, 1938, the Anschluss (annexation) of Austria to the Third Reich was accomplished. This "union" between Germany and Austria was not only in violation of the spirit of the Treaty of Versailles, but a Germany political victory of far-reaching consequence. For generations, Germany had been plagued by internal debate over the unification of the country. In the nineteenth century, Austria and Prussia aspired to hegemony and the unification of Germany. The unification finally took place in 1871, as the climax of Bismarck's political and military campaigns, but did not include Hapsburgian Austria. The age-old dream finally came true only in the Third Reich, under Hitler's rule, and the Germans interpreted it as an expression of unprecedented power and greatness.

German army units cross the barriers at   Jewish refugees in the China Sea.
the Austrian border.

Fascist Italy had a vital interest in Austria's existence and independence. The southern Tyrol area, added to Italy after the First World War, was populated by Germans and it was reasonable to assume that the Germans would make trouble over the situation. In the early years of the Nazi dictatorship, Italy openly declared its opposition to the annexation by maintaining close links with independent Austria. But the Anschluss of Austria was carried out with Mussolini's blessing; Italy had abandoned Austria in favor of tightening its bonds with Germany. The two countries established an alliance which lasted for many years. Some 180,000 Jews lived in Austria, mostly in Vienna. The Anschluss resulted in a drastic change in attitudes toward the Jews of Austria, with the Nazis dealing far more severely with them than they had so far dealt with the Jews of Germany.

Immediately after the annexation of Austria, the issue of the German residents of the Sudetenland in Czechoslovakia arose. Approximately three-and-a-half million Germans resided in the district, which bordered on Austria and Silesia. Czechoslovakia, which had been created after the First World War, consisted of a variety of minorities and ethnic groups, and had made impressive achievements in the economic sphere. It had a democratic government, which allowed the various ethnic groups a relatively large degree of freedom and equality. The country as a whole was considered to be the only success among the countries created after the First World War.

The unrest in the densely-populated Sudetenland began with riot-ing and demands made by the German residents of the area. The de-mands were seconded by the Third Reich, whose intentions were to "protect" the Sudeten Germans. Hitler asserted that Germans in the Sudetenland had the right to be re-united with the German father-land. This undermining of Czechoslovakia's sovereignty had rever-berations all over Europe. The motive behind the move to separate the Sudetenland was Hitler's desire to break up the area in which the country's defense lines had been concentrated, thus making Czecho-slovakia totally dependent on its powerful German neighbor. One of the effects of this action was to render Czechoslovakia's mutual de-fense pact with France ineffective.

In the face of Germany's demands and threats, a campaign of po-litical debate, proposals and appeasement efforts began. England and France were still dominated by those who were adamant on avoiding war, whatever the price, even if it meant surrender. The process of appeasement and surrender by the democratic powers reached a climax at the Munich Conference, which was convened to find a solution to the Sudetenland crisis and to ensure continued peace. The conference was called by the Italian dictator Mussolini, in response to entreaties from many quarters, who asked Hitler to host the conference. Four national leaders participated: Prime Minister Chamberlain of Britain, Prime Minister Deladier of France, Mussolini—"Il Duce," leader of the ruling Fascist Party in Italy; and, of course, the German Führer. In Munich, Czechoslovakia was sacri-ficed in exchange for the short-lived promise of a stable peace. One of the most glaring aspects of the Munich Conference was the decision not to invite Czechoslovakia to participate in the discussions. The representatives of the country whose fate was being discussed were forced to wait outside the conference hall and automatically sign the judgment, which was dictated by Hitler and accepted in its entirety by the confused representatives of the democratic world. Munich put an end to democracy in the small nations of eastern and southeastern Europe. Those countries understood that they could expect no assist-ance or support from France or its allies, and that they must therefore seek protection in the rising power of the fascist countries. Hitler de-clared yet again, as he did after every act of political and territorial ag-gression, that he had no more demands and that once he was satisfied, peace and harmony would reign.

Hitler and Prime Minister Chamberlain during the Munich Conference.

The Munich Agreement was never actually implemented. In March, 1939, the Nazi army marched into Prague, capital of the Czech nation. The central areas of the country, Bohemia and Moravia, were declared a protectorate of the Third Reich. Slovakia became a satellite of the Reich and the remaining parts of the country were parcelled out as war spoils to Hungary and Poland. This act of violence, which resulted in the dismemberment of Czechoslovakia, was a flagrant violation of the Munich Agreement and dashed all hopes which had been pinned on it. Germany's claim of its desire to unify all people of German extraction, a claim which had many adherents spread throughout the territories bordering on Germany, was revealed for the lie that it was when Germany, with force and threats, invaded central Czechoslovakia, populated by Slavs. This led to a turnabout of public opinion in Western European countries, especially in Britain. The attack on independent Czechoslovakia and the failure to fulfill the obligations of the Munich Agreement were overwhelming proof, even to the doubters and pacifists, that Hitler was not interested in "remedying the injustices" which Germany had suffered, but that he intended to wrest control of Europe and perhaps the whole world. The Reich's diplomatic victories, and the conquests it had made by means of threats, reinforced Hitler's status and power and at best merely delayed the inevitable military conflict. This delay worked against the democratic world.

Neville Chamberlain, who was a proponent of appeasement and believed in the purported honesty of Hitler's intentions, changed course under the pressure of public opinion and his colleagues in government. He felt that he had lost valuable time both in the diplomatic field and in neglect and lapses in the area of military readiness. Britain frantically searched for allies and focused its attention on Poland and Romania, Hitler's next potential victims. It showed interest in a defense alliance with Soviet Russia, which during the appeasement period had been left out of the political campaigns. Poland rose to the top of the political agenda.

After World War I, Poland had received a corridor of territory giving it access to the Baltic Sea. This strip of land in the north divided and cut off East Prussia from West Prussia and the only link between them was by sea or by crossing Polish territory. Another problem was posed by Danzig. Danzig was a port city populated by Germans, but the Poles claimed historic rights to the city and saw its port as Poland's vital opening to the sea. The compromise reached in Versailles, making Danzig a quasi-independent city under the protection of the League of Nations, was unsatisfactory to both parties involved, and it is doubtful whether this hybrid could have survived for long.

In any event, the Weimar Republic had considered the arrangement with Poland and the inherent loss of territory as intolerable, but had sought to achieve the remedy by peaceful means. Thus it was to be expected that the Danzig affair and the isolation of East Prussia from the main body of Germany would be exploited by Hitler as an excuse for making more demands. This, however, never came to pass. To the surprise of many, about one year after Hitler's rise to power, Germany signed a non-aggression treaty in February, 1934, with Poland, led by "Strong Man" Marshal Jozef Pilsudski. Hitler publicized the agreement widely, and many of the naive interpreted it as proof of Hitler's love of peace. Everyone agreed that no other regime in Germany would have been capable of making such a bond, and that only a dictatorship, which did not have to account for its deeds and subject itself to public scrutiny, could afford to take such a bold step. Poland and Germany developed close ties in many fields and the influence of the Reich was one of the reasons for the resurgence of anti-Semitism in Poland during the period preceding the Second World War. Poland changed political direction significantly, abandoning its ties to France in favor of the new alliance with Germany. On the international scene, Poland occasionally supported German demands and aggression. Poland also took part in the division of Czechoslovakia and gave its blessing to the surrender at Munich, although far-sighted European statesmen noted that having divided up Czechoslovakia, Hitler would be free to deal with Poland.

Indeed, in early 1939, Nazi leaders began hinting to the Poles that the time had come for bilateral negotiations over Danzig. However, the Poles were obstinate and declared themselves opposed to any change in the status quo. Hitler tried to tempt the Poles with enticing promises (including the promise to solve Poland's Jewish problem by removing the Jews from Europe). The Poles, emerging from their fool's paradise, and having learned from the experience of the Czechs, were beginning to realize that any compromise over Danzig and the land corridor would be only the first step in the process of Nazi domination of their country. The Poles, who were not noted for sophisticated diplomacy or realistic evaluation of their strength, were blessed with a large measure of national pride. They retained bitter memories of lengthy periods of occupation, and were ready for the ultimate test, even if that meant pitting themselves against the armed might of Germany.

The Chamberlain government announced that it was providing Poland with guarantees and had signed a treaty with it, even before any express demand by Germany for the annexation of Danzig and the formation of an extra-territorial corridor. Hitler interpreted the re-assessment as a Polish betrayal and unilaterally annulled his treaty with Poland.

A surprising development which facilitated Hitler's decision to annul this treaty was the signing of a pact between the two dictators, Hitler and Stalin. This pact, known as the Ribbentrop-Molotov Treaty (after the German and Soviet foreign ministers), which was signed on August 23, 1939, freed Hitler from the risk of fighting major powers on two fronts, and left Poland facing the Third Reich alone. During the early years of the Nazi rule, the Soviet Union— which was then represented on the international scene by a Foreign Minister of Jewish origin, Maxim Litvinov—had made efforts to form a European front to combat the fascist and National Socialist regimes. In their rush to find ways to negotiate with Hitler, the Western democracies had treated these proposals with suspicion. The Soviets interpreted this approach as a total rejection of Soviet interests, or the targeting of Nazi aggression against the Soviet Union. Nazism viewed communist ideology and the Soviet state as a principal political enemy second only to the Jews. On the eve of the war, the British and French reached the conclusion that an attempt should be made to renew the dialogue with the Soviet Union, and that the defense of Poland would depend upon effecting a treaty with the Soviets. A delegation of Western countries traveled to Moscow for discussions with a Soviet delegation headed by Marshal Voroshilov. Meanwhile, Poland attempted to appease both Germany and Russia. Although it saw the Soviet Union as the lesser of two evils, it was firmly opposed to a united front with Russia against Germany.

On September 1, 1939, Hitler invaded Poland, which collapsed within a few weeks. On September 3, France and Britain declared war against the Third Reich. The declarations of war were not accompanied by military action, however. The Western powers waited for Hitler to appear on their territory. This came to pass less than a year after the attack on Poland, when the military and moral weakness of France and the neutral Western countries were revealed in all their nakedness. The war snowballed into enormous dimensions, becoming the biggest and most gruesome war yet fought by man.

THE JEWS OF GERMANY DURING THE PERIOD
1933–1939

The Jews of Germany, more than other groups of Jews in Europe, had shown excessive eagerness to abandon their Jewish identity, traditional way of life, and Jewish nationalism in exchange for civil rights and the opportunity to be treated as Germans. The Jews of Germany, prior to the outbreak of war, were undergoing an accelerated process of assimilation, marked by an attempt to fully integrate with the people among whom they were living. Even Orthodox Jewry in Germany, which refused to reform religious life and adhered strictly to tradition, stressed unmitigated patriotism and loyalty to the state. Jewish organizations in Germany still protected the rights of the Jews, but most of their efforts were directed towards clearing paths for involvement with and assimilation into German society. German Jewry refrained from demanding individual Jewish national rights and the

Zionist movement in Germany was a marginal force, consisting mostly of Jews of Eastern European origin, who were regarded by the Germans and the established German-Jewish community as a foreign element.

In the nineteenth century, the Jews of Germany made a unique contribution to the development of modern research in the field of Jewish studies; the "Chochmat Israel" School gave rise to thinkers and historians who illuminated Jewish beliefs and ways of life. Many of them laid the foundations for Jewish studies at many centers of study and research the world over, including the Hebrew University in Jerusalem. In the twentieth century, particularly during the period of the Weimar Republic, the Jews made significant contributions to German cultural, scientific and economic life. Among them were scientists of the stature of Albert Einstein, Fritz Haber, James Frank, Paul Ehrlich, and Otto Warburg, famous writers such as Jacob Wasserman, Arnold and Stefan Zweig, Franz Wefel, Leon Feuchtwanger and Franz Kafka, artists such as Max Liebermann, Max Reinhardt, Kurt Weil, Otto Klempfer, and Bruno Walter, and journalists, critics and intellectuals such as Karl Kraus, Walter Benjamin and Maxmillian Harden. Almost one-third of all German Nobel prize winners during that period were Jews or of Jewish extraction. Jewish-owned publishing houses, such as Ullstein, Mosse and Samuel Fischer, published the best literature and journalism in the country.

The patriotism of the Jews of Germany was expressed most impressively in the First World War. Some 80,000 German Jews enlisted in the Kaiser's army and 12,000 gave their lives on the front. Ernst Lissauer, a Jew, was the author of the "Ode Against The English." Walter Rathenau, a politician and industrialist, raised funds for the manufacture of armaments, while Fritz Haber placed his scientific talents at the disposal of the war effort. All this failed to halt the outbreak of animosity against Jews during and after the war.

There were approximately half a million Jews in Germany before Hitler came to power. They constituted less than one percent of the total population of Germany and only about five percent of total European Jewry. In 1880, the Jewish community of Germany constituted 1.09% of the total population, while in 1933 the figure was 0.76%, a reduction of more than one-fourth. This decline in the numbers of Jews in Germany was the result of a decline in the Jewish birth rate, religious conversion, emigration, and the prevalence of intermarriage, which characterized one-third of all marriages of Jews in the large cities of Germany. Demographers saw these trends, together with the aging of the Jews of Germany, as signs of the gradual disappearance of Germany's Jewish community, with some even claiming that by the end of the twentieth century Judaism would be assimilated and disappear naturally from German life.

In the light of the above, what caused the boundless hate and war of annihilation launched by the Germans against the Jews of Germany in particular and all Jews in general?

It is not easy to describe in general terms the situation of the Jews of Germany and their reactions to the tragedy which befell them when the Nazis rose to power. Many were overcome by desperation and saw the change as the collapse of their world. Others believed that the Nazi regime was but a passing episode, and that one should stand fast and await a turn for the better, which would no doubt come. Zionist Jews and those with strong ties to tradition saw the truth in a clearer light and claimed that Hitler's rise to power was not a momentary quirk of history, but the manifestation of deeply rooted processes and developments in the German people's world-view.

When Hitler came to power, many found consolation in the belief that Hitler, as head of the government, would not be able to act irresponsibly and with the same fanaticism that typified the vociferous and vote-hungry demagogue. Others believed that the rule of Hitler and his cronies would be short-lived and that the Nazi nightmare would disappear just as other governments had during the politically unstable period which had preceded Hitler and the National Socialist Party. Some Jews had such strong and overwhelming ties to Germany that they transcended the nature of the regime and the character of its leader. These Jews were incapable of imagining any future or identity for themselves outside Germany, not being part of the German nation.

In an article on the Jews of Germany of the day, a young German rabbi complained, "For us, the new reality began when we were forbidden to be anything other than Jews. We, products of German youth movements, students, lawyers in the German courts, we have become Jews by decree. Doors have been closed to us, and we stand all alone in the wilderness." Other opinions held that leaving Germany or abandoning it during that period were nothing less than demonstrations of weakness or even hostility and disloyalty, as if by leaving, the Jews were lending credence to the Nazi accusations that their ties to Germany were weak and superficial and that the slightest problem would send them into flight.

Nevertheless, many decided to quit Germany immediately. The wave of Jewish emigration during the first year of Nazi rule, 1933, was the largest until 1938, consisting, according to available estimates, of from 35,000 to 55,000 souls. No precise figures are available, but it was a major movement, carrying with it some ten percent of the entire Jewish population of Germany. Many or perhaps even most of the refugees were, it seems, "Ostjuden," Jews who had come to Germany during the previous generation from countries to the east of Germany, who did not hold German citizenship and were considered to be non-members of and even detrimental to the proper German social structure, not only by Germans but also by some Jews.

Another group, which included some Jews, which fled Germany during the first few months following the Nazi rise to power was composed of activists in the liberal movements, members of the leftist parties, journalists, writers, and artists, whose activities and works reflected firm anti-Nazi attitudes and who could expect harassment and vengeance from the new regimes.

However, the large outflow immediately encountered a significant obstacle, which in time worked against the tide of emigration from Germany. The refugees from Germany turned to neighboring countries, mainly France, expecting to be received with understanding and good will. They believed that France, which had earned a reputation as a country granting asylum to political exiles, would stand by their side because they were refugees from a country and regime which France had good reason to fear. The expectations of the exiles were not, however, fulfilled. They were forbidden to work in France and the other countries to which they fled, and were considered an unnecessary, burdensome hindrance. The few organizations which undertook to care for the refugees from Hitler's regime were isolated, had few resources and were unable to substantially ease the severe physical and social distress of the emigrants. As a result, many— some say more than 10,000—Jewish refugees returned to Nazi Germany, explaining their actions with the excuse that "if we are condemned to die we prefer to die in our own beds at home."

In the beginning, when Germany still had a coalition government and President Hindenburg was still officially the head of the government, the Nazis acted rather cautiously. Attacks against Jews were carried out within the framework of a campaign against Germany's "enemies" in general—leftists and supporters of the Weimar Republic. During the first waves of arrests and incarceration in concentration camps, the majority of those taken were opponents of the regime. Relatively few were imprisoned simply because of their Jewishness. Attacks against Jews—acts of violence, removal of Jews from their jobs, organizations and clubs—began immediately after Hitler's appointment as Chancellor.

A boycotted store, owned by Jews, guarded by SA militiamen.

The first large-scale anti-Jewish move was made on April 1, 1933, when a nationwide boycott of Jewish stores and businesses was declared. The official excuse for the action was that Jews were spreading horror stories about the new regime throughout the world. It was of no avail to the Jews and their leaders that they distanced themselves from what was being written and reported in the foreign press and declared that they had nothing to do with the media in foreign countries. They became hostages in the hands of the Nazis, and were held responsible for the behavior of world Jewry. The special committee which planned and directed the boycott was headed by Julius Streicher, a Nazi leader and editor of the weekly journal *Der Stümer*, and the most vulgar and venomous of the Nazi anti-Semites. Nevertheless, the boycott was carried out not under the auspices of the government, but as an act of the Nazi party.

When the boycott was declared, no time limit was set, and its cancellation a day later came as a surprising relief. The cancellation apparently resulted from the pressure of various parties, particularly those who were responsible for Germany's economic affairs. The general impression of the effectiveness of the boycott was mixed. In the diary kept by Nazi Propaganda Minister Josef Goebbels, he registered surprise at the extent of the boycott. On the other hand, there is sufficient evidence to suggest that in spite of the inspection teams manned by uniformed SA personnel (a type of party police force) placed by the Nazis outside Jewish businesses, many people ignored them and made their purchases as usual. Thus many Jews found consolation in the fact that the boycott did not last more than a day and that many had not heeded it, thereby demonstrating their opposition to the Nazis.

On April 7th, a proclamation was issued for the reorganization of the bureaucracy and the public service. Employees who had entered the public service during the period of the Weimar Republic, and who were considered undesirable by the Nazis, were dismissed. Once again, the attack was not targeted at the Jews alone.

On May 10th, an event took place in Germany which, more than any other action, demonstrated the monstrosity of the Nazi regime. That night, books written by writers who were found unfavorable by the new regime were publicly burned. The list of books burned included the works of Heinrich Mann and Erich Kastner, Sigmund Freud and Karl Marx, Erich Maria Remarque, and Mark and Kurt Tucholsky. The list of writers whose works were banned included Berthold Brecht, Albert Einstein, Leon Feuchtwanger, Andre Gide, Franz Kafka, André Malreaux, Thomas Mann, Ignazio Silone, Jacob Wassermann, Franz Werfel, and Stefan and Arnold Zweig.

Once again, the group of banned writers consisted of both Jews and non-Jews, but it is not difficult to see that while the non-Jewish authors on the list were mostly liberals and leftists, or had criticized the Nazi regime or emigrated when Hitler came to power, the same list included all noted Jewish writers, regardless of their opinions or political leanings. However, as mentioned, this monstrous show, taking place in the country which had given the world artistic and intellectual giants and was considered to be a country which respected and encouraged human enterprise, was a grimly foreboding sign.

The administrative restrictions and changes, and even the waves of arrests, could still be interpreted as emergency measures, a form of transitory "revolutionary" method which would be cancelled after the regime's status became established and strong. However, the book-burning and the banning of writers and their works indicated the advocacy of the use of cultural and social methods to remake mankind in the mold of Nazi ideology and thought. Indeed, Goebbels was not satisfied with the removal of works and the silencing of writers. All fields of art and communication, including theater, radio, press, publishing, arts and cinema, soon became offshoots of the Nazi Propaganda Ministry. This methodical process of enlisting all channels of creativity and art to the service of Nazi ideology took place concurrently with the removal of the Jews from the fields of science, art and the media. Thus many Jews in Nazi Germany lost their jobs and livelihood because they were Jews.

The Nazis refrained, however, from attacking Jewish industrial and commercial enterprises until 1936. The reason for this hesitation was the need for continued stimulation of Germany's economy. The new regime, which was dedicated to eradicating unemployment and which faced heavy outlays in public works and rearmament, was forced to give careful consideration to its status in the international marketplace and was desperate for foreign currency. These motives dictated a policy of protection of Jewish-owned businesses in Germany and consideration of external factors, including Jewish agents and distributors for Germany companies.

Jews interpreted the lack of harm to Jewish businesses and financial dealings as a reflection of the basic policy of the government, which made clear distinctions between commercial and other fields. They assumed that the Nazis would limit their harsh treatment of the Jews when their financial interests and reputation in the business world were threatened. Many Jews also concluded from this that, while they were destined to suffer humiliation and denial of their civil rights under the Nazi dictatorship, which was after all just a temporary plague, their existence and financial standing were nevertheless ensured. An outstanding example of the basics of this school of thought was a case in which a large Jewish-owned department store encountered financial difficulties (Jewish-owned department stores had been a favorite target of Nazi propaganda before they seized power), and it was decided to grant it special assistance instead of liquidating or confiscating it.

The Nuremberg Laws—the "Reich Citizenship Law" and the "Law for the Protection of the German Blood and German Honor"—are considered to have been a watershed in anti-Jewish policy in Germany. These laws were enacted at a Nazi party conference in September, 1935. According to some historians, the Nuremberg Laws put an end to Jewish emancipation and put the Jews back in time to the era before they became citizens with full rights. In fact, the laws are of great significance because they negated the civil rights of anyone not of "Aryan" blood. Thus, the lack of rights was not based on religious inequality or similar factors, but on a desire to remove a category of people who were of "bad blood" from civil society. The laws prohibiting marriage and sexual relations between Jews and Aryans mandated total separation between "bad blood" and the state.

The Nuremberg Laws did not encompass the definition of "Jew." The definition of "Jew" was established a few months later in the first decree pursuant to the Nuremberg Laws, which gave them the validity of constitutional laws. The Nazis had great difficulty defining "who is a Jew." According to their statements and opinions, it was necessary to define a Jew as a person with a certain racial imprint or a certain type of blood. It quickly became apparent that physical characteristics would not suffice as an easy means of distinguishing between Aryans and non-Aryans. Many Jews were fair haired and had "Aryan" noses and facial features, whereas many Germans, including Nazi leaders, had dark eyes and hair, the supposed image of the Jew. It was also difficult to define "Jewish blood" in practical terms, because there is no such thing as a Jewish blood group and there is no difference between the blood of Jews and that of other people.

As a result, the Nazis had no option but to adopt a policy of religious registration and identity, even though Hitler and other Nazi leaders continued to stress that the characteristics of the Jew were in essence not religious in nature but racial. The attitude adopted by the Nazis led to the categorization of people with one Jewish grandparent as half-Jews and quarter-Jews—"Mischlinge," or "of mixed races." Since none of those who became Jewish pursuant to this decree considered themselves Jewish, and were, in most cases barely aware of their Jewish roots, these unfortunates were rejected by the Jewish establishment and were left with no contact or association with Jewish society or the established Jewish institutions.

Paradoxically, not all Jews perceived the full significance of the Nuremberg Laws. The laws denied Jews their full rights of citizenship and placed a barrier between Jews and Germans, but that was a situation which they had been facing for a long time, and the laws merely gave official sanction to the status quo. On the other hand, the legal definition, it was hoped, would create recognition within Germany that the Jews had no official legally-protected status and put an end to the chaos which had reigned until then.

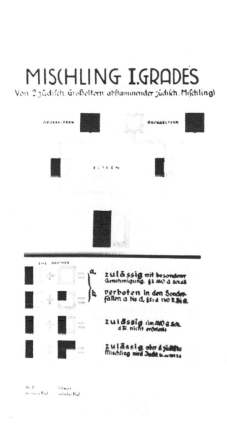

A person's value and his status as a citizen were determined by the percentage of "Aryan" or Jewish blood in his veins.

The large synagogue in Orien (Berlin) going up in flames on *Kristallnacht*.

The interpretation of the Nuremberg Laws and the status of the Jews were discussed extensively. At a meeting of Nazi Party leaders, Hitler stated that "National Socialist legislation provided the only opportunity for achieving a tolerable relationship with the Jews living in

Germany." The Führer placed particular emphasis on the fact that the laws would provide the Jews of Germany with an opportunity for independent national life in all fields, the likes of which were not available in any other country.

This gave rise to the hopes of many Jews that they would achieve a form of internal Jewish autonomy within Nazi Germany, and they made extensive efforts to create independent Jewish community structures. However, the pacifying statements made by Hitler were apparently not intended to create a status quo for the Jews. The purpose of the statements was to placate public opinion in foreign countries, to lower the Jews' guard, and to lay the foundation for measures yet to come. Students of Hitler's methods, which were repeated in the general tactical and political arenas, find forewarning in his statements on the occasion of the enactment of the Nuremberg Laws on September 15, 1935: "The only way to prevent outbreaks of severe and uncontrolled defensive activities by the unruly populace is to solve the problem by legal means. In doing so, the government of the German Reich is guided by the thought that it may be possible, by means of a one-time secular solution, to create a foundation upon which the German people will be able to adopt a tolerable attitude towards the Jews. If this hope is not realized, and Jewish troublemaking in Germany and other countries continues, the situation will be reassessed. . . ."

The threat is buried in the last sentence, and is similar to couched threats contained in speeches made by Hitler on the occasions of the revocation of the Treaty of Versailles and the occupations and annexations which preceded the war. On more than one occasion, Hitler claimed that upon completion of the annexation or occupation, he would have no further demands and that the Reich would be satisfied. However, if one element or another were to continue its hostile activity, the Reich would not able to remain silent and the situation would be reassessed. Hitler expressed the opinion that treaties signed in the international arena should not be taken seriously and that promises made for internal purposes should certainly not be taken seriously. Moreover, the laws themselves did not contain any provision giving the Jews any rights (apart from the fact that on German national holidays the Jews would be forbidden to display German flags, but would be permitted to display their own colors). The talk of "tolerable relations" was intended, at best, to sweeten the pill.

In 1936, when the international Olympic games were held in

Berlin, Hitler made an effort to give the Reich the image of a normal, tolerant, strong and popular country (for which anti-Semitic writings were temporarily concealed and the anti-Jewish campaign was momentarily stilled). That same year, Hitler launched an aggressive political campaign which was targeted against the Jews. We find that every radical step and political achievement made by Hitler was accompanied by an attack against the Jews.

It is possible that the adoption of more severe anti-Jewish policies was not a calculated, integral part of general international policy, but rather that his successes against both internal opposition and international forces gave Hitler greater confidence and freed him from various constraints, enabling him to implement his plans against the Jews. During the initial years of the dictatorship, Hitler was faced by pressures from the radical faction of the Nazi party, which demanded the immediate implementation of far-reaching programs against the Jews. He claimed that he was in no need of encouragement in his anti-Jewish attitudes, but that he felt that the ordering of priorities and proper timing were essential.

In any event, of all the ideas put forth by Hitler and of all the principles he announced, he remained loyal and uncompromising toward only one—his anti-Semitic obsession. Hitler entered into a treaty with Poland which he later annuled and made statements of a clearly socialist nature in the Nazi party platform, but forgot those promises after reaching the conclusion that it was far more important to accept the support of German capitalists in promoting his program. When the time for military engagement drew closer, he befriended the Soviets, in spite of avowed opposition to Marxism and previously declared opposition to Bolshevism. Finally, he brought the Japanese into the Axis, even though they were racially inferior according to his ideology as expressed in *Mein Kampf*. It is only in his anti-Jewishness that there is no withdrawal or substantive change. Enmity toward the Jews and the argument that the Jews were responsible for the war, tragedies and losses suffered by Germany, were never changed or moderated. It is no surprise that rabid anti-Semitism and hatred of the Jews appear in *Mein Kampf*, as well as in the political testament he wrote before his suicide in 1945.

It was also during 1936 that preparations began for future military confrontations. In the autumn of that year, a four-year economic plan was formulated, and Herman Göring was appointed to oversee it. The implementation of this plan signaled a retreat from the line directed by H. Schacht to integrate Germany into the world economy. The Nazis had acted with relative moderation toward the Jews in order to build an economy which placed emphasis on economic independence and aspired to rearmament and preparation of the country for war. Once the economy was placed on a war footing, though, it was no longer necessary to consider the Jews as a factor in international economic relations. Thus an "Aryanization" campaign was launched. Businesses and organizations were taken away from the Jews and placed in "Aryan" hands. At first, the Jews were paid for their property, but later the expropriation of Jewish property was carried out using trickery and coercion. Large, respectable companies such as Krupp, Thyssen and I. G. Farben also took part in the theft of Jewish property and competed with each other for their share of the spoils.

In the propaganda, anti-Jewish legislation, and the process of removal of Jews from all areas of life, a distinction must be made between two contrasting attitudes. The bureaucracy was interested in carrying out anti-Jewish policy through the institution of legal measures, without resorting to violence. In certain government ministries, there were even officials who did not share the Nazi's attitude toward the Jews, and they assisted the Jews with advice and considerate handling of their affairs within the limits of their authority. On the other hand, the party publications, particularly *Der Stümer*, libeled the Jews, accusing them of scheming to dishonor German girls, with the intention of poisoning the blood of the "Aryan" race.

This type of sewer propaganda and venomous hatred was of great importance. *Der Stümer*, with its vile caricatures, had a large circulation and copies of the paper were displayed publicly at railroad stations and street corners. Streicher also published hate-filled books for children and teenagers. Indeed, this form of racist propaganda was common in the *Hitlerjugend*, the Nazi youth movement, and in schools. Jewish children, who continued to attend public schools, suffered humiliation and were forced to attend classes in which students were lectured on the master race and the inferiority of the Jews.

In 1938 there was, to a certain extent, a merging of the two attitudes—the official attitude adopted by the authorities and the brutal anti-Semitism of the masses. The year 1938 was considered to be a turning point, a bold leap forward in the course of the Nazi Reich toward fulfillment of its dreams. It was the year of the *Anschluss*, the annexation of Austria to the Reich, and of the Munich conference, at which Hitler attained the status of world leader in dictating first the framework of the conference and then the fate of the European participants.

These Nazi victories had an effect on Jewish affairs. More anti-Jewish laws were passed in 1938 than during any previous year of Nazi rule. Some of the anti-Semitic decrees were political and economic in nature, while others were intended to humiliate and express the hatred of the masses. In 1938, the theft of the property of the Jews reached a new height. Jewish communities were deprived of their officially recognized organizations and institutions and of their benefits, and synagogues were burned to the ground. Jewish passports were imprinted with the letter "J." All Jewish males were ordered to add the name "Israel" to their names, and all females "Sarah." Finally, after Poland questioned the citizenship of Jewish holders of Polish passports living in Germany, the mass deportation of Polish Jews began, which led to bloody pogroms and unrestrained theft.

A Jewish-owned store in Berlin destroyed by rioters on *Kristallnacht*.

The best-known event of 1938 was the pogrom known as *Kristallnacht* (Night of Broken Glass), in November of that year. A young Jewish man by the name of Hershel Grynszpan, the son of deportees living in France, shot an officer of the German embassy in Paris, who later died of his injuries. In retaliation, Goebbels, with Hitler's blessing, organized a pogrom. In the pogrom, which was carried out on the night of November 9th, 91 Jews were murdered, 191 synagogues were burned or destroyed, 7,500 stores were looted, and 30,000 Jews were thrown into concentration camps, from which only those who could prove that they intended to leave the Reich immediately were released.

Kristallnacht was a turning point in the history of the Jews in Nazi Germany before the outbreak of the war. In the wake of the murders and thefts of that night, the Jews were required to pay a quarter of their total assets as a tax. All Jewish organizations and associations not related to the emigration of Jews representation underwent a process of reorganization which in practice made them forerunners of the *Judenraten* (the Jewish Councils) which operated during the war. As a result, the Jews' desire to leave Germany grew considerably. However, it was at this stage that emigration became most difficult, and asylum became increasingly hard to find. The efforts made following the Evian Conference to find a broad-scale solution to the emigration of the Jews proceeded slowly, and no results of any substance were achieved.

THE REFUGEE QUESTION AND EMIGRATION FROM GERMANY

The Jews who fled Germany in 1933 turned to the neighboring countries, particularly France. They were not given a friendly welcome and were treated as undesirable. These Jews were not permitted to work, and many were classified as illegal aliens to be removed from the country as soon as possible. It should be borne in mind that Jewish emigration began during a period of severe economic depression and unemployment, and the additional people seeking employment understandably caused fear. This in turn led to severe opposition, such as that expressed by physicians in England, who protested the arrival of Jewish doctors as potential rivals. In addition, the countries the Jews turned to for refuge were also acting out of a desire to avoid conflict with Nazi Germany, and support of refugees, particularly emigrés who fled Germany because of political persecution, was seen as a hostile act against Germany.

It is important to note that during the thirties, anti-Semitism spread and became very strong in Europe. Only a few abhorred Nazism because of its racist, anti-Semitic nature and its anti-Jewish policies. Others, including many in Poland, Hungary, Romania and other East European countries, adopted open, vociferous anti-Semitic attitudes, which were guided by Nazi associates and propaganda spread by Nazi Germany in those countries. In some countries, radical anti-Semitic circles interpreted the anti-Jewish legislation and methodical anti-Semitic campaign in Germany as a suitable model for imitation, as well as proof that the methods introduced by the Nazis against the Jews were no longer reactionary or despised, but an effective means of persuading the "unnecessary" Jews to leave.

There is no doubt that the deepening of anti-Semitism, the tendency to follow the example of the Nazi campaign in Germany, and the attitude that the matter of the German Jews was an internal German affair contributed to the closing of the doors to immigration in many European countries, including France and Switzerland. The desire to emigrate was frustrated by the restrictive policy and severe limitations on immigration to the United States. It may well be that the quota system introduced by the United States after the First World War was the result of internal developments, and was not invented in order to block immigration from Germany. In practice, however, the quota system had this effect and, in addition to strong anti-immigration sentiment which prevented the amendment of legislation on this subject, there were also anti-Semitic and pro-German opinions and forces which worked toward preventing the immigration of the Jews. The closure of the United States had an effect on Canada, the Latin American countries and Australia as well. Entrance to Palestine was also severely restricted, according to the British government's laws, particularly in view of the Arab anti-Jewish disturbances which began in 1936. Thus the Jews of Germany were trapped, and although there was still some degree of understanding with regard to Jews living in the Third Reich and some effort was made to help them leave, for the Jews of Eastern Europe, such as the Jews of Poland, who were to be the main victims of Nazi oppression and genocide, the door was almost completely closed.

Immediately after Hitler came to power, German emigré leaders of the Jewish settlement in Palestine, as well as German Zionist activists, had begun to make plans for the mass emigration of the Jews of Germany to Palestine. This exist involved the forfeiture, at least in part, of Jewish money and property as a condition for obtaining entry visas, at the time when German laws forbade the taking of currency out of Germany.

In order to implement the arrangement, the Palestinian delegates and German Zionists entered into negotiations with official representatives of the Reich and came to an understanding known as the "Transfer Plan." According to the plan, the authorities permitted Jews leaving for Palestine to take with them the amount necessary for obtaining entry visas as capitalists. They also agreed to trade part of their property for goods and materials which would be sent to Palestine, so that their owners could then sell them and use the proceeds.

The agreement, which encouraged many to emigrate to Palestine and helped them in practical terms to save part of their property, was the subject of bitter debate in Palestine and among Jews around the world. Many objected to representatives from Palestine negotiating with the Nazis, and many in the Diaspora railed against the fact that while world Jewry had declared an economic boycott of Germany, Jews from Palestine were importing German goods and violating the terms of the boycott. This argument is a practical example of the severe dilemma faced by Jews who wished to promote emigration from Germany, activity which required that negotiations be conducted with the Nazi authorities and even that the terms they dictated be accepted. In total, over 50,000 Jews emigrated from Germany to Palestine within the framework of the "Fifth Aliya" or the "New Aliya," which brought with it businessmen, outstanding professionals in a range of fields, pioneers who were "rich" people according to the standards of Palestine. In 1936, when the "disturbances" began, the wave of emigration slowed, and with it the chances for salvation in this manner.

The problem of emigration and the refugees became an international problem after the annexation of Austria to the German Reich and after Adolf Eichmann was appointed to oversee Jewish affairs in Austria and began to use arrests and deportations to force Jews to emigrate. Moved by the reports and pleas coming from Germany and Austria, in the spring of 1938 U.S. President Franklin D. Roosevelt called for an international conference in order to find a solution for the refugee problem. The United States, which had been granting asylum to persecuted masses fleeing from Eastern Europe since the last quarter of the nineteenth century, had severely limited its immigration policy after World War I, setting quotas which drastically limited the numbers allowed to enter its territories.

In view of the situation in Germany, there were increasing demands that the restrictive laws be changed, or that an exception to the law be made in order to help Jews in distress, liberals, and leftists, who were helpless under Nazi oppression. All requests met with adamant refusal. The invitation to the international conference held at Roosevelt's initiative also stated that the parties which were invited would not be asked to amend existing laws relating to immigration. This statement sealed the fate of the conference in advance. Indeed, the conference, which was held July 6–15, 1938, at Evian-les-Bains, a French vacation resort on Lake Geneva, and in which delegates from 32 countries participated, end in failure. Most countries represented at the Evian Conference claimed that they were unable to absorb large numbers of unwanted refugees. The South American countries, which the United States had expected would become suitable destinations for the refugees, declared one after the other, with the exception of the Dominican Republic, that they were unable to take in refugees in large numbers. The excuses were varied. Britain apparently agreed to participate in the conference on the condition that no demands be made of it to increase quotas of refugees to Palestine.

The world-wide depression impaired the capacity of the countries which participated in the conference to absorb refugees, and deterred them from accepting people who would compete for the few existing jobs. However, it is difficult to avoid feeling the sting of blatant anti-Semitism in the various excuses. Arthur Morse, author of the book *While Six Million Died*, describes the responses of the various countries at Evian as follows:

> Australia, with vast, unpopulated areas, announced: "As we have no real racial problem, we are not desirous of importing one." New Zealand was unwilling to lift its restrictions. The British colonial empire, reported Sir John Shuckburgh, contained no territory suitable to the large-scale settlement of Jewish refugees. Canada wanted agricultural migrants and none others. The same was true of Colombia, Uruguay and Venezuela.
>
> Peru was particularly opposed to the immigration of doctors and lawyers lest such an intellectual proletariat upset the unbridled power of its upper class. The Peruvian delegate pointedly remarked

that the United States had given his country an example of "caution and wisdom" by its own immigration restrictions.

France, whose population already included two hundred thousand refugees and three million aliens, stressed that it had reached its saturation point.

Nicaragua, Honduras, Costa Rica and Panama issued a joint statement saying that they could accept no "traders or intellectuals." Argentina, with a population one-tenth that of the United States, reported that it had welcomed almost as many refugees as the United States and hence could not be counted on for large-scale immigration.

The Netherlands and Denmark reflected their traditional humanitarianism. Though Holland had already accepted twenty-five thousand Jewish refugees, it offered itself as a country of temporary sojourn. Denmark, so densely populated that its own citizens were forced to emigrate, had already taken in a disproportionately large number of German exiles. Within its narrow limits, it would continue to do so.

And the United States, the nation at whose initiative the conference had convened, what would it offer? The answer was soon in coming. The United States, with its tradition of asylum, its vast land mass and its unlimited resources, agreed, for the first time, to accept its full, legal quota of 27,370 immigrants annually from Germany and Austria. That was the major American concession made at Evian.

Until October, 1941, the Nazis generally viewed emigration from Germany as the "solution" to the Jewish problem. The Germans were prepared to allow the Jews to leave, and even encouraged them to do so, but took most of their belongings from them. Of course, the theft of their property acted as a brake and slowed emigration. Hitler learned the lesson of Evian well and the Nazi propaganda machine trumpeted the fact that nobody wanted to accept Jews. According to them, criticism of German policies regarding the Jews merely served the interests of the anti-Nazi countries, but when the democratic countries were asked to take action and allow the Jews to enter, they balked and seemed to have lost their pity and sensitivity.

The Evian conference not only failed to assist Jewish emigration in practical terms, but revealed to the world the desperation of their situation. It was with good reason that Chaim Weizmann complained that the world during that era was divided into two camps: those who wanted to deport the Jews and those who did not want to take them in. The only practical outcome of the Evian conference was the establishment of a new international committee charged with finding destinations for refugees and conducting negotiations with Nazi Germany over the terms of large-scale emigration. The sought-after destinations were never found, and the negotiations, after going through several stages, were finally terminated by the War.

In total, approximately one-half of the Jews of Germany and about two-thirds of those of Austria left the Reich, as well as some 30,000 Jews from the Protectorate, until emigration was banned in October, 1941, and outright murder began. Many of those who left were, in the end, not spared, because they had sought shelter in neighboring countries, such as France, Belgium and Holland. These countries were soon occupied by the Nazis, and the Jews who had fled to them were sent to the death camps to the east.

Could more have been saved? The answer is obviously yes—with a little more goodwill and true readiness on the part of all parties involved, although the various countries had no way of knowing of the horrors the Nazis had in store for the Jews. Moreover, during the pre war years, Jewish leaders in Poland and Romania had complained that they were being discriminated against because most efforts for finding places of refuge were being made on behalf of the Jews of the Third Reich. The logical answer in those days was that the Jews of the Reich were in immediate danger and should be attended to first. (Today, viewing the events with the wisdom of hindsight, the question arises as to whether this policy was correct.) On the other hand, some world Jewish leaders believed that the Jews should *not* leave Germany, or in any case that chaotic flight from Germany should not be permitted, lest other anti-Semitic countries conclude that they could force the Jews to leave by means of persecution and terror. These leaders were of course mistaken, but one cannot ignore the hopelessness of the situation in which they also found themselves. With rabid hatred directed at them at home, but no place of refuge to which to flee, the Jews of Germany and Eastern Europe were trapped in a hopeless, desperate, tragic situation.

JEWS UNDER NAZI RULE
BEFORE THE WAR: SUMMARY

Were Germany's Jews passive and obedient under Nazi rule, and did they accept it without resistance?

A survey of the position of the Jews in Germany raises the questions: Why did the Jews not guess what was awaiting them; Why were their behavior and deeds so naive and characterized by unawareness of the danger about to beset them? These questions are, of course, asked by people who know the end of the tragedy and who survey it with hindsight. The Jews were not alone in failing to fathom the danger of Nazism. We may assume that, were the threat of the Nazi secret program widely known among the world's nations and their leaders, the Polish leader Pilsudski would not have signed his treaty with Hitler at the beginning of 1934, Chamberlain and Deladier would not have gone to Munich, and Stalin perhaps would not have sanctioned the Molotov-Ribbentrop agreement of August 1939. Furthermore, if they had guessed where it all would end, there is no doubt that Mussolini would not have formed the "iron alliance" with Hitler, and the German people would not have followed its leader with yearning souls and closed eyes. We should note that while the Nazis and their leader were successful and victorious, rebellion and opposition were very weak. Resistance to Nazism in Germany, which is written of and publicized much more than its small scale justifies, became a reality not as a result of injustice, the trampling of the law, and the murder of Jews and non-Jews, but from the impending defeat of Germany, when it became clear that Nazism was dragging the German people into the abyss.

Under these circumstances, what could the Jews have known or done? They could not prophesy the Holocaust because it was barbaric and contrary to the patterns of thought, experience, and ethics of the Western world. There had never been a Holocaust, a methodical and determined murder of a people as an expression of ideology, and no sane man could have seriously considered that something of this sort would happen. The truth is that the policy of genocide was not framed by the Nazis until 1941, under circumstances we will describe below.

We sometimes encounter Jeremiahs who made use of terms like *Ausrottung* (expulsion) and *Vermichtung* (destruction). Some grasp at these words and argue: "This person sensed what was coming and sounded a warning." But in fact, if we examine well the context of these predictions, we see that they did not mean the destruction of Auschwitz and Treblinka, but rather the confiscation of property, revocation of civil and human rights, and the prohibition of work and livelihood of Jews because they were Jews.

Even before Hitler rose to power, the Jews had harnessed themselves to the struggle for democracy. It would not be an exaggeration to say that the Jews were among the Weimar Republic's most loyal defenders even in the days when it had few defenders in Germany. Jews wrote of and described Nazism and its leaders. They exposed its lies and the evil and madness in its outward accusations and its inward pride. There may have been a sort of incurable optimism in the reasoning that the evil could be exorcised and the demogogic threat exposed through rational persuasion, or that it was possible, as they said, to kill Hitler with sarcasm, fluency, and wisdom. Realty proved the limited power of the wise. Jews of the German middle class, far from the Social Democrats in their social standing and views, gave that party their votes because they saw it as the last defender of the republic.

Arnold Paucker, author of the book *The Jewish Defense Struggle* during the Weimar Republic, wrote:

> The visits of the *Syndicus* of the CV [the initials of the central association of German Jewry, the largest organization protecting Jewish civil rights], Dr. Alfred Wiener, to industry leaders in the fall of 1932, were among the many attempts to influence thinkers of right-wing orientation. Wiener was armed with CV documents and a letter of recommendation from the banker Max Warburg. They were by no means secret visits, and were reported at the time in the Jewish press, though not in detail.
>
> At that time the CV did not see as hopeless the attempt to explain to industrialists who supported the Nazis "for the good of the economy" the true character of the Nazi party and warn them of the results of putting the government in the hands of political criminals. Hitler had met with the industrialists a few weeks previously, and they had formally expressed their reservations about the Nazis' violence and economic plans. The representative of the Jewish organization therefore believed that he had succeeded in having some influence and hoped that, at least for a while, the strongmen of the right would not allow things to go too far.

Organized Jewish response took different forms. The "Representative Council of German Jewry" was formed in September, 1933, headed by Rabbi Leo Baeck. This was a national umbrella organization which, for the first time in German Jewish history, gathered all the communal and political organizations and factions into a representative and united body. Prior to this, in April, 1933, the "Central Committee for Aid and Rehabilitation" was established. This body provided economic protection and material aid to German Jews. After the boycott laws were decreed on April 1, 1933, and Jews were expelled from public positions in culture and education, many Jewish families were left without an income. The Committee helped them to learn new professions and find new jobs. Jews who left villages and small towns, feeling that a ring of hostility and isolation was tightening around them, came to the big cities, and were helped to find housing and work. The Jewish school system grew and absorbed Jewish children who had left or been expelled from public schools. A cultural and artistic project was established, giving employment to many idle artists. Study and sport clubs for youth and adults were founded in many communities. The principal purpose of this wide-ranging activity was to give the Jews a feeling of belonging and security, and to return them to Jewish heritage and given them the desire to develop a greater understanding of their Judaism.

The Zionist movement developed activities which won over many people. Thousands of young people joined the *HeHalutz* and *HeHalutz HaDati* movements, which trained them for agricultural work and prepared them for life in Palestine. The Youth Aliya Institute was established during the same period and it, together with the settlement movements, saw to the emigration of young people and children to Palestine and their absorption there.

During the early part of Nazi rule, German Jews thought that they would be allowed a sort of internal autonomy with room for maneuver, so long as the Jewish framework was separate from the German. And in fact, while the different German political parties were outlawed and dispersed, the Jews were allowed to remain active in their own political frameworks. The internal Jewish press dared to write freely and print information that the German press would not have thought of publishing.

The Jews emphasized the importance of preserving self-respect, of strengthening the Jewish identity of those far from Judaism, and of self-organization. On April 4, 1933, in the face of the boycott, Robert Weltsch, editor of the Zionist newspaper *Judische Rundschau*, published an article which caused many reverberations: "Wear the Yellow Star with Pride." He wrote, among other things:

> Judaism under attack must reach self-consciousness. Even in these days of greatest emotion, when the stormiest sentiments shake our hearts in the face of the unprecedented economic excommunication

of the entire Jewish population of a great cultured state, we must preserve one thing first and foremost: our judgment. Even though we are at a loss in the face of current events, we must never despair and we must report to ourselves without any self-delusion. In these days we must recommend that the work that was the cradle of Zionism, *The Jewish State* by Theodor Herzl, be distributed in thousands of copies among Jews and non-Jews. . . .

Today they accuse us of betraying the German people: the National Socialist press calls us 'enemies of the nation' and we are helpless when confronted with this charge. *It is not true that the Jews have betrayed Germany. If we have betrayed anything, it is ourselves, our Judaism.*

Because Jews did not bear their Judaism with pride towards the outside world, because they avoided the Jewish problem, they became partners in the degradation of Judaism. . . .

The organizers of the boycott mandated posting signs on boycotted stores showing "a yellow star on a black background." This is a symbol of tremendous meaning. This order was meant to condemn and humiliate, but we accept it of our own volition and turn it into a sign of honor.

Jüdische Rundschau, no. 27, 4.4.1933

JÜDISCHE RUNDSCHAU

Tragt ihn mit Stolz, den gelben Fleck!

"שאוהו בגאון, את הטלאי הצהוב", מאמרו של רוברט ולטש בביטאון הציוני

4 באפריל 1933 , *Jüdische Rundschau*

"Wear the Yellow Star with Pride," by Robert Weltsch, in *Judische Rundschau.*

The various Jewish organizations gave priority to helping young people emigrate. The preference given to young people was not the result of the possibility that emigration would be limited. It was felt that young people were more sensitive to humiliation and more exposed to feelings of inequality and loss of identity within Germany. True, organized Judaism, and even certain Zionist circles within it, spoke against surrendering and abandoning Germany. Even some Zionist leaders outside Germany took the same position. They feared that if all Jews were to surrender to oppression and leave Germany, it would serve as an example to anti-Semites in Eastern European countries. If a campaign of oppression were to begin, aimed at forcing Jews to emigrate (and radical-fascist groups in Poland supported such a policy), it would be necessary to find immediate refuge for millions of Jews, a refuge which did not exist anywhere in the world. The most determined reaction against Germany organized by the Jews of the world was an economic boycott of that country. The World Jewish Congress decreed the boycott, and organizations were established to supervise it in, among other places, the United States and Poland.

Even in the planning of the boycott there were disagreements and problems which would continue to accompany the Jewish struggle and eventually paralyze it. The serious contradiction between the "transfer" agreement and the boycott was one problem. German Jews feared the boycott as anti-German activity on an international scale, putting them in a position of being responsible and liable for punishment. In Poland the authorities were tolerant and even somewhat encouraging to the Jewish boycott, but soon, as relations with Nazi Germany became closer, it was prohibited. A debate over the boycott was conducted in the United States among Jews and in the general public. A few Jewish public figures argued that the boycott could boomerang and lead to boycotts in America itself. Parts of the Zionist movement were afraid to support the boycott publicly lest it lead to the prohibition of the widespread Zionist activity in Germany. Without a doubt, an organized and comprehensive boycott would have attacked the Nazi state in a soft spot—the rehabilitation of the economy and the elimination of unemployment. Could such an organized boycott have been effective enough to bring the Nazi regime to its knees or topple it? It is hard to answer such hypothetical questions. In any case, it is clear that tightening the boycott would have led to harsher conditions for Jews.

The irony is that the Nazis declared that the Jews were a secret world power of great strength, but the Jews at that time were actually weak and helpless as a nation and an ethnic group, and the governments of enlightened countries and organized society abandoned them completely.

THE WAR AND THE JEWS OF POLAND—1939–1941

Not all the Jews of Poland fell into the clutches of the Nazis when the war began on September 1, 1939. According to an agreement between Germany and the Soviet Union, signed in the last week of August, 1939, and as a result of the secret treaty between the two new allies to divided Poland between them, the Soviet Union seized over forty percent of the area of eastern Poland, which had a large Jewish population. Many Jews (300,000, according to some estimates) fled from areas occupied by Germany to the Russian zone. The Germans saw in the Jews of the occupied zone the personification of the typical physical, procreative, and moral characteristics of the Jews. The German occupied zone was divided into several districts, the main district being the western region, which was annexed to the German Reich, and included the city of Lodz, the second largest city in Poland and the largest Jewish center outside of Warsaw, as well as Upper Silesia, which had a large Jewish population. Central Poland became a kind of annexed zone, which the Germans called the "General Government of the Occupied Polish Territories," and later simply the *General gouvernement*. This area was also controlled by the Germans, and the senior bureaucracy consisted of veteran, fanatical Nazis, whose appointment to these positions was interpreted as a reward for loyal service to the party. The administration was headed by a Governor General, Dr. Hans Frank, a lawyer and a member of the Nazi leadership.

The Nazis in Poland introduced a regime of oppression of the Jews which far exceeded anything they had done previously in Germany or Austria. The Jews of Poland were a prime target, and because the Poles had been deprived of governmental authority at all levels, there was no need to request their assent or consider their views about the Jews. The war freed the Nazis from their last constraints, which had required them to heed the opinions of the rest of the world.

A series of decrees and humiliating measures were imposed on the Jews. In November, 1939, Jews in the *General gouvernement*, both males and females aged 10 and over, were forced to wear a white arm band with a Star of David on their upper sleeves. (The yellow Star of David was not required in Germany until September 1941.) Among other restrictions, Jews were forbidden to travel by train, change housing without permission, open schools, or pray in public.

However, the most tangible and harmful decrees were those relating to finances, or ways of making a living and acquiring the necessities of life. The Germans immediately announced that they would confiscate all businesses or factories owned by people who were absent (i.e., those who had fled), and any unsuccessful business or factory. This rule applied to all Poles. However, in the case of Jewish businesses, *all* were classified as unsuccessful and were consequently confiscated and placed in the hands of trustees.

At a later stage, Jews were required to register their property and were permitted to keep only their clothes and utensils for personal use. Jewish bank accounts were frozen, and Jews were permitted only to make weekly withdrawals of sums which barely sufficed for subsistence. Each Jew was permitted to hold the sum of only 2,000—2,500 Zlotys (approximately $25).

The construction of the Warsaw Ghetto wall, October, 1940.

The only work that Jews were permitted to do was slave labor for the Germans. The hunting of Jews in the streets began during the very first days of the occupation. The captives were forced to carry loads, clear the ruins of bombed buildings, clear snow from the streets or clean the barracks of the German soldiers. One of the first decrees published by the Governor General in November, 1939, imposed upon the Jews, the obligation of working for the Germans. Responsibility for carrying out the decree was placed in the hands of the police and the SS. The orders issued by the SS Command and the police stated that the Jews were to work for two years as an "educational measure," and that if that period proved insufficient, it would be extended when it expired. On the basis of these orders, all Jewish males aged 14 to 60 were to work for the Germans for a number of days every month. Over the course of time, Jews were taken to work camps, and thousands of youths were sent to build roads, dig ditches and drain swamps. A high proportion of the deportees died from exhaustion, hunger, and poor sanitary conditions. The Jews were not paid anything for their labor. In rare cases, the *Judenrat*, or Jewish Council, was required to pay the workers out of the taxes they collected from Jews, but the paltry wages were not enough to survive on.

As time passed, the German rulers became aware of the fact that most Polish Jews were skilled workers in various fields, whose labor could be exploited for military purposes. The Jewish authorities also wished to employ the Jews in professional fields, assuming that they would thereby succeed in saving as many as possible from deportation to labor camps, and hoping to refute the Nazi claims that the Jews were parasites. Above all, in consideration of such efficient labor, the Nazis would be forced to provide for the essential needs of the laborers and their families. Later in the Nazi campaign, the *Judenraten* grasped at the hope that intensive skilled labor would enable all or part of the Jewish population to be spared deportation to the death camps.

During the early stages of the occupation of central Poland, from September, 1939, to the spring of 1942, Jewish worries and struggles were centered on the difficult task of existence, on withstanding the hunger, deprivation, and infectious diseases which withered and wearied both body and soul. The policy adopted by the Germans in regard to the Jews was to leave them to their fate, with complete indifference and disregard for human life. The struggle to exist required the enlistment of all mental faculties.

How did the Jews fight for their lives, and in what ways was the indomitable will to live which permeated the Jews of the ghettos expressed? It appears that the most common solution was disobedience, non-acceptance of the decrees, and the evolution of clandestine operations in order to stay alive.

Aharon Kaplan, a Jewish teacher who was imprisoned in the Warsaw Ghetto—the largest of all ghettos, which for a long period numbered from 400,000 to 450,000 residents—wrote in his diary in April, 1940:

> God Almighty! How do you feed all these people? They are forbidden to pursue any business or profession. . . Everything is firmly shut, everything broken and in ruins, all sources have been blocked, and our lives are filled with humiliation and shame, since there are streets where the sidewalks on the left or right side are out of bounds to Jews, with a sign in oversized lettering attesting to that fact. Yet in spite of everything, the masses live, the masses are awake, the masses treat the decrees of the mighty occupier like dirt and do all within their power to outwit them, to delude the enemy, doing everything in secret, and the Lord provides their needs.

Elsewhere in his diary, as early as 1939, Kaplan gave a practical example of the methods of "outwitting" and disobeying the decrees of the enemy:

> . . . an edict was pronounced forbidding any single Jewish household from holding more than 2,000 Zlotys. Any amount in excess of this sum must be deposited in a bank, and if he needs money he is given no more than 250 Zlotys per week. The sincere Jews of Germany would no doubt have stood in line on the very next day to fulfill the bidding of the Führer. But the Jews of Poland refused! They did not deposit a penny. No Jew has a penny more than 2,000 Zlotys! All these idiotic decrees, which are indicative of a low level of intelligence and unbridled sadism, are jokes to the Jews of Poland.

The Jewish response was not limited to violating the prohibitions and disobeying orders. The initiative and adamant decision to fight was focused on the search for and use of various means for forbidden work and business activity. In other ghettos, such as Lodz, the Jews were completely cut off from the outside world. That was in fact the objective of establishing the ghettos—to isolate the Jews and keep them completely separate from the surrounding Poles and other peoples. The ghettos were not all built at the same time, but by the end of 1940 there were ghettos in many Polish cities with Jewish residents.

The *Judenraten* had a strong effect on the economy of the ghettos and the struggle to exist. The *Judenraten* were established at the very beginning of the occupation in all cities and towns with Jewish residents. The intentions of the Germans in establishing them were clear and unequivocal: to appoint a responsible administrative body for the Jews which would be obliged to accept and implement all the decrees and demands of the Nazi rulers. To the Jews, the structure and operation of the *Judenraten* were more complex. Many Jews who became members or leaders of the *Judenraten* did so in response to requests or pressures from the Jews themselves. Many had also been involved in Jewish public life before the war, and joined the *Judenraten* in order to continue to serve the public in times of hardship.

Thus the *Judenrat* as an institution was caught between two evils. Changes took place over time in these institutions and in their structure. The weaknesses and, as time went by, the estrangement and severe distortions apparent in the *Judenraten* were the result of the conflict between the opposing interests. There were also a few *Judenrat* heads who ruled harshly—who, drunk with the power given to them, began to believe that they were able to fulfill a historic mission if they could find some way of communicating with the Germans and fulfilling their wishes. One example is the head of the *Judenrat* in Lodz, Mordecai Chaim Rumkovski, who adopted a policy of discipline, meticulous adherence to the rulers' orders, and severity towards the Jews. The approach adopted by Rumkovski was the reason, or one of the reasons, for the tight seal around the Lodz Ghetto. In most ghettos, including the Warsaw Ghetto, the *Judenraten* acted differently. The head of the Warsaw Ghetto, Adam Czerniakow, who committed suicide when the Nazis demanded that he deliver Jews for deportation, attempted to obey those decrees which were inescapable, while not intervening in the internal affairs of the Jews so long as it was not essential.

In spite of the prohibition against contact with the outside world, the isolation of the ghettos was not complete. Clandestine contacts were maintained by forbidden means. Underground organizations flourished in many ghettos. Workshops functioned, and Jews invented clever schemes to convert wastes into raw materials from which a range of tools and materials could be made. Used clothing, underwear and bedding sold by the penniless ghetto residents were dyed in clandestine workshops and worked into new products. Parts of crashed aircraft and smuggled scrap metal were used to make aluminum utensils and cooking pots, and the covers of old accounting ledgers were used to make suitcases. Items such as they daily necessities, clothes, and even toys were smuggled from the ghetto to Poles on the "other side" in exchange for food. But the Poles were not the only beneficiaries of the clandestine labors of Jews. The German army also discovered that if it wanted to obtain urgently needed equipment—beds, furs, shoes, knapsacks or brushes—the ghetto had the capacity to quickly and efficiently supply them. Thus the army began to circumvent official institutions and authorities, prohibitions and bans, and approached Jews directly in order to acquire their needs illegally. Thus, according to one historian, "Primitive flour mills and factories producing oil, soap, knitted goods and socks, leatherware, chemicals, and pharmaceuticals functioned in the ghetto in secret, using substitutes for rubber and wood to manufacture synthetic soles, buttons and stationery, etc."

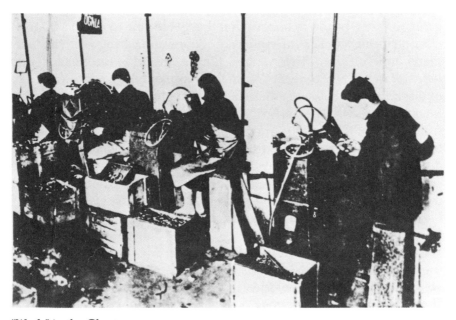

"Work" in the Ghetto.

In the east, immediately after the attack against the Soviet Union in the summer of 1941, when the mass murder of Jews began, the manufacturing activities in those places were pointed to in an attempt to prove to the Germans that in terms of their own interests, it was not worthwhile to eliminate the Jews, and that their genocide meant killing the goose that laid the golden eggs.

Clandestine manufacturing was to have provided the Jews with means for bartering for food, while work in factories and workshops under the supervision of the *Judenraten* and the Germans was to have protected the Jews and provided them with the minimum of food necessary for survival. All food had to be brought in from outside the ghettos. It was not possible to manufacture substitutes for food, or to create something from nothing, and the attempts to grow vegetables in the vacant parcels of land in the ghettos were but a drop in the ocean of hunger and want.

The Germans handed out food vouchers to the entire population, but official rationing was also conducted according to racist principles. Germans were given a relatively varied diet of 2,613 calories per day and Poles were given food which provided 669 calories per day, while the meager allotment of the Jews provided a mere 188 calories per day. Thus those who subsisted only on the official rations were doomed to a quick death from hunger and malnutrition. The Jews also had to pay for their meager rations, and the poorest Jews, mainly refugees who wandered from place to place, found it difficult to accumulate the few pennies necessary to redeem ration coupons.

The main food supply which supported ghetto internees was smuggled to the ghettos from the outside. Smuggling, particularly in Warsaw, went on day and night, over roofs and through cellars, walls, and the barbed wire surrounding the ghettos. There were many professional smugglers who not only lived off their pursuit, but became wealthy from the business of transferring food from the Polish side and smuggling valuable family heirlooms out of the ghetto in exchange. There were also many "small time" smugglers, people who worked for the Germans outside the ghetto and, upon returning to their homes inside the ghetto, brought with them—hidden on their persons—a little bread and vital food items which were enough for their family and perhaps a neighbor. Women and children would leave the ghetto through tunnels or secret passages to bring food for the survival of their near and dear ones.

Smuggling food and other necessities into the Warsaw Ghetto.

Those who have chronicled the history of the Warsaw Ghetto say that there was not a single day without some form of smuggling from the very first day of the ghetto's existence until its destruction. Unfortunately, it seems that there was also barely a day that smuggling did not extract a heavy price in victims. People were killed, wounded, and beaten. The true heroes of the smuggling episodes were the young children who often begged for food among the Poles and went without food themselves in order to bring nourishment to younger brothers and sisters. Every day, the bodies of children clothed in rags who had paid with their lives for wanting to live could be seen near the ghetto walls. A public figure in the Warsaw Ghetto said that after the war a monument would have to be erected in the heart of the former ghetto, to be dedicated to the nameless young child—the smuggler of the Warsaw Ghetto.

The clandestine production and smuggling activities were unable to satisfy the shortage or eliminate the hunger. Some 100,000 people died mostly of hunger and disease from the day the Warsaw Ghetto was established until its liquidation. The truth is that alongside the dead and hungry in the streets of the Warsaw Ghetto were restaurants and businesses where premium food and drinks were served, with gay entertainment. Not many had the means and the insensitivity to indulge themselves, but there were such people, and their existence was all the more strange against the background of the terrible hunger and deprivation surrounding them.

Starving children in the streets of the Warsaw Ghetto.

It may be that this phenomenon, which was minor in the ghetto landscape, was somehow, paradoxically, only natural under the circumstances prevailing in the ghettos. In a place where hunger and death abounded, and everyone was occupied with the endless fight for survival, one might have expected fighting to break out between all, that the weak would be trampled, that crime and violence would rage and that the strong minority would dominate the helpless masses. Some say that this was actually what the Nazis had hoped for, to destroy man's basic humanity, his belief in the Creator of man and mercy on earth, human solidarity and the right to life of every human being.

Did this kind of moral sterility and dehumanization take place in the ghetto? The answer is a definite no! The ghetto was indeed a focus of hunger, deprivation and death, but the Nazis failed to extinguish the flame of humanity from the dark alleys and dying bodies. The Jewish family continued to exist and maintain to the full the invincible bonds which had been formed over many generations. In the compact family structure, efforts were at all times channelled to supporting the weakest and most needy. When a father was no longer able to function or disappeared from the family and ceased to be the natural provider, it was the mother or one of the children, often the very young, who shouldered the burden. Caring for the family was the task which gave them energy and the will to live.

There was hardly any crime in the ghettos, at least no serious crime. In the Warsaw Ghetto, only one single case of murder was recorded, which was the result of a squabble between smuggling partners. In the Lodz Ghetto a man was tried for killing another man in a fight between criminals, but these seemed exceptional and out of place among ghetto residents. What this means is that even people who were hungry and whose heightened senses were focused on a single desire—to obtain food—did not sink to the extreme step of taking another's life. Although one case of cannibalism was recorded in the Warsaw Ghetto, it was an exceptional phenomenon and was perpetrated by a poor woman driven to insanity.

In the ghettos, the Jews became ever poorer. Whoever still had property would exchange it for vital food, but the capital remaining from the past slowly ran out and everyone knew that time, like the gold watches they had sold, was running out mercilessly. Under these conditions, it was to be expected that everyone would cling to their possessions like a lifeline, refusing to share with others. There indeed were such instances, but it was not the dominant trend in the ghettos. Not only did welfare and mutual assistance organizations continue to exist in the ghettos, but their activities even grew and expanded considerably. Free kitchens had a bowl of soup for the hungriest and a crust of bread for any needy child. In some ghettos, "house committees" were established. These committees—an original ghetto innovation—cared for the poorest of residents. In Warsaw, house committees formed a welfare organization, which later gave rise to many public activists. Buildings whose residents were relatively well off adopted poorer buildings and refugee hostels. From every large family event, and from every festive banquet in the ghetto, the celebrants tithed a share for the poor. Of course, in the larger ghettos, even organized activity and support of the poor were unable to put an end to hunger and death from starvation. In smaller places, however, this effort prevented deaths and provided the minimum necessary for each and every person.

It appears that, over time, in most ghettos a kind of permanent reality was formed. The weak and unprotected ceased to be, and manufacturing activities were bartered for goods which were distributed to a large percentage of the residents. It seemed that in spite of everything, the Nazis would not succeed in murdering the Jews by methods of internal warfare, or as one historian described it, a method of "indirect murder, murder without bloodshed."

A kind of everyday routine came into existence, an everyday struggle simply to exist, and many firmly believed that the majority would survive and live through the difficult times to pick up the threads of life anew in the future. Throughout the war, even when the Germans marched from one glorious victory to another, most Jews were steadfast in their belief that it would end with the downfall of the Nazis.

What was the source of their faith? It was in no way common throughout Europe. Among other nations, there was always a percentage of the population who were convinced that the Nazis would win the war and that their total victory was just a matter of time. These included people who saluted the Nazi victories and cooperated with the victors because of their shared ideology as well as others who opposed the Nazis but viewed their final victory as inevitable. There is no way of knowing if this invincible faith of the Jews stemmed from the belief that the Jews would survive only if the Nazis were vanquished, or because they were unable to imagine the possibility that all Jews would be wiped off the face of the earth. Others, perhaps even the majority of world Jewry at that time, were apparently reinforced by their profound belief that the world could never be turned into a wilderness with neither God nor man asserting himself.

The tragedy which befell mankind was a low point, a dark night in history which would soon pass, and which could in no way be the new order of things. This unshakable belief, which stemmed from deeply-held Jewish and humanistic values, did not waver even in the face of impressive victories like the fall of Paris and the advance of Nazi soldiers to the gates of Moscow, times when self-confidence was low and the progress of the war seemed to indicate that the Nazi version of the "new order" was taking root throughout Europe and threatened the entire world.

Ghetto Jews everywhere struggled hard and long to survive. We call this struggle "the sanctification of life." This term does not appear in any documentary material or diary of the Holocaust period, but was reported by Dr. Nathan Eck, a Holocaust survivor, who was also a member of the political underground in Polish ghettos. Eck writes in one of his books:

> We knew all too well, from the very beginning of the occupation, that the enemy planned to do away with us; it had declared so openly before the war began, and we knew that they were more than just empty words. We may not have imagined what was to come, that is, the mass murder. We thought that we would be subjected to living conditions in which it would be impossible to survive. We told ourselves that no other people would be able to survive under those conditions, but that we would, in spite of everything! . . . and the ghetto showed what it could so. Interest in lectures and talks was common among ghetto residents, and there was a concept called "sanctification of God's name." One felt in one's heart that something was about to happen and preparations were made to meet it bravely. Reports of massacres were received from several towns. That is when Rabbi Yitzchak Nisenbaum's words of wisdom began to circulate in the ghetto: This is the time for the sanctification of life and not for the sanctification of God's name by death. In past ages, our enemies wanted our souls, and Jews sacrificed their bodies to sanctify God's name. Now the enemy demands the bodies of us Jews, so we must protect them and save our lives. Indeed, thereafter the residents of the ghetto were overcome by a forceful will to live, drawing on unseen resources, the likes of which have never been seen in normal times.

Rabbi Yitzchak Nisenbaum was a leader of the religious Zionist movement and one of the few leaders of Polish Jewry who remained in that country instead of leaving with the flow of refugees before the outbreak of war or during the first few months of the occupation. Not much, however, is known about Rabbi Nisenbaum's deeds during the occupation and the underground, and Eck's words are a rare testimony to the man's public influence.

There is a significant difference between the meaning of "sanctification of God's name" and "sanctification of life." The commandment to sanctify God's name is one of the fundamental obligations of every Jew. The sanctification of God's name is not a phenomenon unique to Ashkenazic Jews, but is firmly rooted in Jewish tradition since the days of the Second Temple. Professor Ya'akov Katz has written: "They knew that their fate had been sealed in heaven. After that, they just accepted their fate, not because there was no way to escape, but because it was God's will, which could never be understood, nor its wisdom doubted, by mere mortals."

Although it is doubtful whether those sanctifying God's name themselves were able to fathom why they had been chosen for their fate, those who relate their deeds are free to do so. They felt that they were the chosen, that they were unique in their inner strength to withstand the tribulations, and thus they were duty-bound to atone for the sins of past generations and those who would follow them. They believed that the rewards for their sacrifice were in store for them in the world to come. The holy books relate that those sanctifying God's name do not feel any pain when dying and that the path to heaven is open to them. In previous times, many European Jews had chosen to take their own lives in states of communal ecstacy and spirituality. It reached the stage where the European religious leaders found it necessary to warn that sanctification of God's name was permissible only as a last resort, when there was no other option and all means of escape had been closed. In so doing, they wished to halt the excessive enthusiasm of those sanctifying God's name, who saw their death and martyrdom as a rare privilege.

The twentieth century was not a period which glorified the sanctification of God's name, not only because "in past ages, our enemies wanted our souls, and Jews sacrificed their bodies to sanctify God's name. Now the enemy demands the bodies of us Jews, so we must protect them." The truth is that the generation was different. The true, burning faith which had supported those who earlier had sanctified God's name no longer prevailed, and if it still existed it was not very common. There was even a trend among Jews in western and central Europe to abandon their religion, if that price would suffice to save them from the clutches of the Nazis and their allies. Thus, for example, in Hungary, when in 1938 and 1939 the Hungarians enacted anti-Jewish legislation restricting permission for the Jews to engage in certain professions in which they had a proportionately high representation, many thousands rushed to convert, since at that stage those who were not Jewish by religion were not bound by the regulations.

The meaning of the struggle for life, or the "sanctification of life," was that the enemy's decrees, which were designed to deprive the Jews of their means of livelihood, should not be obeyed and that the edicts depriving the Jews of their right to study, pray, or work as free men and to live in freedom should not be accepted. The obstinate fight by the Jews to protect these rights is worthy of the title of "sanctification of life." This concept encompassed the smuggling of food into the ghettos, and the development of clandestine factories.

The "sanctification of life" was expressed in the existence of Jewish educational institutions at the time that the Germans closed down the schools and declared that Jewish children did not need to study. Secret groups were established in the ghettos for study in various formats. Teachers gathered small groups of students, who continued to study according to their regular curriculum. The diaries of children which we now have express their enormous will to learn.

A children's choir in the Warsaw Ghetto.

The risks and efforts involved in studying during times of deprivation took the ghetto children to new worlds of knowledge, freedom, and creativity. The Germans banned the works of Jewish writers, and the very possession of books was a real danger to Jews, but this did not prevent mobile libraries from springing up in the ghettos. People continued to read books, which gave them hope and an insight into the world of freedom. The Nazis prohibited the Jews from listening to music written by German composers, but orchestra were formed in the ghettos, in which famous instrumentalists played, believing rightly that the great artists were not the property of the Third Reich but of all humankind. The Germans forbade the Jews to pray or gather for public prayer, but Jews met for devotion in private homes every day, pouring out their hearts in prayer to their Creator.

On March 10, 1940, teacher Chaim Aharon Kaplan, author of the Warsaw Ghetto diary, wrote:

> Fortunately, the occupier is not aware of what Polish Jewry truly is, nor of its vital energy. According to logic, we should all be dying. According to the laws of nature, our fate is death and total extinction. How can an entire group of people feed itself when it has no means of livelihood? Not a single profession or trade has been left open to us! Even now we are not on equal terms with the laws of nature. We are imbued with some mysterious, unseen force, keeping us going beyond all the laws of nature. If it is impossible to live from what is permitted then we will live from what is forbidden, and it is no shame to us. What is permitted is but a matter of convention and what is forbidden is also a matter of what everyone agrees on. Thus those who do not consent to the agreement are not bound by it, especially the permitted and forbidden of a barbaric occupier, treating life in its image, according to its thieving, murderous instincts. . . . The Jews of Poland, humiliated and repressed, downtrodden, and despised, love life and refuse to leave the world before their time. Say what you will: the will to live in deprivation as horrible as ours is the direct result of an unseen, mysterious force the precise nature of which we do not yet know. It is a wonderful life-giving force with which only the stronger of our people have been blessed. . . . We were left powerless, but so long as this vibrant force remains within us, we shall not give in.

The ghetto Jews revealed a large degree of solidarity and mutual assistance. However, it would not be true to say that the Jews were always on their best behavior and that there were no ugly, despicable incidents or that there were no cruel Jews who remained indifferent to the suffering and deprivation of others. There were shameful, gruesome incidents and saddening, repulsive acts. In the Warsaw

Ghetto, hunger-stricken Jews lay in the gutters while indoors people ate their fill, and laughed and played, according to the standards prevailing at the time. There were also informers in the ghettos, people who maintained contact with the enemy and reported to them everything that took place inside. In the Warsaw Ghetto there was even an entire ring of spies, operating under the auspices of the Germans. Some members of the Jewish forces in the ghettos were enemy agents or suspected agents. In some ghettos, the heads of the Jewish Councils, such as Rumkovski in Lodz and Merin in the town of Zaglembia in the district of Silesia, kept strict control of the Jews and were subservient to the enemy, fulfilling their every demand.

Hunger and deprivation were processes. Those who until recently had been normal people had eaten sparingly but enough to keep their bodies going, taken care of their personal hygiene, revealed interest in their surroundings and occupied themselves with some form of work, but were destined after a month or two to decline to the level of hunger and want, refraining from begging for food but on the verge of breakdown. There were many who arrived at this final stage, begging for food while crying bitterly, until they became almost a nuisance. These poor helpless creatures reminded all who heard them that a similar fate awaited them sooner or later. Thus, at a certain point the house committees simply collapsed under the combined weight of the burden, when the numbers of the needy exceeded by far those who were able to help them, be it to the slightest degree.

In central Poland, there was an aid organization which was affiliated with a branch of the Joint Distribution Committee, an American-Jewish aid organization. The local heads of the organization, guided by local conditions and considerations, were people who had been active in communal work before the war and spared no effort in their toil to provide help. As in other cases, this organization also operated on two levels. On the one hand, it was a legal organization recognized by the authorities and even received some nominal funding from them, while at the same time it was active in the underground.

Yitzchak Gitterman, an outstanding activist in the ranks of the Jewish self-help organizations, did not hesitate to support the fighting organization when the time came. When visited by a representative of fighters from Bialystock, Chaika Grossman, who asked for money to buy arms, he acceded to her request. She wrote in her memoirs that her happiness was twofold. Firstly, she had received money to arm the organization, and secondly, she had received the money from Gitterman. Accompanying Gitterman in his work, as his trusted assistant from before the war, was Emanuel Ringelblum. Ringelblum concentrated on providing assistance to the most needy places— house committees and public kitchens—but at the same time he was the light and life of an undertaking to produce a documentary and a memorial, and was also an avid supporter of any clandestine cultural activity.

In the spring of 1940, the Joint Distribution Committee faced a severe crisis. The financial reserves which had remained from before the war were slowly running out and the funds received from the American "Shefa Fund" were not enough for even one daily portion of watery soup for the hungriest at the public kitchens of the ghettos. The heads of the assistance organizations were in need of extensive resources in order to continue with their work. They approached wealthy Jews who had succeeded in hiding some of the property that they had accumulated before the war with the proposal that they give them some of their money in exchange for the promise that the money would be returned to them after the war in American currency. They were not empowered to make these promises and to bind the JDC thereby, but the terrible deprivation forced them to undertake the responsibility.

There were many doctors in the ghettos, but the epidemics reaped a deathly toll. Many of the sick were unable to pay for medical help, and those who were more severely stricken were even less able to afford to pay doctors or buy drugs, thus doubling their degree of suffering. It is on this subject that we find in diaries and memoirs descriptions of doctors refusing to accept payment for their treatment and help, who even spent some of what little they had to buy vital drugs or a little food for their patients.

These stories bring to mind Janusz Korczak, who was a doctor, writer of children's stories and father to many orphans. As a reputable doctor and successful writer, he spent a large portion of his time in the poor neighborhoods where Jews and Poles lived. During the War, Korczak was already an old man, disappointed and embittered. All that was left to him was his orphanage in the ghetto. Korczak became a caring father to his orphan children. He would make the rounds of the ghetto alleys, visiting individuals and institutions, asking, begging and demanding aid, fighting for his orphans and succeeding in preventing the cold hand of hunger from entering his orphanage.

Hungry children in the Ghetto.   Vaccination of children in the Refugee
                                        Center, 2 Mila Street, Warsaw.

Nevertheless, most of the cohesiveness, loyalty and trust of the Jewish family remained steadfast in the face of time. This unifying power and devotion was of inestimable value during the Holocaust period. Poverty, deprivation and humiliation are natural breeding grounds for arguments and dissent, for the release of egocentric impulses and the erosion of social structures. The survival of these structures is dependent upon a stable environment and the maintenance of social criticism, making demands on individuals to provide examples and leadership. In the ghettos and camps, people sometimes had the feeling that the earth had changed, that the word of God and the law of man had ceased to exist and that a new order of might had taken control of everything. Signs of the germ of erosion and loss of morality were evident. In ghettos, there were incidents of callousness and indifference to the suffering of others. People turned their backs on family and friends. Yitzchak Katznelson, the noted writer of the Warsaw Ghetto, lamented:

Don't you know us, recognize us? Have we
    changed so?
Are we so different? We are the same Jews
    we were,
Even better. . . Not I! I don't compare myself
    to the prophets—
But all the martyred Jews taken to their death,
    the millions murdered here—
They are better. They have suffered more and
    were purified here in exile.
How can a great Jew of long ago be compared
    with a small, simple, common Jew
In present-day Poland, Lithuania, Vohlynia?
    In every one of them
A Jeremiah wails, a tormented Job cries, a
    disillusioned king intones Ecclesiastes.

The memorial literature of survivors, diaries and testimonies, give rise to a picture indicating that incidents of cruelty or irresponsible behavior were rare, and that even if such incidents drew attention, it was not they that determined the nature of the life of the majority. We read and hear of Jewish mothers who went without food in order to feed their children, women who risked their lives daily to bring food for their families, and children who became smugglers, creeping through to the Aryan side and returning with a little bread or potatoes for their families.

Works dating from those days tell of young children who were the sole survivors of entire families, where the older of the two children would undertake the task of feeding the younger. People were never alone, not even in the camps. Broken families held themselves together, the strong supporting the weak, with both finding solace and a reason to live in their mutual bond. At times, people in the camps forged deep friendships with people whom they met on nearby bunks or at work, forming relationships which to a certain extent substituted for their lost family ties. Many who suffered the horrors of the camps and survived owe their lives to such friendships.

Chapter 2

Youth Movements in the Polish Underground

From the beginning of the war the Jewish youth movements were the vanguard of the underground, a moving and active force. In discussing the range of Jewish youth movements, we are speaking not only of the natural phenomenon of young people being the first to become alerted to danger and the first to courageously fight for the general good. The unique nature of the circumstances and the period of Nazi-occupied Europe indicate that something more than this was at work.

Even before the war the Jewish youth movements were independent and dynamic. Youth groups such as *HeHalutz* engaged in what was termed "pioneer" activity, aimed at preparing young people for life on communal agricultural settlements in Palestine. They and the Betar youth organization organized illegal immigration to Palestine and transferred agricultural training programs from Germany to other countries. It was they who stood among groups of self-defense which organized themselves in the face of anti-Semitic pogroms in Poland and other places. The older generation, raised and educated in a period of liberalism, fostered hopes for the new social order and its attitude toward Jewish society, and was not able to comprehend the danger inherent in Nazism and totalitarianism. Even thought the youth movements did not understand the full danger the Nazis presented, they were nevertheless more aware of events and their possible consequences, and tried to encounter this reality in new and unconventional ways.

Tosia Altman.   Yitzhak Zuckerman.

The youth movements were prepared for difficulties from a practical point of view. During the first weeks of the invasion of Poland, party leaders of all factions (from the Communists to the Revisionist Zionists) fled from the area captured by the Nazis to the zone occupied by the Soviets. Youth movement leaders also moved eastward among the refugees. But after putting down anchor wherever they stopped, they began to give thought to the members left behind under German occupation. Mordecai Anielewicz, later to become commander of the Warsaw Ghetto, was among the first to demand that youth leaders return to Warsaw and assume control of the underground movement. The adults, the senior figures in the movements, had abandoned the city and left young people lost in the storm raging about them, some of the youth movement leaders argued. Mordecai Anielewicz presented this demand to his fellows, gathered in Vilna, Lithuania (which between the wars was in northeastern Poland). Similar discussions among members of the *HeHalutz* movement took place in Lvov, southeastern Galicia, and led to like decisions. Tosia Altman, Yosef Kaplan, and Mordecai Anielewicz set out to Warsaw from Vilna; Yitzhak Zuckerman, Tzvia Lubatkin, and Frumke

Plotnicki came from the south. All of them later stood at the head of the underground in occupied Poland and were among the founders of the Jewish military organization in Warsaw and its branches in other Polish cities.

What did youth movement members and refugees do at the outbreak of war? At first they tried to break through the German and Soviet lines and blaze a path to Palestine. There were attempts to establish a route from Poland to the Black Sea coast of Romania, and from there to the land of Israel. The first to cross the border were captured. Shmuel Broder, a member of *HeHalutz* paid for this with his life, and others sat for years in Soviet prisons. Only a handful succeeded in making it over the border and arriving in Palestine. When it became clear that the southern route was impassable, they turned northwards to Vilna and the cities of Lithuania. Lithuania was, from November 1939 to June 1940, an independent country with limited internal freedom. The Jewish refugees who gathered there, including members of youth movements, students and rabbis from *yeshivot* (seminaries for Jewish religious studies), and political activists, tried to take advantage of Lithuania's status in order to use it as a point of departure to Palestine and the free world. In July, 1940, Lithuania was annexed by the Soviet Union, but the refugees still tried to obtain exit permits, and the Soviet authorities surprisingly did not prevent them from passing through Soviet territory as long as they had such permits and emigration destinations. Four hundred fifty-three Jews left Lithuania in the period up to April 1940, and of these 406 went to Palestine. They left with legal exit permits, aided by Jewish institutions around the world. In the summer and autumn of 1940 about 1,200 more embarked from Odessa and Istanbul. This second wave, however, included hundreds of Jews whose permits had not been obtained properly, and were therefore able to leave only thanks to daring, dexterity, and invention.

An example of such dexterity can be seen in a rescue operation initiated by the refugees themselves, who found they could leave by way of the Far East. The organizers of this operation were *yeshiva* students, and notable among them was Dr. Zorach Warhaftig, one of the leaders of the *HaPoel HaMizrachi* movement and later a minister in the Israeli government.

During this period the Dutch consul in Kovno, Lithuania, indicated his willingness to give, to Jews to applied to him, permits certifying that the bearers would be allowed to enter Curaçao in the West

Indies. He did not ask his government for permission to do this, and he decided to dispense with the formal requirement of obtaining the permission of the Governor of Curaçao. Those who received such permits then needed to obtain Soviet transfer permits. These were granted despite the Soviet "closed door" policy, but with the condition that the refugees obtain permits from a country bordering the Soviet Union. In this matter the refugees found an unexpected savior in the person of the Japanese consul in Kovno, Sempo Sugihara, whose job was apparently to keep abreast of political developments in the area. The refugees applied to him in desperation and asked for Japanese permits. Sugihara, who was granted the title "Righteous Among the Nations" by the Israeli government after the war, asked his superiors in Tokyo. Even before receiving a reply, however, he gave a permit to every refugee who applied and had a certificate of destination. Even after being instructed to stop, Sugihara continued to grant the permits, issuing a total of about 1,600. When, with the annexation of Lithuania to the Soviet Union, the foreign consulates were ordered to close, they accepted the help of refugee volunteers in order to make out hundreds of permits before the deadline.

We have told the stories of the Kovno-Curaçao and Kovno-Japan routes at length because thousands of Jews were saved in this way. It was possible because of the initiative and inventiveness of trapped people coupled with the goodwill of authorities from the free world and their willingness to take unconventional measures. Unfortunately, there were few other episodes like the Japanese escape route. Such rescue attempts were repeated only in occupied France, and in Budapest in the summer of 1944, when in a daring operation involving Raul Wallenberg, the Swedish and Swiss embassies saved thousands of Jews from being sent to Auschwitz by granting them diplomatic protection.

Those who volunteered or accepted the call to return to the areas under German occupation were forced not only to part from their friends and give up hope of going to Palestine, but also knew that from then onwards they would suffer humiliation and persecution. Despite this, they were not deterred from fulfilling their obligation.

The sources at our disposal show that young people, youth movement members who remained in the German zone, did not wait for orders from the headquarters but began to organize and act on their own. Even so, it is doubtful whether the Jewish underground, and especially Jewish resistance in the ghettos, would have achieved the range and dimensions it did, had part of the leadership not returned from the east.

Before telling the stories of the youth movements in the underground, we will survey the status and influence of these movements before the war. Youth movements must be distinguished from youth divisions of political parties. Movements like *HaShomer HaTzair* and *Akiva* were typical. They were not associated with parties; they developed their own ideologies. The leaders were young people only a few years older than the other members. The educational philosophy of these movements was focused on character development, scouting, ideological activity, and a system of units or small cells characterized by internal discipline, comeraderie, and obedience to the instructions of the movement. Other than the evening and weekend activities, the groups or units attended summer and winter camps, where the education was concentrated and intensive. The special nature of Jewish youth groups can be best demonstrated by comparing them to similar groups in the rest of the world.

Youth movements formed in different European countries during the twentieth century. They were committed to returning to nature, fostering the experience of youth, and expressing inner truth, free of what they saw as hypocrisy and falseness disguised as bourgeois social manners. Youth movements were, however, generally only for young people. As their members aged, they abandoned the movement and generally adopted the customs and way of life of their parents. The European movements, and especially that of Germany, did not always contribute to tolerance and democracy. Their graduates tended to associate themselves with totalitarian philosophies.

The Jewish Zionist youth movements were completely different, especially those founded with the goal of immigration to Palestine. For their members, association with the movement was not to end when they grew up—it was meant to be a way of life. Several of the movements—*HaNoar HaTzioni, B'nai Akiva, HaShomer HaTzair, Gordonia, Dror*—instilled the desire to live in communal agricultural settlements in Palestine. The young people joined the movements and trained themselves for a communal way of life, and saw this preparation as the most important part of their membership in the youth movement. When the war broke out this changed, since the normal means of preparation and the way to Palestine were blocked.

Before the war, the Polish Zionist youth movements did not take an active role in local public and political life. Their major concern was to prepare themselves for life in the Land of Israel. Exile in Poland was for them only a transition stage leading to the fulfillment of life on a kibbutz, or of a different life style in Palestine. But when the war broke out the members of the youth movements could no longer isolate themselves from what was happening around them. They had to give their full consideration to events of the day. This involvement increased until the youth movements became the leadership and vanguard of the underground.

What were the ways in which the underground youth movements acted in Poland?

Their first steps were to gather their committed membership and renew their activity, now in the underground. Adult party members were not sufficiently prepared or willing to take action at a time of danger. Only small groups of committed loyalists of the large parties were active. At the start, most of their underground activities involved material help—helping their members defend themselves from hunger, illness, and labor camps. The question then arose whether a political party dedicated to a moral and political philosophy should do more than see to the material well-being of its members. In the wake of discussion and mediation on this question, the parties began to involve themselves in propaganda, obtaining information on political and military developments, and taking political positions within the reality of the war and the underground. The political parties in the underground remained active in the field of social help and political education until the beginning of the stage of extermination.

In many places the youth groups had not dispersed and some had continued to meet and function, waiting for direction from the leadership on involvement in a nationwide underground movement. Tosia Altman, one of the leaders who returned to Warsaw from Vilna in order to renew his movement's activity, wrote in April 1941 in the underground newspaper *El-Al* about those first days or renewal:

> On dark nights someone began driving a wagon over rain-washed roads to the town of Zaglembia and the poor villages of Polesie. In the evening someone would tap on the windows of darkened houses, and when the door opened and the tired guest was brought into the warm house, eyes opened in wonderment and joy and their mouths formed a single word: "the leadership." Had there really been? With no interruption? We are not alone? Impatient, drilling questions meant to expel what had been. Memories of activities, of

dances, of debates were recalled so that they might live. . . The taps on the windows became more and more frequent. Most often the doors were opened with warmth, and the next day saw illuminated faces, believing, sure faces in action. It was not always necessary to tap on a dark window. Sometimes one came upon a lit room, a circle of heads around a lamp. And proud words: "There is no need to give us encouragement. We began ourselves. While your houses were still crumbling and burning, we had already resumed activity. Believe us—we can go on." With hearts full of pride, they sent out a wave of warmth, a wave which began spreading to the disconnected cities of the Reich, arriving at the Lodz ghetto, closed in expectation of its destruction. It was a wave which warmed and filled people with hope. Afterwards, letters began flowing to mailboxes. Today Kielce, tomorrow Staszow, the next day Miedzyrzec, and Siedice, and on and on. "The family is well, works, makes a living, the young people work, the adults work. We are studying Hebrew." Then came the council in Warsaw. . .

Yitzhak Zuckerman, among the leaders of the fighting underground in occupied Poland, compared the parties with the youth movements in the following words:

I was both a party man and a youth movement member. I thought that, in the period we are discussing, the parties excelled in only one area—in social work. In every other area connected to the work of the underground, from its beginnings in 1940, . . . the underground seminar in Warsaw in the middle of that year and ending with the underground press which then began to appear, the party people were not among the initiators, nor even among the pushers and planners. In all these things the youth movements led the way.

An internal document of the *Dror* movement sets out the timetable for work within the bounds of the *General gouvernement*:

1. September 1939 to April 1940—period of locating members of the movement.
2. April 1940 to November 1940 [until the ghetto was sealed off]—reorganization and training of the youth movement. [Work reached its height.]
3. November 1940 to June 1941 [beginning of the German-Soviet War]—concentration on underground activity in the large cities.
4. June 1941 to present [the document is dated May 1942]—the struggle to get out.

After the first stage of "locating members of the movement" and re-establishing communication, there were council meetings and gatherings in Warsaw involving representatives of the underground's branches in provincial cities, and plans were made for underground activity and war. It is fitting to mention here the first important achievement of the youth movement underground—breaking through the Nazi grip on the ghettos—was accomplished in part because of their isolation from other Jewish communities. The Nazis forbade Jews to ride the trains or to leave their homes without permission. The centers of the underground movement did not acquiesce in this decree of isolation and initiated visits by messengers and representatives throughout the occupied area. This wide-ranging activity became established and developed until there were national gatherings and seminars in Warsaw. The youth movement underground thus became an organization with a system of cells spread all over the country. This character gave the movement the ability to evaluate circumstances and act on a larger scale than any other Jewish organization in the occupied country. Youth movement messengers, the great majority of whom were girls, disguised themselves as Poles and conveyed, at great personal danger, underground material from cell to cell. They filled a vital role in their movement as the only link between the various besieged and isolated Jewish centers. The importance of this unique mission was especially evident after the extermination campaign began.

In his words of appreciation on the work of the messengers, written May 1942, Emmanuel Ringleblum notes:

> These heroic girls—Chaika Grossman, Frumka Plotnicki, and others—are a subject worthy of a great author: heroic and brave girls who travel to and from the cities and towns of Poland. They have Aryan documents, and they are like Aryans—Poles or Ukrainians. One even wears a cross, from which she is inseparable, and in the ghetto she feels its absence. . . . They are in unsurpassable danger each day. They pin their hopes only on their Aryan appearance and on the kerchiefs which cover their heads. They take the most dangerous missions upon themselves and carry them through without a word, without hesitation. If someone must go to Vilna, to Bialystok, to Lvov, to Kovel, to Lublin, to Chystochowa, to Radom, etc., to smuggle forbidden items such as illegal publications, material, money—they do so as if it went without saying. If members have to be rescued from Vilna, from Lublin, or from another city,

they take on the mission. Nothing will keep them from doing so, nothing stops them. If it is necessary to make connections with a German responsible for the train, to make it possible to travel out of the *General gouvernement*, limited to those who possess special passports—they do so simply, as if it were their profession. They pass through cities where no representative of any Jewish institution has been, such as Volhynia and Lithuania. They are the ones who first brought news of the tragedy in Vilna. . . .

Many of these messengers sacrificed their lives and all traces of them were lost in the whirlpool of those times. They remained faithful to their mission to the end. They never revealed addresses, names, people.

Among these messengers were some non-Jews. The most outstanding was Irena Adamovicz from a leading Polish family, a devout Catholic and an activist in the Polish Scout movement. A few years before the war she and a few other Catholic Scouts became close to *HaShomer HaTzair*. It is difficult to understand what attracted Poles, who had a powerful patriotic link to their motherland and to their religion, to a Jewish youth movement which preached pioneering settlement in the land of Israel, and which in addition advocated a radical leftist ideology. It is reasonable to assume that the atmosphere of the youth movement, the feeling of friendship, youthful joy, and the open and honest questions about man and society, the love of books, and the deep link to Polish literature and culture were the factors which drew Irena and her Catholic friends to *HaShomer HaTzair*. Irena and her friends visited *The Hachshara's* training camps, learned a bit of Hebrew, and became partners in the achievements of the pioneer movement, party to both its joys and its concerns. During the war Irena Adamovicz worked as a social worker in Warsaw and her connections with the members of the youth movement deepened through the link with the underground. Heniek Grabowski and Alexander Kaminski, central figures in the publication of the official newspaper of the fighting arm of the Polish underground, also had warm feelings for the movement to settle Palestine and for Jews in general, and stood by their side during their most difficult trials. Irena Adamovicz traveled from place to place and passed on materials and information. She sometimes even took an active role in instruction. She was the first to reach the Kovno ghetto in 1942, and told them of the horrible suffering of the Polish and Lithuanian Jewish communities. Leib Garfunkel, a Zionist activist who was a member of the

Kovno *Judenrat* and who, along with the head of the *Judenrat*, Dr. Elchanan Elkes, was a dedicated servant of his people, wrote in his memoirs about Irena Adamovicz:

> Her tremendous desire to give moral support to the prisoners in the ghettos is what brought her in 1942 to the Vilna, Kovno, and Shavli ghettos. She sat for an entire day with a small circle of Zionist activists in the Kovno ghetto and spread before them the story of the torture of the Jews of Warsaw, Lodz, Lublin, Cracow, Lemberg, Bialystok, Grodno, Vilna, and others. The guest related and described everything with emphasis, colorfully, with a fullness that only special people are able to achieve. Even though she was extremely pessimistic about the future of the Jews of the ghettos—and horrible reality corroborates her pessimism—Irena wove words of encouragement and comfort into her story. It was a great day for the Zionists who sat with her and heard her long and shocking story and who gave her details about life in the Kovno ghetto. They presented the ghetto to her and showed her its most important institutions: the *Altstahnrat* office, the hospital, the orphanage, and more—everything, of course, in total secrecy. The next day she left for the Shavli ghetto. A few weeks later Irena Adamovicz again visited the Kovno ghetto, related her impressions of the Shavli ghetto, and completed her story of the fate of Polish Jewry. She parted with her conversants with exceptional friendliness and warm goodbyes.

It is only fitting that we should relate the rest of Irena Adamovicz's story. She did not establish a family of her own, and for years cared for her elderly and ill mother. After the war she renewed her connections with her Jewish friends. She maintained contact with kibbutz members and was even invited to visit Israel. During her visit she was awarded the title "Righteous Among the Nations," and a tree was planted in her honor. She toured the country, taking an interest in people and their actions. Everything aroused her curiosity and her unquenchable desire to know and understand. Upon returning to Poland, filled with impressions of Israel, she found no rest. She made frequent visits to the Israeli embassy in Warsaw, wrote letters to friends in Israel, and sought out every Israeli who came to Poland. This enthusiasm aroused the suspicion of Poland's Communist authorities, and the secret police arrested her. We do not know how Irena Adamovicz was interrogated, what she was asked and with what methods they tried to wring answers out of her. We know that she ended her life in a psychiatric hospital, frightened, refraining from mentioning her Jewish friends and Israel.

Emmanuel Ringleblum.

We will now return to the work of the underground youth movements. Once the ranks were united there was regular activity. The young people would meet in private houses or in hiding places outside, in the summer. Most of their activity, however, was in the public kitchens, which functioned under the sponsorship and funding of the Jewish Social Aid organization in Warsaw and in the Warsaw ghetto. At the head of this public body stood the Polish "Joint," which bore the major part of the cost. Yitzhak Gitterman, Emmanuel Ringleblum and other leaders of the "Joint" in Warsaw in those days knew about the underground activity conducted in the kitchens, and supported it with all their hearts. During the day the kitchens gave meager meals to the hungry, and in the evening they hummed with underground business. Meetings were held there, secret libraries were stored there, and underground newspapers were printed there. Ringleblum and Gitterman were involved in all areas of the underground's activity. Later on urban kibbutzim of youth movement members were established, and they lived together in the public kitchen. Youth movements also busied themselves with matters that occupy young people in normal times. They read forbidden books, had conversations, discussions, and literary debates.

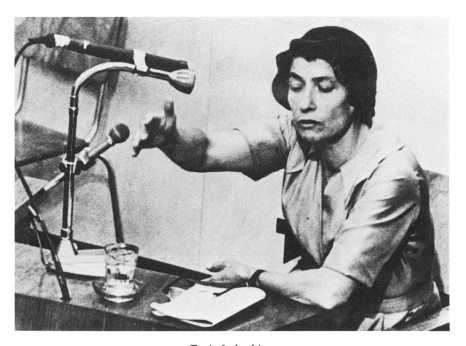

Tzvia Lubatkin.

They dealt with cultural questions and learned about socialism, great artists and writers, discoveries which enriched man's intellect and his material life, Palestine and kibbutzim. Tzvia Lubatkin wrote in her memoirs:

> Once we began wide-ranging cultural activity, we discovered that we had no literary or historical material for the leaders. New books did not come out in the ghetto, and old ones were hard to find. In this area as well we were forced to create out of nothing. So we began large-scale literary activity. The first book published by *Dror* was a literary-historical anthology: *Pein un Gvura in der Yiddisher Geshichte in Licht von der Kegenvart*, that is, *Suffering and Heroism in Jewish History in the Light of the Present*. The book was printed on a mimeograph machine. At times of low spirits and despair we wanted to give

young people a sign and an example from the stories of heroism and defense from the nation's history. When we started, we had neither a typewriter nor a mimeograph machine. We sweated and slaved until we obtained printing equipment. Once the Germans passed by and heard song wafting through our window. They didn't like it: How can the Jews dare to sing? They broke in and we barely managed to hide the printing machine. They went through all the rooms and were in shock: So many Jewish youths! We said: "They're refugees!" The Germans interrogated us, searched us, checked every hole and crack. Miraculously they passed by the printing room and did not go in, and so we were saved.

A young girl, Aliza Melamed, wrote in her memoirs at the height of the war:

> Our brigade was born on the day of the war, and it was called *Be-esh*. Each group stood with its leaders, each one symbolizing in its name its birth in molten flame: *Avuka, Zikim, Lehavot, Shvivim, HaSheh, LaMarom*, and we all listened to the words of Mordecai Anielewicz: "We are in the midst of filth and degeneration. From this dirt our war begins. We must not forget that the hardest war is the war against ourselves: not to become accustomed to and not to adjust to these conditions! He who adjusts ceases to distinguish between good and evil, and he becomes a slave in body and soul. Whatever happens to you, remember always: Do not accustom yourselves! Do not adjust! Rebel against that reality!"
>
> Sometimes Shoshana, one of the leaders from the *Tel-Amal* Regiment, would come to lecture to us. Shoshana was for us a symbol of the realization of pure beauty and pureness of soul. Toiba Szayngnt from *Tel-Amal* would also come to us. It was so pleasant to look at him as he sat among us wearing workers' clothes and lecturing on astronomy. After a hard days' work he would take us to far worlds among the wonderful stars on high.

One of the greatest difficulties the youth movement members faced was the need to become used to giving up their free, liberated behavior—singing together, hikes—all of which expressed the bubbling spirit of youth, of young people whose hearts were overflowing with ideas and experiences. Gusta Davidson, an activist in the *B'nai Akiva* movement in Cracow, wrote of this in her diary while in the Cracow prison:

> We were warned a hundred times: Do not gather in groups. A hundred times we made the same decision: We will no longer gather!

But as soon as two members met in the street, another and another would join them and very soon they walked in a long line across the entire width of the sidewalk, and their wild hair, bare and clear faces, their sure and measured march, drew the attention of passersby, who never knew their thoughts and purposes. They knew very well that they should not behave as they did, but when they were together, they felt themselves so strong, to the point of fearlessness of both known and unknown enemies.

Before the war, the youth movements took no notice of the material and economic conditions in which their members lived, and a member's home life was kept separate from his life in the movement. Social life in the movement was characterized by full equality, but during the war the movements were forced to consider the need for food. The movement kitchens distributed soup to the most hungry. Members who were able regularly invited a friend from a hungry house to meals. In some groups there was a sort of collectivization of food—that is those in whose houses there was still food brought portions for others, and those who had nothing at home brought crumbs. Regularly, sometimes once a day, there were communal meals.

All these efforts could not overcome the troublesome problem: Was it possible to rise above severe disadvantage? After all, when hunger exhausts and demands the attention of all the senses it is impossible to continue to dream and speak of the world beyond the walls of the ghetto and the problems meaningful to human beings in normal times. Thus the question arose whether the youth movements should seek after all young people, both hungry and well-fed, or whether they should concentrate on those who had the necessities to allow them to think abstractly and deal with questions of the soul.

In the beginning, up until the mass extermination campaigns, the youth movements were no different from the rest of the public. Both hoped to survive the war and preserve the physical existence of the nation. They hoped to achieve this goal, whether by legal or illegal means, and in this matter there was general agreement among Jews in the occupied countries. But youth movement members and their leaders were not satisfied only with saving the body, but wished also to preserve their simple spiritual image. The underground newspaper of *HaShomer HaTzair* gave this explanation:

> Poverty and complete economic depression will pass when the political conditions change, but the nation will not rise from its spiritual poverty if its youth remains wounded and degenerated, because only we, aged 13–18 today, can be those who are destined to lead the Jewish masses to another, better future.

Degeneracy spread among some of the young people in the ghetto. The lack of law and social order challenged the moral order, and selfish and inconsiderate behavior became common. A few, who had not yet been affected by the troubles of the time, chose to confine themselves to their social class, to give themselves over to the enjoyment of the moment, to sink into gluttony, wild sex, card games and dances, to forget the street, death, and the hungry crying for help. In contrast to them, at the bottom of the social scale—which always moved downward—were those who had been defeated by the war and by hunger. There were those who were close to death, and those who joined together as lawbreakers, ready to commit crimes (although there were no murders) in order to obtain food among Jews in the occupied countries. Other young people, also at the bottom of the social scale, worked as smugglers and were thereby able to bring a crust of bread to their families. The poverty and hunger experienced by these people forced them to adopt customs and ways of thinking alien to their customary way of life.

This sad reality found its expression in the youth movement newspapers. The February–March 1941 issue of *Neged HaZerem* published the following in its column on educational problems:

> The increasing severity of living conditions has had a tremendous effect on youth. Today it is only in rare cases that a family occupies more than one room, and this gives children a gross and distorted picture of sex among adults. . . . The worsening economic and housing situation has caused a huge decline in the authority of parents. The father, who does not earn a living for his family, the pressured couple, always arguing—these are the elements which bring the child to lack of respect for his father and mother. It is clear that such a boy is prey to the trap of the slogan "grab and eat," and that the absence of care and authority brings about a rejection of all conventions, excessive card-playing, smoking, wild dancing and sexual abandon. In short, Hitler's policy has destroyed the most essential part of the nation. Under these conditions we have taken upon ourselves the task of rescuing our youth from these dangers. Our role is to educate a vanguard to continue pioneer work in Israel. . . . In

general our leaders have understood that under existing conditions we cannot even dream of taking in poor children and educating them. These children first and foremost need bread, clothing, and shelter, and can be educated only in these matters. Establishing this unfortunate fact is not in line with our position on the social question, but that is the way it is. Our ranks necessarily consist of young people from the *petit-bourgeoisie* who, while they have become destitute, still do not live in total poverty, thanks to what remains to them from the past.

Another approach and a different tone can be found in the newspaper of the *Dror* movement, the members of which were from the more common strata and the activities of which were much less centered on intellectualism and ideological and spiritual molding of members than was *HaShomer HaTzair*. The following appeared in the May–June 1941 issue of *Dror*:

If we depend on our youth, it is not because of youth's tendency to simplify things. We have not drawn our future leaders from among youth who were looking for self-sacrifice. We did not demand sacrifices. We demanded spiritual strength, courage of the soul and daring, as much as is necessary to sever oneself from one's former life and search for new life. We looked for character, will-power, and a sense of responsibility. This can be found in young people of all classes. We will not give up those young people who, for material reasons, cannot come punctually and regularly to discussions and meetings. We will not reject the hungry because they think only about eliminating their hunger. We must see that their situation is eased and allow them to come our way. We take in all those who are willing to accept the path of realization of settlement in Israel. In our opinion, we cannot reject a person who has become a Zionist, a Socialist, a pioneer, because hunger pushed him to do so. If a person can discover a way for himself through hunger and suffering, we must honor this and take him with us.

HaShomer HaTzair and *Dror* were the largest youth movements in the underground, and in Warsaw each one had close to 1,000 members. The debate and dilemmas expressed by the above quotations were general and were conducted within each movement. Each of the youth movements worked with a membership which strived to retain the necessary strength to exist and struggle. The loyal, senior nucleus tried to help under all conditions, and the new members were almost exclusively those not suffering from severe hunger. The circle of potential candidates to join and remain in the youth groups was, therefore, very small.

During the war there was an attempt to renew agricultural training. In the past this had been a step in preparing members for kibbutz life in Palestine. It brought together people who had previously met only for social activity and ideological discussions.

There were various factors which brought about the attempt to re-establish agricultural training during the war. The first was the desire to reclaim the agricultural land and buildings which the youth movements owned before the war. *Dror* worked in this direction with great energy. It received the Grochow farm near Warsaw and a group of pioneering members of the movement settled there. With time, farming skills became valuable for other reasons as well. When the Germans started taking young people to labor camps, the youths were given a choice: to be taken for forced labor or to work in a Polish agricultural village in need of laborers—the Polish laborers having been taken themselves for forced labor in Germany. This allowed members of organized groups from the different youth movements to move to Polish farms and agricultural estates. In some places they encountered difficult conditions and harsh treatment, but in others the treatment was tolerable and occasionally even friendly. In those places where the attitude of the locals permitted, a sort of youth movement colony was established. After work there were activities, discussions, and evenings of singing and dancing. During work itself, the stronger tried to help the weaker and together they produced the quotas demanded. The most urgent questions among groups sending their members to these farms were whether the workers were demanded to perform impossible labor, and whether they were given enough food to enable them to put out the strength required by the work. In some places, such as the Cerniakow farm, members of *Dror* found such helpful conditions, and in time the farm served as a shelter during the mass deportations of the summer of 1942.

The *Betar* movement managed to get almost all of its members out of Warsaw, as well as people who were not members but signed up to go with *Betar* members for agricultural work close to the town of Hrubieszow. This was an estate that before the war was owned by a Jew with sympathies for the Revisionist Movement. He had lost his land during the invasion, but still had some say in what happened on the farm and arrived in Warsaw in order to organize a youth brigade to work there. Conditions were tolerable and allowed the movement to conduct communal activities. Moreover, the young people there stayed for an extended period and not only for a short season. The luck of the young people in Hrubieszow, who enjoyed a relatively peaceful life there, did not last, however, and they were eventually deported together with the rest of the Jews in the area. Only a few of them managed to escape alive.

Agricultural training camps were established in Cracow, in Zaglembia, and in Zarki, near Canstokowa. For a time, there was a training camp in Lodz under the control of the forceful head of the *Judenrat*, Mordecai Chaim Romkowski. There were also settlements and agricultural plots in the area of Marisin, at the edge of the ghetto. Groups of young people of all political persuasions, Zionist and non-Zionist, found room in these camps and settlements, conducted social and communal life, fostered the movement's unity, and studied.

Chaika Klinger writes in her memoirs, *From the Ghetto Diary*, of the farm in the Zaglembia area:

> The farm was a three-kilometer walk from the city and had lain fallow for 30 years. . . . A series of meetings of *HeHalutz* were devoted to discussing the share of each movement in the farm. The question was whether to accept people for training in accordance with the old proportional system set by the *HeHalutz* leadership with regard to the majority and minority tendencies among the youth groups, which had been set before the war for Poland as a whole. . . . The debate was conducted according to the traditional routine: Organizations which had no candidates for training demanded that the number of places allotted them be increased, purely for honor's sake. Meanwhile, members of other organizations were dying of hunger. These people saw going to the farm as a matter of life and death. . . . We began without any experience, without tools and equipment, without means. Each day groups of young people left the city, shovels over their shoulders. The dead fields came to life. We still had neither horse nor plow. We hoed with our shovels. We stood in a straight row, 20 boys and 20 girls, wearing shorts, and step by step, with measured rhythm, we pounded the land. . . . In the city there is hunger, plague, illness; you see not a scrap of sky, but you see an abundance of Germans. . . . Every young person in the city takes his work clothes off immediately after work and runs to the farm. At the farm there is happiness, laughter, the joy of youth. It is good to see the young people in their shorts working and rejoicing noisily. You can breathe fresh air here, and see few Ger-

mans. . . . We held memorial evening for Herzl and Bialik. We all sat in the field. Far into the stillness of the night we sang *Tehazekna* ["Be Strong"]. We condemned and called for rebellion against Fascism, against the great injustice wrought on the Jewish people.

An important and daring chapter in the life of the underground was the appearance of the underground press in Warsaw and Cracow. The information was distributed to the public and reached, by dangerous means, the provincial cities and towns as well as the big cities. This secret press was a joint project of all the underground organizations and divisions, political parties and youth movements. Since the regular press had been silenced, the only Jewish newspaper which appeared, once or twice a week, was a mouthpiece of Nazi propaganda. Neither the German nor the Polish press told the truth about political and military events. Jews were forbidden to have radios, and received almost no news of the outside world. Under these circumstances, there was great need for reliable political and military information. The truth was a ray of hope and a drug that strengthened the Jewish population, easing its oppression and depression. The youth movement papers were not satisfied with merely passing on the news surveys heard on secret radios, or in giving political commentary. The underground newspapers were full of cultural matters, ideology, and attempts to evaluate political and cultural developments in the world. They also told of events in the various ghettos and in the Zionist movement. The youth movement newspapers published news from Palestine, chapters of Zionist history and of the history of the *yishuv*. The political debate conducted on these pages was sometimes reminiscent of the heated arguments held before the war, trumpeting outdated opinions and doctrines. But there was also a stance of the underground that was shared by all its shades and divisions. The historian Emmanuel Ringleblum makes this clear:

> The war forced the Jewish public to face extremely important questions. It was necessary to bring the pre-war political relations to an end, and create a united front from left to right: Hitler's struggle against the Jewish population was one of destruction. It was directed against all levels and all classes of the Jewish public as a whole. Nazism did not differentiate between Zionists and Bundists. They were both hated equally. In accordance with this, it was necessary to establish a battle line for the Jewish public. It was necessary to establish a national front against the Fascist German powers of

destruction. The Jewish population was faced with cardinal questions: To be or not to be? No single person could take the responsibility for important problems like these. An answer to the problems life presented could be found only together. The institution of party consultations between all movements was not given a name, but it became an established body consulted by the "Joint," by the social self-help organizations, and often by the community (the *Judenrat*) itself.

The *Bund* party and its youth section excelled in the field of underground journalism, and this party was among the most active bodies in the political underground. The party had many dedicated members active in the underground, but managed to preserve its independence and kept its distance from the various Zionist factions. The newspapers were mimeographed on thick paper and an effort was made to make them esthetic. The large size of the pages and the thickness of the paper made it difficult, however, to keep them hidden and to pass them on in secret.

The only newspaper to be printed in the ghetto was called *HaMedina* and was published by the *Betar* movement on the occasion of Jabotinsky's death in 1940.

Various tricks were used to camouflage the character of the newspapers. The *HaShomer HaTzair* newspaper, *Iton HaTnula*, for example carried a Polish masthead reading "The Agricultural Survey," and dated from the 1930's. The Bundists were aided by their Polish socialist colleagues in shipping their newspaper to the provinces. The Poles turned to a member of their party, a woman suffering from cancer, and asked her to carry the forbidden newspapers. She was captured on her first trip and the names and addresses of the subscribers were discovered on her. As a result of this failure the *Bund* leadership in the city of Piotrkow-Trybunalski, an area where the party was strong and controlled the *Judenrat*, was arrested.

The young members of the underground in Poland did not at first claim for themselves responsible decision-making positions in the Polish Jewish community. During the first period they saw themselves as members of youth movements which should defer to the older and more experienced parties and their decisions. Only gradually did the influence of the youth movements in the community and their range of activities grow. This process was aided by the weakness of the parties and their need for someone to take control. Zivia Lubetkin wrote in her memoirs:

When I summarize the activity of our movement, which had a completely different direction, I must mention one serious mistake of ours: If we had immediately, with the German invasion of Poland, achieved the same consciousness imprinted on us at a later stage—the realization that we ought to take responsibility upon ourselves not only for young people and for the settlement movements, but rather for all public and political life in the Jewish community—the condition of the Jews might have been very different. But we were an educational movement dedicated to realizing settlement, and we worked among the youth. We did not feel within us enough power to act among the Jewish community as a whole. We reasoned that those tasks were meant for others. There had been, among the Jews, people with public experience, and they claimed to stand at the head of political life during the war as they had before the war. . . . It was only later that we recognized that the situation required us to take the leadership of the Jewish community into our hands.

The underground organ of *HaShomer HaTzair, Neged HaZerem,* in its May 1941 issue, proclaimed: "The role of the movement, as a public force in the ghetto, has grown not as a result of intentional activity in this area, but because of tension and momentum in internal activity and the breaking down of all the Jewish political parties."

In 1947, Yitzhak Zuckerman, recalling the underground activity of his movement and of the Jewish Fighting Organization, argued:

If we had seen, if we had understood, if we had been able to turn history back to 1939, I would say: Immediate revolt! because then we had much more strength, many more young people; because we were much more upright and had much more human feeling; because our hearts then had much more energy; because we had many more weapons; because we had many more soldiers; because we had much more hope.

It is doubtful, however, that a revolt could have been led at that time. In 1939, no person of healthy mind could have guessed the intentions of the Nazis, and despite the abilities of Zuckerman and his friends to persuade and enlist, it would have been difficult to bring people to revolt. Even if they had been able to, they had no soldiers, no weapons, and therefore no hope of achieving their desired results. Would an uprising of a few Jews in 1939, even if they had know the future, been beneficial in the long run, prevented what was to come, or brought effective help? It is doubtful. It might even be best to say flatly that there was no such chance. Such an action, doomed in advance to failure, could at the most have made destruction come more quickly, to justify, as it were, Nazi propaganda.

Ringleblum presented an argument similar to Zuckerman's. In his biography of Anielewicz, Ringleblum wrote that Anielewicz told him, close to the fall of the ghetto, that he regretted and was troubled by the years the youth movement had wasted in educational activities. If they had know, from the start, all their energy could have been concentrated on the effort to prepare for the coming test in battle.

Again, this was an unrealistic regret, and it overlooks the strength and positive morale that the educational activities inspired in the young people, the ability of the movements to close themselves off in their own spiritual world, to stubbornly hold onto values and norms despite what was happening before their eyes—these were their most important assets, and it gave them the strength to endure the first years of the war. Ringleblum writes in one of his entries after a lecture before a seminar of *HaShomer HaTzair* group leaders: "As I looked at the exuberant faces of young people thirsty for knowledge, I completely forgot the war. The seminar's work was done directly opposite the German guards stationed at the ghetto gates. The members felt so good that they would often forget that a war was going on in the rest of the world."

This was what mattered—the fact that the youth movements preserved a human, fresh, and loyal public, one that behaved and acted as if there were no war. Hundreds and thousands of these youth group members did not lose their human dignity and their spiritual and social character, despite the war and the inhuman conditions of life in the ghettos. This was the great achievement of the youth movements.

Chapter 3

The Armed Resistance—From Conception to Organization

Until the war broke out, Nazi policy was to bring about the maximum amount of Jewish emigration from the Reich. When the war began, however, this policy was exchanged for one based on the principle that the Jews should "disappear." How the Jews would disappear and where they would go was not made clear. Expressions like "evacuations" (*evakuierung, aussiedlung*), "removal" (*ausschaultung*), "removal of the Jews" (*Entjudung*), and "purification from Jews," (*Judenrein*), grew more common, with the implication that "solving the Jewish problem" was no longer restricted to the Reich. The anti-Jewish line had become a political element applied to all occupied countries which strove for a Nazi "New Order" in Europe, with one of the major Nazi goals being to conquer the world. In May 1942, Hitler said:

> All Europe must eventually be cleansed of Jews (*Judenrein*). This is necessary because there will always be a certain percentage of extremist Jews who will have as their goal the elevation of Judaism. It is not desirable to push the Jews into Siberia, because their ability to adjust to difficult climates will strengthen their health even more. Better, in light of the fact that the Arabs do not want them in Palestine, to send them to Africa and put them in a climate in which any person with resistance would suffer, and in so doing bring to an end any further encounter with European society.

In September, 1939, Reinhard Heydrich, in charge of the SD and the solution of the "Jewish question," had already ordered that the

Jews be taken from small towns to the large cities near the railroad lines. His instructions also said that the concentration of the Jews in the cities was only a step along the way to the "final goal" (*endziel*). By the spring of 1940, a plan to concentrate masses of Jews in the Lublin area was considered and experimented with. The proposal was raised without examining the problems of housing, feeding, and employing so many people there. The plan was abandoned after Hans Frank, Governor of the *General gouvernement*, succeeded in persuading the Reich authorities, among them Göring, that "he had enough Jews of his own" in the *General gouvernement*, and there was no room for additional Jews. In the second half of 1940 the Madagascar plan was proposed—the deportation of European Jewry to a sort of concentration or prison camp on the island off coast of Africa. The written proposals detailing this plan left no room for doubt: The intention was to deprive the deported Jews of their money, revoke their citizenship in European countries, keep them in conditions of slavery, and turn them into hostages so that Jews in the rest of the world, who had not yet come under Nazi rule, could not act against the interests of the Reich. It is clear that the Madagascar plan was meant not only to isolate the Jews from the world outside the island, but also to destroy them physically, if not by killing them all at once, then in a gradual way. The Madagascar plan was not carried out however, despite the interest Hitler and the senior officials of the Reich displayed in it. The plan was filed away because the Germans did not have a free sea line to use in the mass deportation. German documents mention the plan on occasion long after its was rejected as impracticable.

The turning point came in 1941, during Nazi preparations for the Barbarossa Operation—the invasion of the Soviet Union. It seems reasonable to assume that, in accordance with Hitler's basic assumptions as expressed in *Mein Kampf*, the Soviet Union would sooner or later become prey to Nazi expansionism. Eastern Europe was the Prussian target area for expansion and so was also a target of the Nazi military catechism. Invasion of the Soviet Union was also an ideological and political move. From Hitler's point of view, the battle against the Soviet Union was one of the missions of National Socialism; a lightning stroke at the heart of international Marxism and the "Jewish Bolsheviks." The preparations and strategies approved for this struggle were sharper and more extreme than anything the war had so far known. This battle, which was a struggle between two world-views, would go on until final victory.

Leading up to the attack on the Soviet Union and during the Eastern Campaign itself, concepts like "Jewish Communists" and "Jewish Bolshevism" became expressions used in Nazi propaganda and military operations. Four "operational divisions" (*Einsatzgruppen*) were established during the planning of the Barbarossa Operation. The four divisions were composed of personnel from the different branches of the police, and each consisted of between 500 and 1,000 men. They were headed by senior officers from the SS and men who held academic degrees, and who were authorized to take on tasks outside the range of activity of previous campaigns. Instituted by Hitler, a special agreement was made between the *Wehrmacht* and the SS to the effect that operational units in the Barbarossa operation would not be under army command, as they had been in the past, but under the command of the SS. The army was to aid these units with supplies and services and, as it turned out, sometimes by providing military support. The instructions given to the operational divisions were that they were to kill various enemies, such as Communist activists, terrorists, those who held Communist ideas, inciters, and Jews. The German historian Helmut Krausnick has stated that these instructions left no doubt that the object of these units in killing Jews was directed "solely against their biological existence as Jews." The army took an open part in the murder operation. The infamous "Commissar's Order" of March 13, 1941, issued by the high command of the *Wehrmacht*, stated:

> In the operational area the army receives *special tasks* from the *Reichsführer* of the SS and from the Führer, deriving from the decisive struggle being conducted between two opposing political ideologies. *In the framework of these tasks the Reichsführer of the SS acts independently and on his own responsibility.* The army received an order to turn over political commissars from the Red Army to the SS, for execution.

These instructions were brought to fruition as expressed in the field reports of the operational divisions. These units, reinforced by members of the local population—Lithuanians, Latvians, and Ukrainians—went from town to town, kidnapped large numbers of Jews and charged them with provocation, and then all trace of those taken disappeared. Only weeks or months later did the Jews remaining in the towns hear of the improvised murder sites where the prisoners were massacred. These locations—Ponar near Vilna, Romboli near Riga, and Babi-Yar near Kiev—were the sites where soldiers slaughtered masses of unbelieving Jews, entire families and villages. Mrs. Rivka Joselewska, a survivor of one of the death pits, gave evidence at the Eichmann trial in Jerusalem:

> When we arrived at the place we saw naked people. We still thought this was only torture. I wanted to see, to find out, to be sure. I walked around and looked at what was under that mound, that platform, what was in the hole, in the pit. It became clear and I knew. I saw that rows and rows of people who had already been shot to death were lying there. About 12 people were there . . . it was very hard to walk, the children suffered. We exchanged them. People carried their children and the children of others in order to delay the end, to put off the torture of the children. The parents, the fathers and mothers bade their children goodbye . . . They brought us, shoved us towards the pit. We were already naked. My father did not want to undress completely and remained in his underwear. His turn to be killed arrived. They told him to undress. He did not want to undress and remained in his underwear. They beat him and he did not want to. They tore the clothes off him and shot him. I saw! Afterwards, my mother's turn came. She did not want to be first. They took her anyway. Pushed her and shot her. Afterwards it was Grandmother's turn, my father's mother. A woman of about 80. Afterwards, my aunt, my father's sister. She also stood with babies in her arms. . .

On August 1, 1941, an order was issued from SS headquarters saying that from that date onward, operational unit reports would be passed on for Hitler's examination. From these reports we learn of the role these uniformed gangs played in the so-called "cleansing" of occupied territory of the enemies of the Third Reich. *Einsatzgruppe A*, stationed in the northern part of occupied Soviet Union, reported on February 1, 1942, that in the space of the previous four months the *Einsatzkommando 3* (an arm of *Einsatzgruppe A* responsible for the Baltic countries and the Leningrad salient) had murdered 1,064 Communists, 56 partisans, 653 mentally ill people, 44 Poles, 28 Russian prisoners, 5 Gypsies, 1 Armenian, and 136,421 Jews. An earlier report from *Einsatzkommando 3* itself, dated December 1, 1941, indicated that of the 240,000–250,000 Jews in Lithuania there were only 34,000 left, in the ghettos of the cities of Shavli, Kovno, and Vilna, and that the Jews who were still alive were "working Jews." Commander Karl Jager reported that he had considered liquidating these

Jews as well, but was forced to give up the plan because of the pressure he received from various German authorities in need of workers. By the end of 1941, it is estimated a million Jews had been murdered in the massacre campaign of the *Einsatzgruppen*. This wave of murder was the first stage of Hitler's "final solution," the plan for the extermination of European Jewry.

Babi-Yar.

The opening of the eastern front made the anti-Jewish policy more extreme—from a plan to deport Jews from Europe it became a plan of mass murder—and Hitler repeated on several occasions the threats he had first made in January 1939, that the war would end with the elimination of European Jewry. The precision with which Hitler used expressions and terms teaches that these were not outbursts of anger in propaganda speeches, but the expression of an object or plan of action deeply entrenched in his consciousness. It is reasonable to suppose that the difficulties which Hitler and his army encountered in their advance into the Soviet Union, the failure of the *blitzkrieg* method which had up until now been the recipe for German-Nazi victory, the inability to conquer the main cities of the U.S.S.R., and the signs of defeat which were beginning to show in the ranks of the German-Nazi army provoked the Führer's desire for revenge and destruction, and he redoubled his attack on the Jews. We may assume that this had an effect on the extent of the operation and on the stubbornness and consistency with which it was carried out.

Up until the beginning of the mass murder, the Jews did not respond with force, and certainly not with armed resistance, since they knew that any such attempt would bring about the collective punishment that they had already experienced a few times under Nazi rule. More than anything else the Jews knew that, as a people, an ethnic group, they could not achieve anything by armed uprising. Their fighting power could not seriously harm the great and powerful Nazi enemy. The Jewish underground in the Nazi-occupied territories had neither weapons nor links with the local underground, which could have guided them in such a struggle. It was natural that the Jewish underground concentrated, for the most part, on the struggle for physical existence and on the spiritual image of the Jew. The change or turning point came with the beginning of the mass murder campaign.

The first place in which an armed Jewish force was organized was in Vilna, the "Jerusalem of Lithuania." Vilna had been a thriving Jewish community for more than 300 years, a center of Torah, study, creativity, politics, arts, and culture. During the nineteenth century, Vilna was the site of the great dispute between the Gaon of Vilna, Rabbi Eliahu Ben Shlomo Zalman, and Chabad, the Hassidic movement led by Rabbi Schneur Zalman of Liadi. The Gaon was not only a great Torah scholar and precise even in his observance of the smallest religious obligations, but also wrote a book of grammar and allowed the study of "external subjects" like mathematics and geography. Vilna was also a center of the Jewish enlightenment, and the first Hebrew press was brought there from Grodno, after which Vilna became known for the books printed there. Vilna eventually became a center for study of the Hebrew language, and produced a crop of young Hebrew writers and poets, and a modern Jewish theater. Vilna was also home to YIVO—an institute for the Study of the Yiddish language. Towards the end of the nineteenth century, it became a Jewish political center for the Zionist movement on the one hand and the *Bund* on the other. Modern national and social ideas spread from Vilna to the Jewish cities and towns in central Poland. During the period between the wars, Vilna was no less important. Its streets and alleys took pride in the important Jewish institutions housed there, as well as Torah scholars, writers, and public figures.

At the beginning of the war there were already many Jewish refugees in Vilna, and those who did not succeed in getting any farther gave the Jews in Vilna additional strength during the struggle with the Nazis. Vilna had been under Polish control, but at the beginning of the war the Soviets overran part of Poland and annexed Vilna as well. When the Nazis invaded Vilna there were 60,000 Jews there, about 30 percent of the population of the city.

Yitzchak Wittenberg, commander of the underground in the Vilna Ghetto.

Mordecai Tenenbaum-Tamarov, commander of the rebellion in the Bialystok Ghetto.

Starting in July, 1941, a series of "actions" occurred in Vilna, as the Jews were put into ghettos and required to carry various documents, and the *Judenrat* was founded. Close to two-thirds of the city's Jews were murdered in these "actions." The mass murder was carried out by the *Einsatzgruppen*. In December, 1941, when the murder of Vilna's Jews halted for a time, only 20,000 Jews remained. All the Jews taken from the ghetto were brought to a site near the city, Ponar, where they were shot and thrown into vast pits. A few individuals who succeeded in escaping from the convoys to Ponar returned to Vilna and told of the fate of those taken from the ghetto. The horrible reports were at first met with disbelief, then accepted as the harsh truth was verified and became known to all.

Zionist youth movements which operated in the underground during the period of Soviet rule were reorganized with the beginning of German domination. In addition to concern for mere survival, the question of defense against German arrests was raised with the utmost urgency. The movements discussed the significance of events and considered what should be done in the face of the "actions," the expulsions, the deportations, and the news of the massacres at Ponar.

Active in Vilna at the time was Mordecai Tenenbaum-Tamarov, one of the outstanding leaders of the *Dror* movement who later made his way to Warsaw. He worked hard to discover what was happening and to find a way out. He sent two women from his movement on missions: Tamar Sznajderman to Warsaw and Bella Chazan to Grodno. Bella Chazan reported upon her return that Grodno, which had also been under Soviet control, had not experienced "actions," expulsions, or deportations.

Mordecai Tenenbaum-Tamarov later stood at the head of the Jewish armed resistance in the Bialystok ghetto. A short time before falling in the revolt, he wrote a sort of will addressed to the General Workers Organization (the *Histadrut*) and the United Kibbutz movement, both in Palestine. In his message he said:

> The first "action" was in Vilna. In the space of a few hours, dozens of our members were taken out. From that day on we had "action" after "action." There was a month of relative quiet—and then a week of pogroms. We searched for the reason for this in the local government, in the attitude of the Lithuanians, and so on. On quiet days, we did the work. On days of pogroms, we guarded our people, the social activists of the Jerusalem of Lithuania. . . There was also an attempt at getting out of Hitlerdom; with German cars to Libau in Latvia, and from there—in the winter— over the ice of the Finnish Sea to Sweden. Anton Schmidt, may his name always be remembered for good, a German from Vienna, risked his life to save hundreds of Jews from the Vilna ghetto and was a loyal friend to the movement. . . We transferred our activists to Bialystok (the work of Schmidt), and there we established the center for Lithuania, Polesie, Volhynia, and Eastern Galicia.

The ambitious plans to break through to another country were never realized. The active nucleus of *Dror* was transferred to Bialystok. We may assume that the belief that events in Vilna had

their source in local conditions and the desire to spare the movement's branch in Vilna further shocks were the main motives for this
move.

At the same time a Jewish armed resistance organization began to
form in Vilna. It was notable for the amazingly accurate evaluations it
made of its situation. Abba Kovner, among the leaders of *HaShomer
HaTzair* in Vilna, along with a group of his comrades, found shelter in
a Catholic convent of the Sisters in a suburb of Vilna. This group ana-
lyzed the situation and labored to work out what steps should be
taken. Rozka Korczak, one of the activists who took part in these discussions, recorded Abba Kovner's words at a meeting in the convent
at the beginning of September 1941:

> It is still hard for me to explain why Vilna flows with blood, while
> Bialystok remains peaceful. Why did it happen this way and not in
> another? One thing is clear to me; Vilna is not only Vilna. Ponar is
> not an episode. . . We face a well-considered method, still a secret
> to us. . . Everything that has happened until now means Ponar—
> death! And this fact is still not all the truth, which is immeasurably
> greater and deeper. The destruction of thousands is no more than
> tidings of the destruction of millions. Their deaths are our com-
> plete loss. . . Is there any escaping it? No! If the method is consis-
> tent here, flying from place to place is only an illusion, and every
> illusion is lost. . . Can there be a possibility of rescue? Cruel as it is
> to answer, we must give the answer: no, there is no rescue. The an-
> swer should be made clearer: for tens or hundreds of Jews, there
> may be rescue. For the nation, for the millions of Jews under the
> Nazi yoke—there is no rescue! Is there a way out? There is a way
> out: *the way of armed resistance.*

On the night of New Year's eve, 1942, a gathering of all members of
the Zionist settlement-oriented youth groups was held in Vilna, and
Abba Kovner's declaration was read there. The declaration was
drafted after discussion and hesitations among leaders of these
groups. The declaration, read in Yiddish and Hebrew, included the
following words:

> Jewish youth! Do not trust those who deceive you! Of 80,000 Jews in
> the "Jerusalem of Lithuania," only 20,000 remain! They have torn
> our parents, brothers, and sisters from us before our eyes . . . of
> those taken through the gates of the ghetto, none have returned. All
> ways of the Gestapo lead to Ponar, and Ponar is death! . . . Hitler
> plots to destroy all of European Jewry, and the Jews of Lithuania

have been chosen to be first in line. We will not be led like lambs to the slaughter! It is true that we are weak and defenseless, but the only answer to the murderer is armed rebellion!!

Abba Kovner and a group of partisans from Vilna.

The first questions this declaration raised were whether Kovner and his colleagues knew of Nazi plans, and whether the fact that "Hitler is plotting to destroy European Jewry" was something they learned from some source. They had no such definite knowledge. The uncompromising and determined statement was the fruit of sense and wisdom alone. The reality was that the government's actions were not advertised to the public, and the media did not discuss these questions. The Jews received no information about what awaited them, and were forced to learn of their fate from experience, from reading the map of reality with sober eyes, and trying to understand from this the mysteries of the future. The facts stated in the declaration were of this sort, daring to speak of the death waiting for all. It offered no way out of this horrible situation in which the Jews were trapped: it only emphasized that there was no escape. Flight from Vilna was not a solution, because "the Jews of Lithuania are the first in line." The only answer to the murderer was, therefore, armed resistance.

It was not just one movement that conceived the idea that there was no point in abandoning Vilna, and that preparations should be made for armed resistance to further attempts at expulsion. The idea awakened and activated groups of young people of all political persuasions, and created a basis for rapprochement and identity among them, a common foundation for the first armed resistance movement.

On January 21, three weeks after the declaration was read, representatives of Vilna political parties and youth movements met and decided to establish the United Partisan Organization of Vilna (FPO) and begin preparations for an armed uprising. The fact that activists of different parties and movements, from the Communists to *Betar*, came together indicates that the founders of the organization felt that the emergency required maximum unity of forces, despite the differences and ideological disagreements. A short time after the organization was founded, a group from the *Bund* also joined. The charter of the FPO stated that "the most important goal of the organization is to prepare for mass armed resistance to any attempt to destroy the ghetto." Three people were appointed to the joint command of the organization: Itzik Witenberg, Communist chairman of the command; Josef Glazman, *Betar*; and Abba Kovner, *HaShomer HaTzair*.

Haim Lazar, of *Betar* and a member of the FPO, notes in *Destruction and Revolt*, his book on Vilna, that

> Josef Glazman wanted another force, which would unite youth from all the movements. It was clear to him that, in a time of danger, there was no justification for dividing forces. The enemy does not distinguish between one Jew and another and does not check his party card. It is absolutely necessary that a united Jewish force stand against him.

Even in Vilna, however, there was not a complete unification of the underground forces. Another organization called *Kvutzat HaMa'avak*, made up mostly of those members of *Dror* still in Vilna and commanded by Yechiel Schejnbojm, was founded some time later. Members of *Betar* who had not joined the FPO or who had left it, as well as people unassociated with any other group, also joined this second organization. In other ghettos as well, including the Warsaw ghetto, there was also not full unification of the fighting forces, although both in Vilna and Warsaw there was in the end general coordination of the preparation and operations leading to the uprising. It should be noted, nevertheless, that the opposing political forces in the Jewish community never achieved more unity than during the organization of the struggle in the ghettos.

Josef Glazman, one of the leaders of the underground in the Kovno Ghetto.

Aharon (Dolek) Libeskind, one of the leaders of the underground in Cracow.

The FPO did not limit itself to organizational activity and preparations for the struggle in Vilna alone. It attempted to spread the idea of armed resistance to other Jewish communities. The conclusion that what they were facing was not a local pogrom but a general process threatening all the Jews of Europe obligated them to warn others. It was only natural that the people of the movements in Vilna should turn to their comrades in other cities and ghettos. Even before messengers were sent out, representatives of the Jewish underground in Warsaw arrived in Vilna. Up until the German invasion of the Soviet Union, Warsaw had been cut off by the German-Soviet border from the areas in the east that had been annexed by the U.S.S.R., including Vilna. After the German invasion, an effort was made to establish contact between the separated parts of Poland. The first representative to arrive in Vilna was Heniek Grabowski, a Pole with links to the Zionist movement in Warsaw. Afterwards, representatives of the different youth movements began arriving. There was secret and frequent communication through messengers between Vilna, Bialystok, Warsaw, and Kovno.

The links between Warsaw and Bialystok were the most important. Warsaw was the focus of the Jewish underground, the base for the leadership of movements and parties, and the terminus of communication lines with Jewish communities all over Poland. There was wide public support and, on occasion, participation in the activities of the underground in Warsaw. The underground in Warsaw, however, did not easily accept the ideas and warnings of its sister organization in Vilna. Many saw them as empty panic, and believed that the disaster which had hit the Jewish communities in the east, within the Soviet Union, was the result of disorder and instability in the areas close to the front, or German revenge on the local Jews, whom they saw as Soviet collaborators. Public figures refused to believe that what was happening in Lithuania, Byelorussia, and the Ukraine was more than a local phenomenon, and would not believe that the slaughter in the east was an indication of a Nazi extermination campaign. It was clear that an attempt by the Jews to put together an armed force would bring about severe retaliation from the Nazis, worse than other conquered nations would suffer, so the preparation for battle and the collective punishment it would bring was liable to turn into an immeasurable disaster. The most important objection, which prevented clear understanding of the situation, derived from their disbelief that a central European country with a tradition of culture and a lawabiding citizenry would be able to conduct a mass murder campaign against an entire nation which had done them no evil. After all, the Jews in occupied central Poland (the *General gouvernement* and annexed areas) had been under German rule for two years by this time, and while it had brought them the humiliation and starvation of the Jews in the ghettos, and had brought about the deaths of tens of thousands of people, there had been no methodical mass murder.

As noted, the Jews of Warsaw, including its leaders and public figures, wished to see the frightening news of the mass murders as a phenomenon that, no matter how horrible, did not touch on Warsaw's Jews and did not endanger them directly. In a report written by Yitzhak Zuckerman in 1944, dealing with the activities of the

Jewish Fighting Organization and on the revolt in the Warsaw ghetto, he noted:

> On Pesach 1942 the liquidation of the Jews of the *General gouvernement* began. The first victims were the Jews of Lublin, and soon thereafter the Lublin district. They took them to Belzec (a death camp set up 90 km. north of Lvov, on the road to Warsaw), where they were killed in new gas chambers built specially for this purpose. The Jewish underground press published detailed descriptions of this mass slaughter. But Warsaw did not believe! The human mind could not understand that it is possible to destroy tens and hundreds of thousands of Jews. They decided that the Jews were being taken to do agricultural work in parts of Russia conquered by the Germans. There were comments that the Germans had begun making the Jewish petit-bourgeoisie productive! . . . For two and a half years, after all, the Germans had already carried out many expulsions of Jews: from Cracow, from Lublin, from the Warsaw district, and from the Reich. Of course, these expulsions involved many deaths and much bloodshed. But complete extermination?

There were indeed people who believed that the reports of events at Ponar were true, but said "it is no more than a caprice of the local authorities." The German authorities in the *General gouvernement* did not give equal treatment to the different city and two ghettos until death made them all equal. The reaction in various places to the news of the extermination of the Jews was "nothing like that could happen here!"

In contrast to the hesitation and the avoidance of the truth displayed by older members of the underground, it was clear to the members of the Zionist youth movements that the liquidation of the Jews of Vilna was the beginning of the extermination of Polish Jewry. This judgment was given even more force when, in January 1943, the few survivors of the Chelmno extermination camp, near Lodz, arrived in Warsaw and told of the mass murder of Jews conducted in the gas chambers of that camp since December 1942. The spring of 1943 brought news of the deportations from Lublin and the operation of the death camps. The horror, which had seemed limited to a defined and far-off geographical area, began to look like an immediate danger.

In March, 1942, representatives of the movements and parties in the underground had met for a consultation. At the meeting, Yitzhak

Zuckerman suggested, in the name of the *HeHalutz* movement, the establishment of a fighting force, the election of a public body to lend support during its organization for battle, and a request for aid from the Polish underground. Among the participants in the meeting were Shalom-Stefan Greik of *Poalei Tzion*, Hirsch Berlinski of *Poalei Tzion Smol*, and Blum from the *Bund*. The plan was vetoed, according to some of the participants, by the representatives of the *Bund*. They argued that they did not support separate Jewish action, including Zionist groups, since they considered themselves to be part of the general Polish socialist camp. The Zionist youth movements were disappointed, because they had been particularly interested in the participation of the *Bund*, which had links with the non-Jewish underground in central Poland, which was in turn under the direction of the Polish government in exile in London. The organizers of the Jewish underground had hoped through these channels to obtain weapons, communications, and guidance for the establishment of an armed group. The refusal of the *Bund* prevented, at that stage, wider organization in the Warsaw Ghetto. Both the *Bund* and *Poalei Tzion Smol* were parties which managed to adjust relatively well to underground activity, and their work in the Warsaw underground was impressive.

The settlement-oriented Zionist youth movements invested much effort, in vain, in trying to create links with the fighting arm of the Polish underground. There were two reasons for the Poles' lack of enthusiasm for ties to the Jewish forces. The first and most important was the belief of central figures in the Polish underground that the Jews were not an integral part of the Polish nation and that the Polish nation did not therefore need to concern itself with them. Neither did the Poles believe that the Jews could fight, and they treated them with open contempt. The second reason was that the Polish underground functioned in accordance with a long-range master plan. According to this plan, comprehensive military action was to begin only when political and military circumstances were appropriate, that is, when both the Germans and the Russians had exhausted themselves. Then the Polish forces would join the battle, liberate Poland, and fix its political future and territorial boundaries. According to this plan, limited action before the decisive confrontation at the right hour was not desirable. The Jews and their proposals appeared at a time when the Poles were not interested in armed resistance. The impatience of the Jews did not fit in with the plans of the Polish underground, and were therefore totally rejected.

One aspect of the extermination campaign against the Jews did, however, make the Poles uneasy: many of them asked themselves if the murder of the Jews was not the first stage of an operation which would later be turned against all or part of the Polish nation. This threat required the attention of the *Armia Krajowa* (AK). In November, 1942, after the huge deportation from the Warsaw Ghetto, the high commander of the armed forces of the Polish underground, General Stefan Grot-Rowecki, issued the following order:

1. The Polish public has been displaying disquiet with regard to the extermination of the Jews by the occupier, fearing that after the end of this operation the Germans will begin to liquidate Poles in the exact same way. . .
2. In the event that the Germans do make such an attempt, they will encounter active resistance from us. Regardless of the fact that the time for us to revolt has not arrived, the units under my command will enter battle to defend the life of our people. . .

Most Poles were therefore ready to act promptly and with their full strength, but only to defend Polish lives.

Members of the pioneer movements, who had initiated the meeting in March, 1942, did not despair. Aid came from another direction. At the beginning of 1942, the Communist Party of Poland reorganized itself, after having been disbanded close to the beginning of the war by the Comintern. Most of its leaders had been murdered in Stalin's purges. This party was interested in organizing anti-Nazi military activity immediately, and one of the paratrooper-messengers from the Soviet Union, a Jew named Pincus Kartyn (in the ghetto he went by the name of Andrzej Szmidt) arrived at the ghetto and took upon himself the task of organizing an armed organization there. The framework he set up called "the Anti-Fascist Bloc," was joined by *Poalei Tzion Smol* and *Poalei Tzion ZS*, as well as some of the left-wing youth movements. The bodies joining this force did so, among other reasons, because of the great sympathy they had for the Soviet Union, then stubbornly blocking the Nazi advance, but mostly because they hoped that the elements acting in coordination with the Soviet Union could supply vital weapons and guidance for the establishment of a broad-based Jewish organization. It became clear, however, that the Polish Communists had no direct links with Moscow. They were outcasts among the Polish people. They had good intentions with regard to the Jews, but they had no arms, and all they gave the new Jewish organization was a single pistol for training. Escape to the forests to join the partisans was discussed but not realized. The plan failed because close to the date of leaving the ghetto, Szmidt was arrested and the military force ceased to function. The only achievement of the "Bloc" was the establishment in the ghetto of the first unified organization to try to form a fighting force.

Even during this period the leaders of the Warsaw ghetto did not think that deportations would ever reach the ghetto. David Vdovinski, the leader of the Revisionists in the ghetto, related that at the end of April, 1943, two members of *Betar* from Lublin came to him and told him that "the Lublin ghetto had been destroyed." Vdovinski brought these young men to Czerniakow, head of the Warsaw *Judenrat*, and they repeated the story for him. Czerniakow thought they were exaggerating, and refused to take any action since the Germans had promised that three ghettos—Warsaw, Radom, and Cracow—would be allowed to remain. Other officials to whom Vdovinski suggested the organization of self-defense also rejected his idea.

Czerniakow wrote in his diary that rumors reached him from different sources that deportation was impending. On July 20, two days before the beginning of the deportation and three days before his suicide, Czerniakow asked the Germans to explain. He turned, naturally, to those same Germans with whom he had been in communication during the previous three years. Despite the impassable barrier which then existed between Jews and Germans, Czerniakow had succeeded in settling with them many matters affecting daily life in the ghetto, and had reached an understanding with them, having discovered a ray of humanity among a few of the German officials. Czerniakow wrote the following in his office diary on July 20:

> At 7:30 in the Gestapo office, I asked Mende whether there was any truth in the rumors. He answered that he had not heard anything about it. Afterwards I went to Brandt. [The two worked in the Jewish Affairs Office of the Gestapo and were at that time making final arrangements for deportation. They played a central role in the deportation when it was carried out.] He answered that he knew nothing of the sort. As to the question of whether it might nevertheless happen, he answered that he knew nothing. I left full of doubts. I turned to his supervisor, the Commissar Boehm. He said that it

was not his office, and that Hohemann (Heimann) could tell me
something about the background of the rumors. I noted that according to the rumors going around, the evacuation was to begin
today at 7:30 p.m. He said that he would certainly know about it if it
were true. I had no choice but to go to Shürer, assistant director of
the third division. He expressed shock at the rumors and argued
that he also knew nothing about it. In the end I asked if I could no-
tify the public that there was no reason for fear. He said I could and
that all the rumors were nonsense and unfounded. I ordered Lejkin
[acting head of the Jewish police] to announce this through the local
stations.

On July 22, 1942, when the great deportation from the Warsaw
Ghetto began, there was no fighting organization prepared to resist,
and there was not even a united framework of all the underground
forces ready to resist. On the second day of the deportation, an urgent
meeting was called, attended by representatives of all the underground organizations and by public figures. The subject for discussion was reaction and the organization of the underground forces in
the face of the deportation. According to reports from the meeting,
the representatives of the political groups, including the *Bund*, supported the establishment of a resistance organization, with the objections coming this time from public figures holding positions of
authority. Yitzhak Schipper, an historian, public figure, and senior
Zionist activist, argued that it was the fate of the Jews to pay a high
price in lives during troubled times. It was a painful price, but they
continued to exist and perform their calling. An attempt to resist
would only turn limited troubles into total destruction, God forbid,
and wipe out the Jewish people completely. For this reason, revolt
should be avoided even at the height of the deportation. Another person whose opinion was important in influencing the gathering was
Alexander Zisha Friedman, one of the leaders of *Agudat Yisrael*, the
ultra-religious organization. Friedman argued that the nation ought
to put its trust in divine benevolence. God would not abandon his
people. Rescue would come. It was forbidden to use violence when it
would be fruitless; the result of such violence would necessarily be
tragedy. With no unanimity of opinion, the meeting dispersed without reaching a decision, and the assumption was that more discussion
would follow.

Emmanuel Ringleblum, who saw Schipper as his teacher, wrote in
a biographical profile:

On Passover, 1942, the *Seder* service was held in the welfare house
of all the Zionist movements at 13 Zamenhof Street. Schipper gave
an enthusiastic speech on self-defense should there be deportations
from Warsaw. . . . He called on Jewish youth to take an example
from Jewish history, the Maccabees, or from the rebels against the
Tsar in 1905, and so on. The Jewish youth of Warsaw had to be
ready to defend Jewish honor. A few months later, when the liquidation campaign began in Warsaw, it was the very same man,
Schipper, who opposed resistance. In the meetings between all the
different groups, Schipper sided with Zisha Friedman, the most enthusiastic supporter of passivity, and his contention that resistance
to the enemy would bring about disaster to the entire nation.

During the first days of the deportation, there was also an attempt to
create cooperation among different Zionist-Socialist groups, but this
did not succeed either. Everything was lost in the deportation and the
hopeless attempts to escape from the Germans, the Ukranians, and the
Jewish police. On July 28, 1942, representatives of *HeHalutz,
HaShomer HaTzair, Dror,* and *Akiva* movements met and decided to
found the "Jewish Fighting Organization" (ZOB or AIL). By November,
1942, the organization had broadened to include most of the Jewish
underground troops in Warsaw, except for the Revisionists and *Betar,*
who established an organization of their own. The AIL command was
composed of Mordecai Anielewicz (*HaShomer HaTzair*), Commander,
Organization Division; Yitzhak Zuckerman (*Dror—HeHalutz*), Deputy
Commander, Armaments; Mark Edelman (*Bund*), Intelligence;
Yochanan Morgenstern (*Poalei Tzion ZS*), Finance; Hirsch Berlinski
(*Poalei Tzion Smol*), Planning; and Michael Rosenfeld (*Communist*). The
central representative of the group on the "Aryan" side of Warsaw was
Arien Wilner, "Turek," a member of *HaShomer HaTzair*. The Jewish
Fighting Organization, like the FPO in Vilna, hoped to influence other
Jewish communities in occupied Poland and encourage and urge them
to establish fighting forces themselves. In this framework, Mordecai
Tenenbaum-Tamarov went to Bialystok and assumed direction of the
armed resistance there. Connections were also made with the
Czestochowa Ghetto and the Cracow underground. The AIL also in-
fluenced the armed resistance in Bendin-Sosnowiec in Upper
Silesia.

The deportations from Warsaw lasted about six weeks. During this
period some 280,000 people were taken from the city and sent to the
Treblinka death camp—in other words, at least 80 percent of the Jew-

ish community in Warsaw. The deportation was conducted as a continuous hunt for people during all hours of the day and night. At first the Germans claimed that they would take only those who did not work steadily in one place, which could have been interpreted as a desire on the part of the Germans to take from the ghetto people who were a burden on the public. It was said that people who worked in recognized work places were given certificates protecting them and their families from deportation. But the circle of those sentenced to deportation gradually widened. Protection was no longer granted to the families of workers, and, gradually the recognition of work places was revoked and their employees deported. Even work places classified as essential to the Nazi war effort were told to reduce the number of their employees.

Every day there were rumors that the deportations were about to end, and people quoted statistics on the maximum number of people they would encompass. The predictions, however, did not even approach the actual number of deportations. The work of capturing people was performed by German police, uniformed Ukranians, and the Jewish police. During the first stages, the Jewish police played an important role in the deportations. Later on, they became a secondary force in the "action," but they participated in the campaign to the very end. The Jews were hunted constantly. They tried with all their strength to escape from their pursuers and defend themselves and their immediate families, but the ghetto began to empty, and everyone felt that the net was closing in. Many were defeated by hunger and in their despair reported voluntarily, convincing themselves that they would be rewarded for turning themselves in with a bit of bread and jam. Many reported because their families had been taken and they wanted to join them, or because they no longer wanted to live after those close to them had been taken. Orphaned and abandoned children went to the collection point called *Umshlagplatz*.

Under these circumstances, when all the powers of the body and the soul were directed toward escaping the omnipresent trap, it was difficult to activate the fighters and prepare the resistance. One event of importance took place in the inferno: The members of the major factions of the new Fighting Organization left their parents' houses and gathered in a few places, in order to meet the evil together and try to act in the final hour. However, in the words of Yitzhak Zuckerman, "The Fighting Organization was established, but the only weapon the ghetto had was a single pistol!"

The public, caught in a desperate struggle for survival, did not know that a resistance group had been founded in the ghetto, and gave it no thought. During the first days of the deportations, the various underground factions issued a declaration calling on the Jews not to obey the German and Jewish police and to hide and resist the deportations. This declaration was met with disbelief. Many even thought that a Nazi provocation lay behind it, and that passive resistance would give the Nazis an excuse to use more severe methods in the deportations and widen its scope. The Organization was not able to take its first steps until the last days of the "action." On August 20, a member of the Organization, Yisrael Kanal, shot the head of the Jewish police, Jozef Szerynski, a convert to Christianity. The next day the first shipment of weapons was spirited into the ghetto, including five pistols and eight hand grenades, considered by the fighters to be a great store. Factories destined for destruction and houses emptied of their inhabitants were set on fire in order to destroy the property and to keep it from falling into the hands of the Germans.

The deportations ceased during the second week of September. The reduced ghetto was limited to a number of disconnected areas and streets on which central factories were located. Officially, 35,000 Jews remained in the ghetto, 10 percent of the pre-deportation population. Close to 20,000 Jews had managed to remain in the ghetto illegally. Plans for the first revolt in January, 1943, and the great uprising of April, 1943, began to take form.

As noted above, the armed Jewish struggle in the ghetto was dependent to a large extent on help from the local non-Jewish population and on its own underground forces. For hundreds of years the Jews of many countries had lived alongside the local populations in the cities and villages, and had made a significant contribution to the economic life and culture of the lands in which they lived. It was natural that the Jews should expect some help from their neighbors at this fateful time. Sadly, though, very few Lithuanians, Latvians, and Ukranians helped the Jews in their time of need, and there were those who even helped the Nazi murderers and participated in the extermination campaign. While the Polish people did not take an active part in the murder of the Jews, most of them were apathetic to their fate. There were also Poles who helped the Nazis find Jews, and those who were happy to see the Nazis "doing a good job." There were gangs of hooligans who enthusiastically hunted down Jews hiding in Polish cities, robbed them of their property, and turned them in to the enemy. A few Poles, deeply shocked by what was happening, tried with all their strength to help Jews escape, and gave them weapons.

As has been discussed, the military command of the Polish underground was not interested in taking any real steps to help the Jews. Nevertheless, the murder of millions of Jews led some members of the Polish underground to consider that some day the matter would be investigated, researched, and made public. There were also indications from London that not only the Jews, but also central figures in the Allied leadership wanted to know what the Poles, and especially their underground, were doing in order to help the Jews. It is only right to note that there were people within the Polish underground who expressed their disgust with the lack of action, and demanded to go to the help of the Jews for both human and religious reasons. Given this, the leadership of the Polish underground felt that it was obligated to take some steps, even if merely symbolical, to help the Jews.

So, in September, 1942, the Jewish Fighting Organization in Warsaw was recognized as a body operating under the sponsorship of the Polish underground. The Jews also received a small number of arms at this time, though with much hesitation. The Jews were forced to obtain most of the ammunition themselves. They had to plan the struggle, train the fighters, and stand alone on the battle lines. It is interesting that in January, 1943, at a time when most of Polish Jewry had been destroyed and the remnants were calling desperately for assistance, General Grot-Rowecki, the supreme commander of the AK military organization in the Polish underground, sent the following telegram to the Polish government in exile:

> Jews from all sorts of groups, including Communists, have contacted us recently and are asking us for weapons, as if we had full armories. As a trial, we took out a few pistols. I am not at all sure that they will use these weapons. I will not give any more weapons, since, as you know, we have none for ourselves.

In this short telegram we find several of the excuses and motives which guided the Poles. First, it is "they" and "we." Second, the highest military figure, responsible for the security of the Poles, does not believe that Jews will use weapons and that they mean to fight. Finally, he argues that he himself has no weapons. The ten pistols delivered then to the Jewish Fighting Organization are presented as a significant portion of the armory of the Polish underground, which had tens of thousands of rifles and pistols, and hundreds of machine guns.

The Jews were forced to fight in the face of the murder campaign in their communities, while the Poles had their own strategic and political considerations. In the last days before the outbreak of the revolt in the Warsaw Ghetto, Polish officials tried to prevent an uprising in the ghetto and suggested transferring the fighters and their weapons to the forests, where they could carry out a partisan struggle under the sponsorship of the AK. The answer of the Jewish representatives was a firm "no."

Yitzhak Zuckerman who, during the revolt, was the representative of the Jewish Fighting Organization on the Polish side of Warsaw, submitted an oral report in May, 1947, of the discussions among members of the Polish underground:

> I will relate, as an example, two meetings during the revolt with the *Armia Krajowa* and the *Armia Ludowa* (which was under Communist influence). I met with a man named Hajcuch, one of the "righteous among the nations." He told me: "I will open the gate for you and bring you to a man who heads the all-powerful Polish detective force." I met with the man. He introduced himself to me as Grandir Karol. I told him: "Bring us weapons! Bring us help!" He answered, and this was during the first days of the revolt, that he was ready to get our company of fighters out of the ghetto. I told him: "The company will not leave the ghetto as long as they have more than the one bullet they need in their rifles to commit suicide! I demand weapons in order to continue to hold out in the ghetto! I demand, for the second stage, when the revolt begins to falter, that you prepare, in advance, vehicles and people to get out those of our men who remain alive. And I demand houses in which to hide the fighters who leave the ghetto." He did not agree, and said that he was ready to get our people out of the ghetto immediately, and I did not agree to that. The man added: "There is fear among the Poles that the revolt will expand beyond the streets of the ghetto and that the Poles will rise up. That is what the *Armia Lodowa* wants. So I warn you: if that happens, and if you cooperate with the *Armia Lodowa* and it comes to your rescue—we will stand against the ghetto!" So our conversation ended.

The Jewish fighters in Vilna met with a similar attitude on the part of the Poles. Rozka Korczak, one of the women members of the Vilna underground, wrote that

> the answer to our request to the FPO for weapons was, and this after various delays and excuses, that according to the order received from the Polish government in exile in London, it was forbidden to give weapons to Jews in the areas bordering the Soviet Union. There was a fear, so the Poles argued, that the Jews would aim these weapons, in time, against the Poles who would fight the Soviets.

> Mordecai Tannenbaum stated in his diary in the Bialystok Ghetto that the members of the armed Polish resistance saw every act of resistance involving direct war against the occupying power as a provocation. "The time has not yet come! We need to keep our reserves for the right day!" The Polish government will tell us when to take out the weapons!

It is only proper to note that the Communists and leftists (the *Armia Ludowa*) were sympathetic to the efforts of the Jews to create a fighting force and defend themselves. However, as noted, these groups were of limited usefulness and could do no more than offer friendly relations and minimal material support.

The ghetto rebellion was a struggle initiated by the Jewish underground, and looked to the general Jewish population for support. One of the Jewish scholars of the Holocaust and author of an important book on the *Judenraten*, Isaiah Trunk, has dealt widely with the question of the attitude of the *Judenraten* to the idea of armed resistance. He reached the conclusion that there were three types of *Judenrat*, or three different positions the *Judenraten* took with regard to fighting in the ghettos: *Judenraten* who objected in principle to fighting; *Judenraten* who favored fighting; and ambivalent *Judenraten*.

The negative attitude is clear. The positive attitude applied for the most part to *Judenraten* in relatively small communities in the eastern districts of pre-war Poland. These took an active part in and in some cases led, uprisings against the "actions," and urged the Jews to break out of the ghetto and escape into the nearby forests. This type of struggle was intended as an act of resistance making escape possible. We will discuss this type of resistance in more detail later on.

As for the third approach, the ambivalent *Judenraten*, Trunk had in mind the *Judenraten* of Vilna and Bialystok. In these two places there

was a certain amount of contact between the *Judenrat*, or more accu-
rately, the heads of the *Judenrat*—Ya'akov Gens in Vilna and Efraim
Barash in Bialystok—and the underground. In Bialystok there were
close relations between Barash and Tenenbaum-Tamarov, and in
Vilna, up to a certain extent, there were such ties between Gens and
some members of the resistance organization. This understanding
and trust existed, however, only up to a certain point. These *Judenrat*
leaders desired close relations with the underground as long as the
positions and ideas of the two sides did not openly clash. When it became clear to the heads of the *Judenraten* that the preparations for the
uprisings were in full swing, and that the organizations were smuggling weapons into the ghetto and maintaining contact with partisan
groups in the forests in preparation for the coming test, they reversed
their position and became sharp opponents. This was inevitable because the *Judenraten* in the large ghettos assumed that working and
negotiating with the Germans was the only way to save Jews. Gens
opposed the exit of young Jews from Vilna to join the partisan units in
the forests on the grounds that this would deprive the ghetto of its
most desirable and efficient work force and would leave the Germans
no reason not to destroy it.

The dispute between the *Judenraten* and the fighters became con-
crete in a few events in the Vilna and Bialystok ghettos. The entente
between the *Judenrat* and the FPO in Vilna was violated after Gens
sent his police to carry out a deportation "action" in Oshmiana, a
town near Vilna. Gens instructed Glazman, an employee of the
Judenrat, to leave for one of these places on a mission and Glazman
refused. Gens tried to arrest Glazman, and he was sent, bound, to police headquarters (June, 1943). Along the way, however, members of
the FPO attacked the police and Glazman was freed by force. After
this violent clash between the *Judenrat* and the resistance, the two
sides met to clarify the matter and Glazman was sent for a time to a
work camp as a compromise. Some time later Glazman left the ghetto
for the forest at the head of a group of partisans.

More serious and decisive was the clash between the two sides in
the Witenberg affair, on "Witenberg Day" in the Vilna ghetto. On July
8, 1943, Gens announced that members of the Nazi security police
had come to the ghetto and demanded that he hand Yitzhak
Witenberg over to them. Witenberg was commander of the fighting
organization in Vilna, and his name was apparently known to the
Nazis, not because they had heard of his activity in the ghetto, but

because arrested Lithuanian Communists said that he was active in a Communist group in Vilna. The FPO faced a dilemma. Gens said he had no say in the matter, and that if Witenberg were not turned over the entire ghetto would pay the price. On the other hand, it was clear that if the resistance organization handed over an officer it would not only deal a severe blow to its reputation, but also greatly weaken its morale and ability to take action. When the debate became heated, Gens turned to the inhabitants of the ghetto, who supported handing over Witenberg. In the end, Witenberg was delivered to the Germans and committed suicide without revealing anything of the activity of the organization. The events surrounding this, however, had far-reaching consequences on the organization's future in Vilna.

In Bialystok, Barash accused the fighters of having taken funds and property from the *Judenrat*, and Mordecai Tenenbaum was forced to hide from a man to whom he had been personally close to some time.

Clashes with the *Judenrat* and the attitude of the public to the fighters and to the idea of resistance had a major influence on discussions of whether it was preferable to fight in the ghetto or to escape to the forests to engage in partisan warfare. The most important factor was whether local topography was favorable to guerrilla warfare and whether there were already other partisan groups in the area. At the end of 1942 and the beginning of 1943, partisan units under Soviet control formed in the forests of Lithuania, Byelorussia, and the Ukraine (around Kovno, Vilna, Minsk, and other cities). These units were disciplined and some of their Soviet commanders displayed an openness to Jewish recruits, especially during the early period, when they found it difficult to fill their ranks from among the local population. This development meant that in these places there was some possibility of escaping to the forests. The possibilities were many fewer, however, in central Poland and in the annexed areas of western Poland where there were only a few thinly-forested areas and few established partisan bases. In Vilna, and to a certain extent in Bialystok, an important factor in deciding to escape to the forest was the assumption that the ghetto population would not support the fighters in their dispute with the *Judenrat*, and neither would they lend support in armed conflict.

A second resistance group active in Vilna, known as the "Yechiel (Sheinbaum) Group," or the "Struggle Group," saw the forests as the major battleground from the beginning. Dr. Marc Dworzecki wrote in his book, *The Jerusalem of Lithuania in Rebellion and in the Holocaust*:

> This organization differed from the FPO in its strategy and evalua-
> tion of the possibilities for resistance in the ghetto. Their feeling was
> that the conditions of the ghetto, composed of a few small streets in
> the center of the city, in the heart of a population unwilling to assist
> in the struggle, would not allow a realistic revolt. For this reason,
> Jewish honor, the desire to take revenge upon the enemy, and the
> desire to save as many Jews as possible demand getting as many
> people as possible into the partisan ranks in the forest.

It is not surprising that the Yechiel Group, formed after the FPO and without the FPO's clear political and organizational identifications, emphasized the opportunity to save lives. In January, 1942, there were developments in Vilna, not considered by the founders of the FPO, which strengthened the possibilities of carrying out rescue operations. After the terrible bloodshed of the second half of 1941, the Jewish community in the Vilna ghetto enjoyed relative stability for two years, giving rise to expectations and hopes of survival. And large concentrations of disciplined partisan forces under Soviet control were interested, especially at first, in enlisting Jews into their ranks, began forming in the forests in the middle of 1942.

This situation made its mark not only on the Yechiel Group, but on the FPO as well. On April 4, 1943, the FPO charter was read to the fighters in Vilna. To the question of how the FPO would act in the event of the partial destruction of the ghetto, the charter answered: *"The FPO will enter battle when the overall existence of the ghetto is in danger . . . The FPO will act when such an 'action' indicates the begin-ning of the end, without considering the extent of the 'action.'"*

To the question, "Should we not go to the forests immediately?" the answer is given as a series of clarifications: "No! The desire to go to the forests immediately testifies to a misunderstanding of the idea of the FPO. . . *The idea behind the Jewish Partisan Organization is a social-national one*, to organize the Jewish struggle and to defend our lives and honor."

For this reason, immediate escape to the forest without defending the ghetto in battle was opposed to the principles of the FPO. The clarifications go on to state: "Our escape to the forest will be *as a result of battle*. After we accomplish our mission here, we will take as many

Jews as possible and continue our struggle against the murderous enemy as part of the partisan movement."

It is clear, then, that in the spring of 1943, the FPO conceived of its goals in two stages; the first was the battle within the ghetto, which was a national obligation. The condition for beginning this battle was that the German "action" be the beginning of the end—that is, the first stage of the total destruction of the ghetto. The reason for this reservation was that the *Premature* action may bring premature destruction." Likewise, the FPO's goal was not a fight to the death in the ghetto, but rather *"defense, struggle, and rescue."* The battle in the ghetto was not meant to be the end; it was to be a war against the enemy in the name of defending national life and honor. When this mission was accomplished, the time to leave the ghetto and continue the struggle in the forest would come. At this stage, the FPO was to do its best to take along as many of the residents of the ghetto as possible. The struggle against the enemy would continue in the forest under new conditions, in a wide, general framework, and this path of struggle offered some chance of survival.

Doubts about the FPO philosophy were expressed pointedly in a discussion held by the *Dror* kibbutz and members of the *Poalei Tzion ZS* party in Bialystok in February 1943. Mordecai Tenenbaum-Tamarov opened the discussion:

> We can do two things; decide that, with the deportation of the first Jew from Bialystok, we will begin our "counter-action," that tomorrow no one will go to the factory, that during an action it will be forbidden for any of us to hide. Everyone will go into action. We can ensure that not one German leaves the ghetto alive, that no factory remains whole, and that while it is not impossible that after this some people will remain alive, the fight will be to the last man, to death. On the other hand, we can decide to go to the forest. We must examine the possibilities. Two went today to prepare a place for us.

Tenenbaum did not present a two-stage plan, as did the FPO charter in Vilna. He presented two possibilities: the first being a battle in the ghetto, which would be a battle to the end, although a few might remain alive at its end; and the second being a retreat to the forest, the possibilities of which were being scouted.

Hershel Rosenthal, a member of the *Dror* kibbutz who fell in the Bialystok uprising in August, 1943, spoke during the same discussion of the methods used by the Germans to deceive the Jewish masses and lead them to the death camps. He also thundered against the members of his movement who did not enlist in the resistance at the moment of truth, and argued:

> Here, in Bialystok, it is our fate to be last in this bloody tragedy. What must we do, what can we do? My evaluation is that the objective situation is this: The majority of the ghetto and of our families have been sentenced to death, and our fate is sealed. We have never seen the forest as a hiding place. The forest was for us always a place for war and revenge. But the many young people going to the forest today are not looking for a place for war, and may will live there as beggars and their end will thus be beggars' deaths. Under the conditions in which we find ourselves today, we can expect the same miserable beggar's fate. Nothing then remains for us but one thing, the organization of collective resistance in the ghetto as our 'Musa-Dag' and to add an honorable chapter to the history of Jewish Bialystok and of our movement.

Sarah Kopinski, a member of *Dror* who also fell in the Bialystok uprising in August, 1943, said:

> Of course, to remain alive is more important than killing five Germans. I have no doubt that we will all die in the "counter-action." In the forest, 40–50 percent of our people may survive. It would be to our honor, and in the interests of history. We are still needed! We still have a role to play! As for honor—that is lost anyway. Remaining alive is our purpose.

Chanoch Zeloznogora, a member of *HeHalutz HaTzair* and another martyr of the Bialystok rebellion, said:

> There are no illusions; destruction awaits us here, to the last Jew! Two ways to death are before us. The forest will not save us, and the rebellion in the ghetto certainly will not. We have nothing to do but to die honorably. . . . Of course, the possibilities for revenge are greater in the forest, but we must not go there and become dependent on the mercy of farmers from whom we will have to buy food and life. Going to the forest means beginning active resistance. To do that, we need the necessary weapons. The weapons we have will not succeed in the forest. If we still have time we must find weapons and go to the forest. But if the "action" comes first, we can only react immediately, when the first Jew is taken!

Mordecai Tenenbaum-Tamarov closed the discussion with the following words:

> The position of our members is clear: we will do all we can to take as many people as possible into the partisan war in the forest. But everyone who is in the ghetto at the time of the coming "action" must react the minute the first Jew is taken. . .

As we can see, the form the struggle took was influenced by the circumstances in the different areas of Europe. In the Warsaw Ghetto, after a series of deportations, after the failure of the attempts to get to the forests and find a foothold in them, and in the wake of the formation of the Jewish Fighting Organization, the idea of battle within the ghetto took hold of the fighters. The Fighting Organization in Warsaw no longer fostered the idea of a one-time battle, retreat, escape, and battle outside the ghetto. Moreover, there was determined opposition in Warsaw to a two-track strategy—war in the ghetto simultaneous with or preceding another type of resistance. The planners of the Warsaw Ghetto uprising argued that even raising the possibility of fighting outside the framework of the revolt was liable to detract from the basic goal of the battle, which was to be a war to the end, to the last man. The search for routes of retreat and ways to continue would, in the opinion of the Fighting Organization in the Warsaw Ghetto, make the fighters less willing to hold their positions to the end.

In Kovno, Minsk, and other places the resistance movement was aimed from the beginning at partisan fighting in the forests. The special conditions in these places, the partisan bases in the nearby forests, and the links established between the underground forces and the partisan units outside the ghetto, led the local Jewish undergrounds to feel that going to the forests was an appropriate type of resistance. Later we will speak more about these places, when we deal with partisan warfare and its character.

In Byelorussia and the Ukraine, the Jewish population rose up several times against Nazi "actions" and mass murder. Thousands of Jews fled to the forests, where they found shelter and organized resistance. One type of resistance unique to this area was the collective revolt of Jewish towns and mass escape of entire families to the forests.

The battle strategy in the Cracow Ghetto was different from the struggles of Jewish fighters in other places. The evacuation of Cracow's Jews began in 1940, and was similar to the deportation from the Reich and its annexed territories. It was initiated by Governor

Frank, with the justification that the presence of Jews in Cracow was detrimental to the capital of the *General gouvernement*, and undesirable to high German officials who had to come into contact with Jews.

This was the beginning of the expulsion of Cracow's Jews, whose number at the outbreak of the war was close to 70,000. Even though the Germans were not able to carry out their intentions completely, many Jews were deported, and others were forced to leave the city under the threat of deportation and return only when the threat had passed. During the expulsion of the population from the city and the establishment of the ghetto, the composition of the Jewish population changed, a change which created an atmosphere of uncertainty and impermanence. The pioneer Zionist *Akiva* movement, which was based in Cracow, was the nucleus of the Jewish underground in the city. Two of the leaders of this movement, Shimshon (Shimek) Drengner and Aharon (Dolek) Libeskind, stood out in their display of initiative, independence and originality in the organization of the underground. During the first stages the Cracow underground concentrated on finding escape routes from the area under Nazi occupation. Many proposals were raised and some of them were actively examined, but the results were disappointing.

When the Cracow ghetto was established in March, 1941, links with the outside world were not completely severed. A few individual Jews and underground groups managed to maintain continuous contact with Polish underground groups in the city. The Polish groups which gave the most help to the Jews were the Socialists, and after them the Communists.

This situation in Cracow and in the smaller Jewish communities nearby led the Jewish resistance in Cracow to pursue different means of struggle than in the other ghettos. The Cracow fighters, both the nucleus of *HeHalutz HaLochem* headed by *Akiva* movement, and the group centered around *HaShomer HaTzair*, decided to attack the Germans and carry out acts of revenge outside the ghetto. Some of their important actions were coordinated with the Polish underground. The argument of the Cracow fighters was that by fighting outside the ghetto they did not endanger its inhabitants and did not bring the anger of the Germans on the ghetto. Members of the Jewish Fighting Organization in Warsaw maintained close ties with Cracow. Messenger Hella Schifer of *Akiva* was in steady communication with them and smuggled weapons from Warsaw to Cracow. Avraham Leibovitz, "Laban," a member of *Dror*, came from Warsaw to Cracow in order to act as part of the nucleus of *HeHalutz HaLochem*, and central figures from the Warsaw organization, among them Yitzhak Zuckerman, visited Cracow. The Organization tried to persuade the people of Cracow to abandon their special tactic and fight within the ghetto. But members of the Cracow organizations insisted on their original strategy, a sort of urban guerrilla warfare.

A reliable picture of the central organization of the Jews of Cracow, its members, and its methods can be seen in the surviving copies of the underground newspaper *HeHalutz HaLochem* and from *The Diary of Justina* (Gusta Davidson), the major part of which was saved. In Issue Number 29 of *HeHalutz HaTzair*, April 29, 1943, an article headlined "Speculum of the Future," written by Shimson Drengner, said:

> Given the tragic reality of the Jews, with the existence of the individual dependent on chance and the existence of the people long ago laid low—it is fitting to survey the situation continuously and from every angle. Individual points of view have nothing real in them; this is clear and certain, for every person. From a personal point of view we are all lost! Our chances of surviving are near zero, and destroyed and isolated we cannot put much hope in life. But while we fall as one with all the Jews of Poland, we must make ourselves feel well the historical significance of the hour, and say courageously that our deaths will not bring on the end of the world, and that the history of mankind, and with it the history of the Jews, continues to move along its path, even though our mass graves will already be filled. . . For this reason, even in the face of inevitable death our hearts are with them in the struggle for the future. Every deed of ours paves the people's path to freedom, advances the establishment of an independent homeland. Our starting point is the protest against the evil flooding the world. As payment for the violence which has crushed our people, we report for the struggle for justice and freedom, for the good of the entire nation. We desire to die in this way, so that in the future the shameful death of slaves will not trouble Jews; so that they will not have to recall with shame the Jews of Europe who went like lambs to the slaughter and did not know how to rise to the virtue of courage in order to die in their own defense! Since we are not able to lend a hand to creative construction, we will at least fulfill our historical role here. We must light up a dying nation, erase from its flesh the stain of slavery and put it in the rank of free nations!

Chapter 4

Revolt and Resistance in the Ghettos

At the beginning of 1943, in the face of the advance of the Soviet army on the eastern front, the Nazis ordered the final destruction of the ghettos in eastern Poland, which had been annexed by the Soviet Union at the beginning of the war. In Warsaw, with the largest Jewish population of any city in Europe, a rebellion was created which can by right be considered the fullest and broadest realization of the goals the Jewish resistance set itself.

THE UPRISING IN THE WARSAW GHETTO

The pioneer youth movements in Warsaw adopted the extreme ideas of the underground in Vilna (FPO), and began to organize themselves for what was to come. The position of the underground organizations of the youth movements was not accepted by the political parties and public organizations in the underground, and those groups rejected the idea of establishing an armed resistance movement in the spring of 1942. Instead, an "Anti-Fascist Bloc" was established under Communist sponsorship. This did not last long and did not aid in the arming and training of the nucleus of people which later became the ghetto's fighting organization.

In July, 1942, when the great deportation from Warsaw began, there was no military force in the ghetto. A meeting called by the youth movements proposed opening a resistance campaign immediately. The proposal was rejected on the assumption that the Germans were still interested in Jews as a labor force and that resistance would bring about the immediate and complete destruction of the ghetto. Given the situation and the feeling that they could not persuade public representatives that their hopes for partial survival were illusory, the leaders of the pioneer youth movements decided to establish a smaller fighting organization and begin action on their own. The Jewish Fighting Organization, established on July 28, a week after the beginning of the deportations, was composed of the *HaShomer HaTzair, Dror,* and *Akiva* movements. A command was established, and a delegation was sent to the "Aryan" side of the city to obtain arms and aid and to examine the possibilities for action.

Since the organization was established at the height of the deportation, the community and the individuals within it were under tremendous pressure, and the threat of kidnapping and deportation to the Treblinka death camp lay waiting in ambush on every street. The attempts to convince the public and bring it to rebellion, however, were met with misunderstanding and fear. The first leaflets distributed by the Jewish Fighting Organization, warning that the deportees were being sent to their deaths, a fate without exception, were interpreted as provocation and were met with disbelief. The attack made by a member of the resistance, Yisrael Kanal, on the chief of the Jewish police in the ghetto, Jozef Szerynski, was seen by many Jews as an act of revenge by a Polish underground organization. They did not believe that avengers had risen among them. Nevertheless, the organization's disappointments did not wipe out its central achievement, the preservation of a fighting force during a long and deadly period of deportation. A large group of *Dror* members resided on a farm in the Czerniakow suburb of Warsaw during the deportations and were not affected by them. Members of *HaShomer HaTzair* and a small group from *Akiva* made the painful decision to cut themselves off from their homes and families and join enlisted groups ready for every call and any mission. These groups were less vulnerable than the general public in the ghetto, because they refused to appear when the Germans called.

At the end of August a small shipment of grenades and pistols was smuggled into the ghetto. This minuscule armory seemed to the fighters a powerful tool to be wielded at the right moment at the height of the deportation. A curse of sorts seemed to lie on all activities of the resistance, however. A group of fighters that had escaped during the deportations and made its way to join the partisans was caught on a train. The documents found on them led the Germans to the place the false papers were printed and to the arrest of a member of the command, Yosef Kaplan. That same day, another member of the command, Shmuel Braslaw, tried to liberate Kaplan but was killed in his struggle with the Germans.

Because of the danger, the weapons were to be taken from their hiding place and transferred to a new one, but the young woman who took the mission upon herself was caught by the Germans. So in one day, on September 3, 1942, the organization suffered a heavy blow. A few days later there was a general "selection," which many members saw as an omen of the final destruction of the ghetto. The young members of the fighting organization demanded immediate action and argued that if the hour were allowed to pass, the organization would be obliterated and its aspirations and goals wiped out with the remnant of Warsaw's Jews. A few of the leaders of the group tried to hold back the agitated young people. Yitzhak Zuckerman, a leader of the organization, opposed immediate action and face-to-face confrontation with the Germans without arms and without planning. This, he felt, could end up as an outbreak of anger, swallowed up in the general tragedy, which would not leave any impression on the future. In agreement with him was Aryeh Wilner, the central representative of the organization on the "Aryan" side who had returned to the ghetto on the eve of the "selection." He said that, according to the reliable information he had, the Germans meant to leave ten percent of the Jews in the ghetto for an additional period of time and that the great deportation was about to end. Zuckerman and Wilner proposed that the members of the organization remain in their safe hideouts in order to take advantage of the time before the next and final wave of deportation to obtain weapons, plan an uprising, and train fighters for the struggle. The younger members accepted this proposal against their wishes, and saw it as an additional delay that would bring about the gradual erosion of the organization and its dissolution without a battle.

Yitzhak Zuckerman wrote of this discussion and the atmosphere urrounding it:

> The discussion was opened by a member: We have come too late.
> The nation has died. When there were hundreds of thousands in

Warsaw we could not organize a Jewish fighting force. Can we do it
now, when there are only tens of thousands? We did not win the
trust of the masses. We have no weapons, and we will almost certainly not have any in the near future. We have no power to start
over. The nation is destroyed. Our honor trampled. This small
group can still revive it. Let us go out to the streets tomorrow, burn
the ghetto and pounce on the Germans. We will be destroyed. Our
fate is to be destroyed. But our honor will be saved. Some day they
will come and declare: "youth rose up for this helpless nation, and it
saved their honor to the extent it could."

A few comrades spoke, each in his own way. The ideas were the
same. Despair overcame the emotions. Emotions demanded deeds.
In an atmosphere of total despair it was difficult to voice other opinions. One of the comrades gathered courage and said something
like this: "The emotions are real, but the conclusions mistaken . . .
our hurt and shame are great. But the act they are proposing to carry
out is an act of despair. It will wither without an echo. There will be
but little damage to the enemy. Our youth will die. We have suffered innumerable failures up until now and we will suffer more de-
feats. We must start anew. The 'action' has ended for now. There
may well be days of relative calm, maybe weeks and maybe even
months. Every day is a prize . . . our glory is not yet lost." There was
much emotion. They shouted against the comrade who wished to
delay the last possible action. "If we do not go out to the streets immediately, we will have no power to do so tomorrow. He's clipping
our wings." The debate was hot. The atmosphere glowed. But little
by little there were voices of calm thinking. Proposals multiplied.
This night was a fateful night for the remnants of the Jewish Fighting Organization. We counted and decided to strengthen ourselves
and renew the armed Jewish force. The rest of our powers were applied to this.

In the wake of the great deportation, the Warsaw Ghetto was not
what it had once been. More than 290,000 Jews had been uprooted
from it and almost all of them had been murdered in the gas chambers at Treblinka. Masses of people had been taken from the ghetto.
Whole families vanished as if they had never been. At the time of the
deportation there were rumors, apparently intended to mislead the
Jews, of letters which had supposedly arrived from the deportees, of
places in which they had been seen, of the work in which they were
employed. All attempts to confirm these, to find out the sources of
the information, to discover exactly who had been seen and where,

turned out to be very complicated. In the end it always became clear that someone heard from a Pole who had heard from an unidentified person. The original source was always impossible to locate. At the end of the deportation silence fell, and the cruel truth was made very clear.

The great deportation left between 50,000 and 60,000 Jews working or hiding, divided into three disconnected sections. The ghetto became a work camp, and the Jews were forbidden to walk the streets during work hours. The *Judenrat* was not active for much longer, and it did not direct the life of the Jews. The control of day-to-day affairs passed to the police and the *Werkschutz*, a sort of factory police.

The same impressions and anger appear in all the diaries and memoirs from the short period after the deportation. For weeks all the attention of the ghetto residents was concentrated on evading the net of kidnappers. Then there was a sort of change, a sort of easing of the danger and of the constant fear. But no one fooled himself into believing that the situation was more than a temporary interlude, that the death mark chasing the Jews had been removed. This feeling of the certainty of deportation and death was augmented by the shame and guilt of having allowed one's close ones to be taken without any response, any action. They had saved only themselves. Those taken were those who had depended on the protection of the young and strong. The bitterness grew because of the feeling that the humiliation, the effort, the separation and abandonment of their dear ones had been no more than a temporary, futile escape.

This was the source of the anger and rebelliousness of the remnants of the ghetto. Emmanuel Ringleblum wrote:

> Moratorium—that is the proper name for [the situation] of Warsaw's Jews. Most of the population supports resistance. It seems to me that they will not go like lambs to the slaughter. The remnants want the enemy to pay dearly for their lives. They will attack with knives, sticks, acids. They will allow no more sieges for deportation. They will not allow themselves to be trapped in the streets. . . .

The support of resistance was not itself a guarantee of action, but it persuaded the people and bodies in the underground to put aside their reservations. The fighters acted first and foremost against the heads of the police and the *Judenrat* who had collaborated with the enemy in the deportations and done their jobs diligently, with hardened hearts. On October 29 the members of the Jewish Fighting

Organization executed Ya'akov Lejkin, a lawyer and head of the Jewish police during the great deportation. A month later a death sentence was carried out against Yisrael First, known as a *Judenrat* and German loyalist. Such deeds and others in their wake terrorized the police and the *Judenrat*. It was clear that even if these actions were not meant to directly deter the *Judenrat* from limiting the action of the organization, in the end this was one of the results.

The police and *Judenrat* were forced to restrain their activity; collaborators feared for their lives and hid from the vengeance of the resistance. After awhile, when the Germans complained to the *Judenrat* that the streets of the ghetto were no longer secure, the *Judenrat* leaders answered that they were no longer in control and that the secret organization was the real ruler of the ghetto. This purge of collaborators was apparently a necessary step in preparing the revolt.

In October there were significant changes in the composition and structure of the resistance. Much importance was given to the return of Mordecai Anielewicz from his mission in Zaglembia. Anielewicz, who was the outstanding figure in *HaShomer HaTzair* and one of the heads of the youth movement underground, breathed a new spirit of activism into the ranks of the organization. At the end of October negotiations with other underground organizations were concluded and a broad resistance organization was formed, including most of the groups active in the ghetto: the Zionist factions, youth movements, and political parties including the non-Zionist left—the *Bund* and the Communists. *Betar* and the Revisionists did not join, but established a separate group of their own. The Jewish Fighting Organization (AIL or ZOB) now consisted of two bodies: the military division and the national committee. The first, the major component, undertook the establishment of fighting units, acquiring weapons, and strategic planning of a large-scale resistance operation. The national committee was to grant the organization the authority and backing of the entire underground and allow it to present itself to the Polish underground as the united Jewish underground force. The military division combined all the organizations and political factions, but the *Bund* refused on principle to join that national committee, which it saw as an ideological framework in which it could not take part. As a compromise, the national committee combined all the political bodies in the underground other than the *Bund*, while a coordinating committee included both the national committee and the *Bund*.

The military division was headed by Mordecai Anielewicz and its members were Yitzchak Zuckerman (deputy commander), Marc Edelman, Yochanan Morgenstern, Hirsch Berlinski, and Michael Rosenfeld.

Representatives of the national committee on the Polish side of the city and the chief representative of the organization to the Polish groups, Aryeh Wilner, succeeded in making contact with the AK and obtaining official recognition by the large Polish organization. They also obtained a quantity of small arms and instruction. This aid, important in itself, was far from providing the needs of the organization and certainly did not reflect an effort or real desire on the part of the Poles to help. In a telegram the general commander of the AK sent to London on January 2, 1943, he said that he had "experimentally" given the Jews a few pistols, but "I will not give any additional weapons."

At the stage of the broadening of the Jewish resistance organization and the creation of its wider structure, an additional organization was formed in the ghetto made up of members of *Betar* and the Revisionist movement. We will not deal with the complex question of why, even during the final stage and time of the greatest test, all the different Jewish organizations could not achieve complete unity. It is necessary only to note after a period of conflict between the two organizations, conflict which was liable to do damage to the joint effort, the two groups came to an agreement to coordinate areas of activity, they divided the ghetto into sectors, and in the end, during the revolt, the two organizations fought as one. The second group was called the Jewish Military Union ("*Etzi*") and it was commanded by Pavel Frenkiel (commander), Natan Szulc, S. Hazenszprung, Arieh Rodal, and others. The central figure in the public side of the organization was David Wdowinski. The Revisionist organization had no formal contacts with the AK, but it managed to make links with factions which had loose connections with the central Polish military organization and, through it, the organization received arms. According to the information we have, the Jewish Military Union had a few heavier weapons that the ZOB lacked.

The fighters knew from the experience that deportations or escalations of deportations generally began on Mondays. For this reason Monday was set as a day of alert and readiness. When the second deportation began on Monday, January 18, however, the fighters were not ready for the blow they were to receive. The reason was that the

German police had been busy for a few days kidnapping Poles for forced labor in Germany, and the Jewish fighters assumed that the Germans had their hands full in the Polish sector so they would not bother the Jews.

This "second deportation" was different from the great deportation that came before it. The Jews who remained after the first reasoned that the next deportation would be the final one. However, this was not yet the German intention. We know from German documents that Himmler, in his visit in Warsaw in December, 1942, was angry that there were more Jews than planned for in the ghetto, and ordered an "action" to get rid of the "surplus," estimated by the Germans to be 8,000 people.

The January deportation was not meant, then, to destroy the ghetto completely, but rather to "complete" the previous deportation. The Jewish organizations, however, saw it as final. The Jewish fighting organization did not have the opportunity to convene its civilian institution, the national committee, to discuss the situation. In Yitzchak Zuckerman's opinion, this was actually helpful, because if they had begun discussions, hesitation might have overcome decision. Not only was the committee not convened, but there was not time for a meeting of the different groups of the organization spread throughout the ghetto, so each unit had to act on its own initiative and strength.

HaShomer HaTzair, headed by Mordecai Anielewicz, was on Mila Road, and decided to fight on the streets. The group of fighters assigned to distribute the few arms that there were merged into a long line of Jews being herded by the Germans toward the Umschlagplatz and, at an agreed-upon signal, opened fire, each one shooting the German closest to him. The entire group was made up of 10–12 men and was commanded by Mordecai Anielewicz. These few fighters, armed with pistols, could not stand against a German force, and nearly all of them fell in this engagement, including Eliahu Rozanski and Margalit Landau, who had carried out the death sentence on Leykin. Anielewicz survived.

The Mila battle took a heavy toll, but its importance for the continuation of the struggle was great. The first Germans fell in this battle, and the line of hundreds of Jews being led to the Umschlagplatz was dispersed. The Germans understood that they were liable to pay with their lives in the streets of the ghetto and this brought about a change in their behavior. In addition to the street fighting led by Anielewicz, a group of members of *Dror* also entered battle that day, from a house on Zamenhof Street. This group, commanded by Yitzchak Zuckerman, chose another strategy, defense rather than attack, and decided to engage the Germans in battle when they came to search the house. When the Germans appeared the fighters sprayed them with fire and defeated them. Other organized groups did not take part in battles during the January deportation. Mark Edelman, a member of the *Bund*, wrote in a report after the war that the members of his movement were not concentrated or in a state of alert and therefore could not act, and many of them were taken by the Germans. This second "action" lasted for four days, during which 4,000–5,000 Jews were taken from the ghetto and murdered. Many Jews hid in improvised hideouts. After the first day of the second "action," they no longer obeyed the calls of the Germans to come out of their houses and into the yards to be examined, given papers, and marched to the *Umschlagplatz*.

Warsaw Jews being led to the Umschlagplatz.

The January operations were a prelude to April. The three months in between were decisive in preparing the revolt. The Jews interpreted the second "action" as a German failure. The Nazis intended, they thought, to expel all the Jews and destroy the ghetto, but the Jewish resistance, both the active resistance by the fighters and the passive disobedience of orders by the masses, forced them to halt the deportation and retreat. This seemed to justify defense operations. The Germans were ready, it seemed, to deport and murder without distinction as long as the prey was easy, but retreated in the face of difficulty and bullets. If this were true, then perhaps defense and resistance was a way of escaping, and maybe the resistance could force the Germans to delay or even cancel their plans.

The Jews were, of course, mistaken in their conclusions. The Germans, as we have seen, did not intend to destroy the ghetto but to take out a few thousand of its residents. Not only the Jews, however, misunderstood the actions of the Germans and the significance of the limited deportation action. The Poles and their underground also thought that the Germans had broken off the deportation when faced with resistance, and that this was proof that active fighting could ruin the German plans for oppression and murder. The January uprising influenced the leaders of the Polish resistance, and despite their tendency not to grant additional weaponry and not to strengthen their links with the Jews, they did in the end do so, in a limited way.

The leaders of the resistance did not deceive themselves into thinking that the resistance had changed the Germans' plans or their attitude towards the Jews. The fighters and their leaders knew better than others the role of the extermination program in Nazi ideology and in Hitler's war plans. They had no doubt that if the Nazis had decided for tactical reasons to halt the deportations temporarily, they would quickly resume, ready and willing to carry out their plans regardless of the difficulties they might encounter. The Jewish resistance leaders nevertheless knew how to take advantage of the sentiments awakened by their actions. The reputation of the fighters rose and the doubters in the civilian underground joined the military effort. The Jewish public as a whole supported the anonymous fighters.

The fighters had learned several lessons in battle readiness and strategy. The first was that it was necessary to gather the fighters in places close to their battle positions and to keep them on constant alert. Similarly, the commanders began to design a detailed and exact battle plan. The field was divided into three sectors, each with its own commander. In each sector were squads of fighters with commanders, each with its assigned battle position. From their experience in January, it was clear that while face-to-face combat with the Germans in the streets had served as an important first display of power, its results were harsh in terms of loss of fighters. It was decided to take advantage of the fact that the fighters knew the ghetto and all its hiding places well, and plan a strategy of attacks from hidden positions, with constant movement from position to position. With this, the fighters hoped to gain the advantage of surprise. They took advantage of the fact that almost all the houses in the central streets of the Jewish neighborhood were of the same height and had attics. It was possible to pass from attic to attic and from street to street without being seen from below. The next major concern of the two organizations—the Jewish Fighting Organization and the Jewish Military Union—was to supply arms to each fighter and supply each squad with ammunition. The money needed to buy the arms was obtained by decreeing a mandatory tax on the well-off of the ghetto. Another mission of the two organizations was to carry out punishments and death sentences against collaborators with the Germans. Among those executed by the Jewish Fighting Organization was Alfred Nossig, a talented man who at the start of his public career had been a promising activist in the Zionist movement. He had taken part in original and adventurous diplomatic missions, but in his old age served as an informer for the Germans in the Warsaw Ghetto.

By April the organizations succeeded in arming each fighter with a personal weapon—pistols of various types. It later became clear that the pistols were not suitable to urban warfare, but during the period of armament the fighters were enthusiastic about being able to arm their forces. Each squad also had a heavier weapon, a rifle or submachine gun. These had been obtained in clashes with soldiers wandering the ghetto and in clashes with German forces. With the help of the Poles, a quantity of explosives was smuggled in and these were used to make hand-made grenades and mines planted in a number of key locations in the ghetto. The achievement which in the end fixed the dimensions and character of the uprising, however, was connected with activity outside the organizations, within the Jewish civilian public remaining in the ghetto. Residents began to prepare bunkers within the ghetto. Days and nights were spent at frenzied work in basements and underground. Basements became bunkers, secret entrances were created, and everything was camouflaged. In areas where there were no basements, bunkers were dug. Passages connecting bunkers were dug and the bunkers were prepared on the inside as well. Weeks' worth of food was stored in them, they were connected to water and gas mains, medicines were gathered, and multi-story sleeping berths were built. In some of them there were arms and groups organized around the bunkers were ready to defend themselves if necessary.

In addition, units later called "wild groups" organized themselves. They bought pistols with their own money and decided to defend themselves and fight when the time came. At the same time many turned to the fighting organizations or searched them out. The fighting organizations did not expand their ranks by much, because of the lack of weapons and because of the need to preserve their secret and underground character.

By mid-April the ghetto, and especially the central ghetto where the majority of the remaining Jews lived and in which the greatest fighting force existed, was ready for the battle to come.

The last "action," and the rebellion, began on Monday, April 19, 1943. The commander of the police and SS in the Warsaw district, Oberführer von Sammern-Frankenegg, knew of the resistance organization in the ghetto, although he apparently did not have an accurate picture of the extent of its power and preparations. He had not informed his superiors of what was happening, out of fear that it would be unacceptable to the Germans that he "allowed" the Jews to organize an armed resistance. We may assume that in Berlin there were doubts as to von Sammern's ability to accomplish his mission and that for this reason they sent SS General Jürgen Stroop to command the operation in the ghetto.

April 19 was the first day of Passover in the Jewish calendar year of 5713. The ghetto knew that the "action" was to begin; the fighters were in their positions in the attics and the civilians were in their bunkers. During the revolt which began that day and continued for almost a month, the Nazis made use of a force which included tanks and heavy guns and, on an average day, 2,054 soldiers and 36 officers. They faced a force of about 500 members of the Fighting Organization and 250 members of the Military Union.

The German soldiers who were first to enter the ghetto were greeted by a hail of bullets from well-camouflaged positions and were forced to retreat in disorder. The second attempt to enter the ghetto also failed—two German tanks were set on fire. The battle took on the character of a military confrontation. Stroop wrote daily reports and a final summary of the operation, which were found after the war to contain a detailed account of the revolt.

In his daily report of April 19 Stroop wrote:

> As the units were positioning themselves—a planned attack by the Jews and hooligans; molotov cocktails were thrown on the tank used and two armored cars. The tank burned twice. This enemy attack first caused a retreat of the forces. Our losses in the first action were 12 men (six SS, six Travniki).

The German units entered the ghetto in a military march towards Nalewki Street. Upon arriving at the corner of Gesia and Nalewki Streets the Fighting Organization position at 33 Nalewki opened fire on the Germans. The Germans dispersed, backed up against the walls of the houses and looked for cover in gateways, leaving their dead and wounded in the road. At the same time another German column marched towards the organization's central position at the corner of Zamenhof and Mila Streets, from which the fighters fired pistols and rifles at the Germans and threw grenades. A German tank was set aflame by a molotov cocktail and they were forced to leave the ghetto.

Von Sammern reported to Stroop and admitted that he had failed in his attempts to enter the ghetto. Stroop took command and planned the entry in a sophisticated military way. Towards the end of the day he entered into battle with the forces of the Military Union in Muranow Square. Fierce resistance forced him to halt the battle and abandon the ghetto.

While the Nazis used a well-armed military force, they could not break the resistance of the fighters entrenched in the attack positions. So the Germans began to burn and destroy each house from which they had been fired upon. In this way, after three or four days of battle, they were able to force the fighters to descend to the basements and hiding places. The fighters adopted a partisan strategy, making surprise attacks, and at night most of the area was under the control of the fighters and civilians. The Nazis tried to quell the revolt quickly, which cost them many dead and wounded, partly because of the strong waves the battle was making among the Poles. From the point of view of the Nazis the fact that the city was rising up against them in the middle of an occupied country was an extremely harmful phenomenon.

German shock troops in the burning Warsaw Ghetto.

The great difficulty the Nazis had in suppressing the revolt was not only because of the hundreds of armed fighters who jumped out at them again and again from cracks in the walls and ruins of the houses. The Nazis did not know how to overcome the system of underground bunkers. They were forced to conduct a bunker war and try to attack bunker after bunker. When it became clear to them that this was likely to continue for many months they adopted a new strategy. They began to burn and explode every house in the ghetto in a methodical way. The fire and heat poisoned the air in the bunkers, the food stored in them spoiled, and in many places the water was undrinkable. Despite this the people in the bunkers did not abandon them and the battle continued. General Stroop claimed from time to time in his daily reports that he had succeeded in defeating the revolt, because there were no more signs of resistance and because his operation to burn out the Jews was proceeding as he wished. But the next day there would again be clashes costing German lives.

German soldiers taking Jewish prisoners after the suppression of the Warsaw Ghetto uprising.

The stubborn revolt continued for nearly a month, and both armed fighters and civilians fortified in their bunkers took part. On May 8 the central bunker of the Jewish Fighting Organization at 18 Mila Street fell. Among the 20 fighters who fell there was Mordecai Anielewicz, commander of the revolt and the best of the fighters. On May 16, Stroop announced that the battle had officially ended, and that he was blowing up the synagogue outside the ghetto in honor of the victory. His report concluded with the words: "The Jewish Quarter of Warsaw no longer exists."

Only a few survived from the ruins of the Warsaw Ghetto—a few dozen fighters and bunker hold-outs—who made their way underground to the "Aryan" side of the city. Among them were two groups of members of the Jewish Fighting Organization, one from the central ghetto and one from the shops area. One group arrived in the "Aryan" side by way of a tunnel which connected the central position of the ZZW on Murawowska Street with the Polish side of Warsaw. A ZOB group from the central ghetto was aided by a rescue team which entered the ghetto through the tunnels from the Polish side. Among them was the Jewish fighter Simcha (Kazik) Rotem. A group of fighters left the shops area under the guidance of Shalom (Stefan) Grayek. Regina Fuden (Lilith), a ZOB messenger, distinguished herself in this operation.

"The Jewish Quarter of Warsaw Is No Longer" (title page of General Jürgen Stroop's report).

Mordecai Anielewicz, commander of the Warsaw Ghetto uprising.

On the "Aryan" side, there was a group belonging to the Jewish underground and the ZOB, including Yitzhak Zuckerman, Avraham Adolf Berman, Tzvia Lubatkin, Shalom (Stefan) Grayek, and Marc Edelman, who aided the Warsaw escapees, and who were active in the national committee and the coordinating committee, both of which continued to function among the Jews still hiding in Warsaw and in other places. Among the survivors were also outstanding ZOB members like Tosia Altman, Yisrael Kanal, and Eliezer Geler, but they perished soon afterward. The remnants of the ZOB and ZZW who went to the "Aryan" side, among them Pavel Frenkiel and Leon Rodal, were all killed as well.

There were still hundreds of people fortified in their bunkers under the ruins of the ghetto who did not surrender or turn themselves in even after the battle ended and General Stroop declared that his job had been completed. The people in the bunkers would come out at night, hunt for food and water, make contacts among themselves and, from time to time, take on groups of Germans or uniformed Poles who were guarding the area. Some individuals or groups among these "last ones" succeeded in making contact with the Poles and escaping to the "Aryan" side. Others held on in the bunkers until the beginning of the Polish rebellion in Warsaw in August, 1944.

When the Warsaw Ghetto uprising was put down, men, women, and children from the ghetto were executed on the spot.

Mordecai Anielewicz wrote his last letter on April 23, to his friend Yitzhak Zuckerman, then the organization's representative on the "Aryan" side of the city:

> From this evening we are changing over to a partisan strategy. At night three companies go out with two missions before them: an

armed patrol and getting weapons. You should know that pistols are worthless and that we hardly used them. We need grenades, rifles, machine guns, and explosives.

I cannot describe to you the conditions in which the Jews are living. Only a few will hold out, the rest will die, sooner or later. Our fate is sealed. In all the bunkers where our comrades hide you cannot light a candle at night for lack of air.

Of all the companies in the ghetto only one man has been killed: Yechiel, and even that is a victory. I don't know what else to write you. I suppose that your questions are many, but this time please be satisfied. Peace to you, my friend, maybe we will meet again. The main thing—my life's dream has come to be. I had the privilege of seeing the Jewish defense of the ghetto in all its greatness and glory.

The Warsaw ghetto revolt was the first urban revolt in occupied Europe. It was unique in that it was a popular revolt encompassing all residents of the ghetto in an active or passive way. In this way the Jewish ghetto in Warsaw became a fortification and defended itself against the Nazi armies longer than many independent states in Europe had been able to do.

RESISTANCE IN THE ZAGLEMBIA AREA

Between the two world wars, Upper Silesia was part of Poland; it was annexed by the Third Reich at the beginning of the Second World War in 1939. The Jews in that area suffered during the first weeks of the occupation, but in general they enjoyed conditions much better than those of the Jews in the rest of Poland. Ferdka Mazia, a member of *HaNoar HaTzioni* in the area's underground, related:

Despite the anti-Jewish laws, the economic condition of the Jews was very different from that in other ghettos. There was no lack of housing, there were no plagues, starving people did not wander the streets, there were no abandoned children. The internal organization established welfare institutions. The homeless were housed in large apartments belonging to their own people, they set up an orphanage and an old-age home, aided those without income and organized public kitchens of various types—both for free meals and as inexpensive popular restaurants. . . .

In June 1941, when the eastern territories were conquered and the *Einsatzgruppen* began their operations, ghettos like those in

Vilna and Kovno learned the meaning of extinction. We established a farm for the members of the pioneer youth movements and held a convention of them with the participation of a representative of the Youth Aliya organization in Vienna, Aharon Mencher. . . . In the winter of 1942, when the first declaration calling for armed struggle was published in Vilna, we still skated in the ice rink to music and held meetings and conversations of youth groups and brigades.

There were close to 100,000 Jews in Upper Silesia, living in 37 communities. The two biggest were in Bendzin and Sosnowiec. The ghettos in this area were established only in 1942–43, close to the beginning of the deportations and extermination campaign. The area had a centralized *Judenrat*, headquartered in Sosnowiec, to which the *Judenraten* in the various communities and ghettos were subordinate. This organizational structure was similar to the structures of the Jewish institutions in Nazi Germany and in occupied Central and Western Europe. The head of the central *Judenrat (Zentrale der Judischen Altestenraten in Ostoberschlesien)* was Moshe-Monik Merin, who earned a reputation as one of the *Judenrat* leaders who was harshest to the Jews and most obedient to the Germans.

It is easy to understand why awareness of the need for resistance and the establishment of a resistance organization crystallized very slowly here. Ferka Mazia explained: "Even when the deportations to the labor camps began, we believed that the Germans were drafting Jews for agricultural and industrial work in Germany; just as the Poles had been sent to work, so the Jews would be." The left-wing parties and youth groups criticized the *Judenrat*, but *HaNoar HaTzioni*, which was influential in Zaglembia, believed that there should be negotiations with the *Judenrat* if any benefit might be derived therefrom. Ezriel (Yuzik) Korzuch was appointed head of the *Judenrat's* youth and vocational training division.

In 1942, during the spring and early summer months, representatives of the youth group offices in Warsaw—Eliezer Geller, Tosia Altman, and Mordecai Anielewicz—visited the cities of Zaglembia. They told the members of their reactions to events in Poland, and told them of the dangers to come, warning them to organize themselves.

On August 12, 1942 the deportations from the Zaglembia area began, taking 15,000 Jews. The deportation was carried out to a large extent by Merin and the Jewish police. They aided the Germans in deceiving the deportees into thinking that they were being taken to labor camps.

Chaika Klinger, a *HaShomer HaTzair* activist in the underground, wrote in her *Ghetto Diary*:

> One day the "community" announced the registration of all Jews. Everyone was to report, and there would be nothing to be afraid of. Nothing bad would happen. They were to appear washed, joyful, as if on their way to a wedding. The registration would be carried out simultaneously in each district. This bothered us: if it was a regular registration, why did it have to held at the same time everywhere? Was it not because there would be an "action" and they did not want word to spread from one city to another?. . . . All the Jews reported to the square. On one side stood the Germans and on the other, the Jews. The Jews held notes in their hands. They were sent in three different directions. Suddenly they understood everything. One direction was for those being sent to death, the second for labor camps, and those in the third were free. The Jews began to be afraid to approach the Germans, and the police forced them with nightsticks to arrange themselves in lines and present themselves to the committee. The Germans did not look at the notes at all, only at the faces of those who approached them. The young people—freedom, the old—deportation . . . the children for deportation, the parents—free, or the opposite: children ran after their parents, mothers after their children. They were separated by force, with nightsticks and with rifle butts.

This deportation was a turning point in the consciousness of the Jewish public and destroyed all illusions that "it won't happen here."

Here, as in most places, deportation united the resistance and led to a complete break with the *Judenrat*. At the beginning, the fighting organization was made up of members of *Dror, HaShomer HaTzair,* and *Gordonia,* with members of *HaNoar HaTzioni* joining later.

The organization's first activities were attempts to sabotage the German war effort. Members of the organization who worked in factories manufacturing boots for the German army placed anti-Nazi leaflets in the shoes. Letters supposedly from a German organization telling of the atrocities the Nazis were committing and warning of revenge on the German nation were sent to Germans and factories in the region. Merin apparently got word of these activities and he took harsh steps to halt the organization's activity. Two *HaShomer HaTzair* activists in Sosnovitz, Tzvi Donski and Lifek Mintz, were turned in to the German police.

In their efforts to build a base for armed struggle and defense, the members of the organization encountered difficulties more serious than those faced elsewhere in occupied Poland. The Carpathian Mountains, relatively close to the cities of Zaglembia, could have been an appropriate base for partisan activity. On the other hand, since the entire region had been annexed to Germany and its Polish sector was much weaker than before, the Polish underground was almost inactive. The Jewish fighters tried to make contact with the few Polish underground groups in the area, but the Poles were not interested in working with the Jews. Mark Felman, from Warsaw, helped the organization establish contact with a Pole thought to be a supporter of the PPR (the Polish resistance sponsored by the Communists). This man promised to bring Jewish fighters to partisan bases. Two groups of young people had gone with him before it was discovered that he was a German agent and had turned the fighters over to the Germans.

The difficulty in obtaining weapons and maintaining contact with the centers of Jewish resistance in the *General gouvernement* slowed the pace of the military organization of the local underground. The echoes of the April rebellion in the Warsaw ghetto reached Zaglembia in the spring. They stirred the consciousness of the members of the organization and filled them with pride, but also brought about a careful self-examination and question about whether the heavy price in lives and the final results really justified the uprising. The debate over which tactic to use became fiercer; should there be a revolt and an attempt to join the partisans, or should there be a search for some other form of rescue? The idea of joining the partisans was rejected after the failed attempts to send fighters to them, and the question of rescue and its chances were still bothersome. The remaining Warsaw Ghetto fighters, who had succeeded in escaping to the Polish side of the city, advised their comrades in Zaglembia to exhaust all possibilities for saving lives. In her *Ghetto Diary*, Chaika Klinger wrote:

> Of all the great and beautiful activists only they remained, and life had lost all value for them. The re-examined their values and asked whether the path of sacrifice and tragic death was justified. They did not want us to see them as a symbol obligating us as well. They did not suggest we organize a rebellion. We had to remain alive. At least save a few people from the entire area.

It was difficult to maintain good connections between Zaglembia and the ghettos in the *General gouvernement* but on the other hand, it was easier to make contact with other countries. Non-Jewish messengers from the delegation of the *yishuv* (the Jewish community in Palestine) in Istanbul arrived in Zaglembia, and one of them met in July of 1943 with members of the Jewish fighting group. An important and influential link was established with Natan Schwalb, a representative of *HeHalutz* then established in Switzerland. Schwalb hinted to members of the youth movement that there was a possibility of obtaining South American passports for them, with which they could escape from the Germans. Members of the youth movements were asked to submit photographs and personal information so that the passports could be prepared. The possibility of escape caused fierce debate within the youth movements. The radicals among them opposed it.

There were two other escape routes, both the result of Zaglembia's geographical location and its political status. Zelig Bujak, a member of *HaNoar HaTzioni*, proposed sending young Jews, mostly women, camouflaged as Poles, to forced labor in Germany. The second way was to cross the southern border, relatively close to Zaglembia, into Slovakia and thence to Hungary, which in 1943 was still thought to be a safe haven for Jews.

The results were limited. Only a handful succeeded in overcoming the obstacles. Thirty-four young men and women, most of them members of *HaNoar HaTzioni*, managed to go to Germany disguised as Poles. Only a few of them survived the war. Some of them could not cope with the depression brought on by isolation and loneliness and tried to make contact with Jews in camps for foreign nationals. Those uncovered this way suffered a terrible end. The southern route to Slovakia was not used only by members of the organization. All kinds of smugglers used to take money to bring people who were willing to suffer the dangers of the journey and the uncertainty of their fate. We do not know how many people succeeded in crossing the border and how many were caught. The estimated number of Jews who arrived in Slovakia and received help from the Jewish Community there is in the hundreds and perhaps the thousands. Members of the organization tried to station trustworthy people at the transfer points with the aid of smugglers. One hundred youth movement members crossed the border in this way and arrived in Slovakia.

The use of passports, which brought about a debate over principles, could only, by its nature, serve a small group of people. The preparations involved attracted attention and news reached private people, many of whom offered large sums of money in exchange for the coveted passports. The method was meant to save people with a certain status. It was meant to work in places other than Zaglembia, as well. In Warsaw there was a plan called *Hotel Polski* (after the name of the hotel in which candidates for extradition as citizens of other countries were held), requiring good will, subterfuge, informers, and victims. Two groups left Zaglembia. The first, made up of 17 members, most of them from the *Gordonia* movement, succeeded in surviving. The second group, numbering 34, was divided among the different movements, and was caught and sent to Auschwitz. The names of the passport-holders were known in advance to the Gestapo. There is a theory that Merin wanted to control the passport operation, and when he saw that he could not, he informed the Germans. There is no proof of this, and it is reasonable to suppose that the Germans knew in advance about the passports.

The final liquidation of the Jewish communities in Zaglembia began in August 1943. The fighters, led by Tzvi Brandis and Baruch Gaftek, descended to bunkers which had been prepared beforehand. They attempted to attack the Nazi officer in charge of deportation, but failed. The fighters in the bunkers could not take action and had no communication with the outside. Even communication between the different bunkers was obstructed and dangerous. The bunker which served as an armory was in the area where the Germans gathered the deportees, preventing the fighters there from distributing the weapons to the other bunkers, where there were only a few pistols. Yuzak Korzuch tried without success to organize the escape of *HaNoar HaTzioni* members from the bunkers into the "Aryan" side of the city.

Little is known of how the bunkers were captured. When they were discovered, shots were fired from them and some Germans were hit. The clash did not become a real battle. Many of the fighters and their commanders fell in the exchange of fire. A few were captured and sent to the concentration camps. A handful succeeded in escaping and even surviving.

RESISTANCE IN CRACOW

In contrast to the relative stability which for a time characterized the Zaglembia region, Cracow suffered frequent deportations and population transfers from the beginning of the war. From Cracow it was, however, easier to maintain regular communications with Warsaw and other centers in the *General gouvernement*. The youth movements went underground immediately when the invasion began. Notable among them was the general Zionist youth movement, *Akiva*. This group was stable and united in Cracow both before the war and during the occupation.

In Cracow, as in other places, the news of mass murders, of the resistance movements developing in Vilna and Warsaw, and of the deportation campaign moving steadily from east to west in the occupied areas brought about a revision of the focus of underground activity, from educational and ideological activity to the construction of a fighting organization. The first deportation from Cracow to the extermination camps began in June 1942. The first central organization in Cracow Ghetto, established in August 1942, was founded by members of *Akiva* and included members of *Dror* and of *Akiva Bet*, and was later named "The Fighting Organization of Jewish Pioneer Youth." Its command included four people: Dolek Libeskind, Avraham Leibowicz-Laban, Shimshon Dregner, and Moniek Ajzensztadt. Another organization was established at the same time, centering around members of *HaShomer HaTzair* and including members of other organizations and individuals unaffiliated with any youth group. This latter group was known as *Iskra* ("Spark"), and among its leaders were Hashik Bauminger, Benik Halbrajch, Shlomo Schajn, and Moshe Cukierman.

In October, or according to other sources in November or December, 1942, the two organizations combined into a single framework under a united command composed of Dolek Libeskind, Shimshon Dregner, and Avraham Leibowicz from the general organization and Hashik Bauminger and Benik Halbrajch from *Iskra*. Even then there was not a total unification and the two groups continued to function separately.

The united command also included Golda Mira, who wielded much influence in the organization and activities of the Jewish resistance organizations in Cracow. Mira was older and more experienced than the rest of the activists. She began her career as a member of *HaShomer HaTzair* and switched to the Communists a few years before the war began. When it began, she was in prison serving a 15-year sentence. She escaped, made her way to the eastern sector under Soviet control, and returned to Cracow after war broke out between

Germany and the Soviet Union in the middle of 1941. Upon returning to Cracow she renewed her contacts with the Communists and became close to the underground Jewish organization, both to *Iskra*, in which there was much Communist influence and strong links with the Polish Communist underground, and to the Pioneer Fighting Organization.

We have no reliable information on the number of members in the two organizations. It is said that there were some 100 founding members of the Pioneer Fighting Organization and that the members of *Iskra* numbered about 120. The Pioneer Fighting Organization faced the same doubts other groups of its kind did—whether to adopt a strategy of rebellion together with rescue activity, or do only one or the other. From *Justina's Diary*, written by Gusta Davidson-Dregner while she sat in the Montelupie Prison in Cracow, we know that Libeskind raised this question in a sharp and unequivocal way; he did not negate rescue operations, and those who wanted to chose that path had the right to do so, but their place was not in the ranks of the resistance. The resistance, it was said, was a battle for "three hours in history."

We have already noted that the Cracow underground had a unique conception of its role. Its resistance organization decided not to concentrate on preparing an uprising in the ghetto but on taking the battle out of the ghetto to the "Aryan" side of the city. This decision of the Pioneer Fighting Organization, which apparently applied also to *Iskra*, was adopted for several reasons. The Cracow Ghetto was at that time relatively small, its population changed frequently, and it was difficult to preserve absolute secrecy. The fighters abstained from endangering the ghetto as a result of their activities. The organizations acted within the ghetto in one matter, however—in punishing informers and German agents in the Jewish police who persecuted residents of the ghetto and endangered the existence of the resistance in and out of the ghetto.

The first activity of the resistance was to prepare forged documents allowing their holders to leave the ghetto and to move freely outside. We know that the fighters also sold these documents to individuals as a way of funding purchases of weapons, many of them brought from Warsaw and other distant points. Another important activity was strengthening connections with the Polish underground in Cracow. Mira helped establish contact with the Communist underground which was more willing to cooperate with the Jews than were other Polish factions.

Two groups of partisans made up of members of the Pioneer Fighting Organization left for the forests in the summer of 1942. The first group was made up of five members of *Akiva*, led by Milek Gottlieb. They arrived at the place set up by members of PPR—only to discover that the base promised by the Communists did not exist, and that they had been left to fend for themselves. They tried to survive by themselves, but this turned out to be impossible and they returned. Some time later the group set out again, joined by two additional men, planning to find their way in the forest by themselves. This also failed. Local inhabitants informed on them; two members of the group were killed by the German police and the rest were forced to return to Cracow.

The decision to operate within the Cracow city limits dictated the character of the resistance activity. The activity consisted of terror and sabotage operations hitting against the enemy, its installations, and collaborators. The list of these operations is impressive and some were apparently carried out in coordination with the Polish Communist underground, which was also interested in interfering with the German war effort.

After a series of operations in which there were no heavy losses to the resistance fighters, and which included capturing a German uniform storehouse, attacks on Germans and capture of their weapons and attacks on German garages, a series of simultaneous operations were planned for December 22, 1942, as Christmas approached and the enemy forces were expected to be less alert. The targets were the Ziganeria coffee house, frequented by German officers, another coffee house, an officers' club, and a cinema. The attack on the Ziganeria was executed according to plan and 12 Germans (20 according to another report) were killed. This was one of the most impressive operations of the Jewish underground and was comparable in scope with activities of the Polish resistance. It brought attention and reaction from the German command.

The night after the attacks, the Germans began to arrest members of both Jewish resistance organizations. It became clear that the Germans knew of groups located in apartments in the non-Jewish side of the city. This information was given to them, as far as is known, by Jewish informers.

At the end of April, 1943, came a daring escape attempt by Jewish fighters in the Cracow prison. A group of them being led from the Montelupie Prison to the execution site attacked their guards and overcame them. Two of the fighters—Shimshon Dregner and Moshe Cukierman—succeeded in getting away. At the same time, a group of girls escaped their captors while being led through the city. One of the two to escape was Gusta Davidson-Dregner, Shimshon's wife.

The Dregners were reunited and fled to Bochnia, where the remnants of the organization had gathered. There they renewed the work of the Jewish Fighting Organization, passing the call for rebellion to underground cells in ghettos and Jewish villages in Western Galicia, in the Cracow area.

This renewed activity was highlighted by a series of actions initiated by Shimshon Dregner and his comrades. He renewed publication of the organization's newspaper, *HeHalutz HaLochem*. In a series of articles, he made an impressive and in-depth summary of the organization's operations and its methods, and a piercing analysis of the conditions of Jews under the Nazi occupation and their future after the war.

The group in Bochnia, acting as a partisan unit, issued death sentences to Poles who had betrayed Jews, and called on Poles to aid Jews in hiding. When only a few Jews remained and everyone felt that the war was coming to an end, the last fighters of the Cracow resistance worked on rescuing Jews, and saw this as their most important mission. They, the active nucleus of the resistance, were not concerned with their own safety and in the end fell in action.

An article entitled "The Anniversary of the Founding of the Organization" in the issue of *HeHalutz HaLochem* dated August 20, 1943, states:

> In fact, our mission has been accomplished. As a vanguard we cracked the shell of do-nothingness which formed around the ghetto generation. We showed the world that the Jewish nation knows how to fight for its life and die in the name of justice. We reported for battle against the enemy, and once and for all shattered his illusion that he could murder masses of Jews and escape punishment. We broke the shameful tradition of baring the neck to the knife without resistance. We taught the people to frustrate the intentions of the enemy. We reminded traitors that, despite having sold their souls to the enemy, they would not survive the war, because our movement lay in wait for them. We rose up against the

shame of our history, and we may say with confidence that we achieved our purpose. . . .

Chaika Grossman

Hashik Bauminger, one of the leaders of the underground in the Cracow Ghetto.

REVOLT IN BIALYSTOK

In Bialystok there was for a long time an underground made up of different political factions operating separately, with only loose ties between them. The largest of these factions was made up of members of *HaShomer HaTzair* and headed by Adak Boraks and Chaika Grossman, and it included Communists as well. Mordecai Tenenbaum arrived in Bialystok in the summer of 1942 and made an effort to fuse the different factions into a united underground, but not all the factions were willing to accept Tenenbaum's authority. The Communists, who were themselves divided into several groups, had reservations about Tenenbaum because of his strong connections with Barash. Tenenbaum based himself and acted in the framework of the *Dror* kibbutz, which was a stable underground group. Tenenbaum succeeded in establishing contact both with members of *Betar* and with members of *HaNoar HaTzioni*. Towards the summer of 1943 there was a swift process of unification in Bialystok, and close to the destruction of the ghetto in August, 1943, a resistance organization was founded. The organization lacked, however, the framework needed to merge the forces and prepare them for battle.

The weapons which the Bialystok underground groups had were smuggled in by workers in German warehouses and workshops. This was also the main source for the arms cache of the Vilna Ghetto. In these places there were a large numbers of weapons captured from the Soviets and delivered to workshops for repair, classification, or storage. There were two burglaries of German armories carried out by people from the Bialystok Ghetto in 1943, in which about seven rifles and parts were taken. The parts were assembled and prepared for use in secret hideouts in the ghetto.

The partial deportation from Bialystok in February, 1943, was an important push for the unification of forces and preparation for the revolt. Barash believed that the Bialystok Ghetto, which had an impressive industrial output and supplied the Germans with essential goods, would be saved from the fate of the other ghettos. This belief was based on promises he received from various Germans who worked in the ghetto and had business connections with it. In fact, these interested Germans tried to prevent the destruction of the ghetto, but the decision-makers in Berlin did not respond to the petitions of the local officials. The Nazi political and ideological assumptions condemned all Jews to death, including those in Bialystok. After the deportation in February, 1943, the members of the underground understood that, even though there was a certain tendency to believe the promises given to Barash, Bialystok was no different from other places and the time remaining to it was very short.

The revolt in the Bialystok Ghetto began in the middle of August, 1943, when the Germans began the second "action." At that time there were some 45,000 Jews in the ghetto. The fighters fortified themselves in the larger and stronger houses and thought that many of those who would refuse to obey the German call to report to the authorities would join the resistance. These expectations were not realized, though, and very few people were persuaded to join the fighters. The program, the main part of which was to gather in the houses and engage the Germans when they came to search them, could not be carried out, and the fighters had to improvise another tactic. It was decided that they would station themselves at the head of the line of people going to report to the authorities and attack the Germans face to face, afterwards forcing a way out of the ghetto. There were some 300 people in the ghetto's resistance force. They opened fire, burned factories, and advanced toward the fence surrounding the ghetto.

By the time the Bialystok uprising broke out, the Germans had already learned from the experience of the long and difficult battle in the Warsaw Ghetto. They were apparently prepared for the possibility that Jews might fight, and made their plans accordingly. The burned-out wooden houses of the ghetto left the fighters exposed. The Germans created a wedge between the ghetto population and the fighters and succeeded in surrounding them. Most of the fighters fell in battle, surrounded on all sides by heavily-armed Nazis. Those who were captured alive were shot by a wall, the "Wall of the Seventy-One." Among the fallen were Mordecai Tenenbaum-Tamarov and his deputy, the Communist Yechiel Moszkowicz. This battle was the major military confrontation between the rebels and the Germans in Bialystok, but for several days thereafter the fighters still hidden in the ghetto continued to fight face-to-face with individual Nazis or small teams searching the ruins.

The fighters' last position was in a bunker at 7 Chmielna Street, close to the ghetto boundary. The bunker had three well-camouflaged openings and was connected to a passage which led to the street out of the ghetto. It contained a radio, weapons, and explosives. The bunker served as a gathering place for many of the fighters, and those who wandered the ghetto arrived there. Armed teams would set out from it at night to sabotage the ghetto's factories. On August 19 at 11 a.m., the Germans discovered the bunker and surrounded it with armed men. We do not know how the Germans managed to discover the bunker and expose its entrance. The fighters tried to defend themselves. It took several hours to get them out: by 4 p.m., 72 had been captured. They were then placed along a wall and shot. Seventy-one fell; only one survived the slaughter. Their bodies were brought to the Jewish cemetery and buried in a mass grave.

Chaika Grossman wrote:

> The revolt in the ghetto was put down, and the battles quickly diminished. The Jewish rebels who had not fallen in battle were shot by the Germans at the famous wall on Jurowiecka Street. The "Wall

of the Seventy-One" soaked up the blood and the last cries of the Jewish fighters. The story of the Bialystok Ghetto came to an end, but not the story of the Jewish resistance in the area. A few members of the underground remained in the ghetto, scattered among the ruins. Most members of the underground knew the way to the forest. There was a set meeting place in the forest and the fighters were informed of this on the eve of the battle. Valvol Wolkowiski of the underground command, who had by chance remained alive, wandered the ghetto looking for the remaining fighters. The echoes of the uprising had by that time reached the forest. The farmers passed the news from mouth to mouth, the news that Jewish blood had flown there like water and that many Nazis had been killed. The Forward Unit (a Jewish partisan group, among the first in the forest near Bialystok) was in deep mourning. The sternest men cried, including the commander and the commissar. Their world went dark with the death of their most loved ones—family, friends, the entire ghetto organization. But they did not lose their sense of mission. "Our comrades in the ghetto did their part—we must do ours." The ghetto and the organization had established the partisan unit and maybe there were survivors in the ghetto, maybe fighters would arrive, fleeing the inferno. The Jewish units spent days in expectation. And they arrived. Little by little. One family member and two from the organization. Several came out with Valvol Wolkowiski, two broke through Nazi lines during the revolt, their guns in their hands, and others jumped from the death trains. Partisan teams gathered these remnants wandering the paths and roads. . . .

Mordecai Tenenbaum, commander of the Bialystok underground, had written a letter summing up its story to the Zionist institutions in Palestine:

> We knew there was no way to defend ourselves. The power which had conquered all of Europe and crushed whole countries in a few days could certainly defeat us, a group of youngsters. It was an act of despair, of determination. We had but one aspiration: to sell our lives at the highest possible price.

And in a letter he wrote in February, 1943, to his sister in Palestine he said:

> And now my words have really come to an end. The deportations are to resume the day after tomorrow. If I really wanted to, I could see you again, but at the price of my honor and against my desire. I do not want this. Who cares? You won't cry, will you? It will serve no

purpose. I know that from experience. One line: Mother, Wanda [Tama Schneiderman, his girlfriend] and I.

ESCAPE FROM VILNA

The Vilna Ghetto experienced a series of "actions" in the summer and fall of 1941, the most notable being the massacre at Ponar (see chapter 3), after which only about 20,000 Jews remained. In reaction to these incidents, a resistance movement was born in Vilna, the first of the Jewish resistance movements, called the "United Partisan Organization of Vilna" (FPO).

Prior to the orders for destruction of the ghettos, the Germans had ordered that Jews who could work were to be taken from the Vilna Ghetto and the work camps nearby and sent for forced labor in concentration camps in Estonia. Thus in August, 1942, the Jewish workplaces in the Vilna area were eliminated and about 2,500 Jews were sent to Estonia. The Germans saw to it that the Vilna Ghetto would receive reports that the Jews taken were not sent to death but to work.

On September 1, 1943, the Vilna ghetto was surrounded and Estonian and German police forces were sent into augment the Jewish police. At that time there were about 12,000 Jews left in the ghetto, and the ghetto administration announced its intention to take 5,000 men and women to Estonia. The FPO and the Yechiel Group decided that this was the time for revolt to begin.

The FPO command distributed a declaration that same day stating that

> There is an organized Jewish force between the walls of the ghetto which will begin an armed revolt. Support the rebellion! Do not hide! In the end you will fall to the murderers like mice. Jewish masses! Take to the streets! Whoever lacks a gun will carry an ax: Whoever lacks an ax will carry an iron rod or a stick! For our fathers! For our murdered children! Avenge Ponar! Attack the murderers! In every street and every courtyard, in every room. In the ghetto and outside it.

Rozka Korczak noted that "the declaration did not persuade the people" in the ghetto. Only a small group of young people joined the PPA. The FPO called up its fighters. Its two brigades began gathering at meeting places in key locations, and, according to the plan, these concentrations were to serve as defense posts for the Jewish forces. The second brigade of the organization, under the command of G. Ceplewicz, gathered near the hidden arms supplies and a group of fighters went to bring the weapons to those waiting for them. But even before the weapons arrived, the gathering, the movements of which were apparently known to the enemy, was surrounded and only 25 of its 100 men were able to escape. The fall of the second brigade, which constituted about half of the active force of the organization, was a heavy blow to the fighters. The major part of the remaining force fortified itself in a house at 6 Strasznn Street. A force commanded by Yechiel Schejnbojm took up the forward position at 12 Strasznn Street.

Estonian and German police marched through the ghetto and made arrests. Gens, head of the *Judenrat*, promised the German authorities that he would supply the quota of people for deportation if the armed police forces would leave the ghetto. Gen's clear intention was to prevent the armed clashes expected when the Germans and Estonians approached the fighters' positions. Towards evening the police approached the forward position and found themselves under fire. They returned fire. Commander Yechiel Schejnbojm was killed in this clash.

The next day the Germans did not enter the ghetto. They left the work of gathering the Jews slated for deportation to the Jewish police. The Jewish fighters were thus prevented from battling the enemy. The Jewish police gathered the people, some by persuasion and others by subterfuge.

The *Judenrat* and the Jewish police apparently succeeded in persuading the Jews of the ghetto that this was not deportation for death but rather transfer to labor camps. Korczak assumes:

> It is possible that, were the ghetto to have been faced with a single certainty—destruction—the spark fanned by the FPO might have burst into the flames of revolt and armed defense. But instead of Ponar, it was a transfer to labor camps, carried out by Jews. Instead of immediate extermination—the hope of liberation as the front approached. And at a time when the masses of Jews were leaving the ghetto on their way to the train—broken and bowed, but not completely in despair—the organization remained alone and isolated within the emptying, dying ghetto. All the plans, all the purposes, all the prayers of the FPO came to naught.

The organization had to decide on a plan of action. Abba Kovner, commander of the FPO, presented its command with two possibilities: to begin the battle at the height of the deportation, break through the walls and flee to the forest, or to remain in the ghetto during the "action" and organize the fighters' exit to the forests at the conclusion of the deportations.

The command chose the second way.

Escape had actually begun much earlier, and by August, the escape to the forest was in full gear. The fighters joined up with the partisan units in the Narocz Forest, with the encouragement and aid of the FPO and the Yechiel Group. Estimates are that in August, 150 to 200 people let the ghetto to join the partisans. Between September 8 and September 13, 100–150 FPO fighters left the ghetto through the sewage canals and made their way to the Rudniki Forest, among them Abba Kovner and the organization's command. The FPO's plans to escape to the forests together with masses of Jews came to naught. Rozka Korczak describes the flight through the sewage canals as follows:

> We were 150; could we pass? From the head of the line came the order, passed in a chain by one person to another: "Follow the light!" "Forward!" The pale illumination of the flashlight showed the way and we advanced. My shoulders brushed the narrow pipe. I could not move my hand. The person walking in front of me announced: "Six minutes ago we passed the ghetto's boundary." Mechanically, I pass the news to the person behind me. Snatches of thoughts, distant memories, pictures from books I read as a girl were floating and rising in me—but all these were overcome by one single thought— not to get my gun and the ammunition tied on my chest wet, not to fall behind. The pipe, with a diameter of more than a meter, ended suddenly and a round pipe continued in its place, smooth and only 70 centimeters across. I crawl. The sewage covered my clothes. Sweat bathed my eyes. "If it rains, we won't make it," I suddenly remembered Shmuel Kaplinski's comment. The file halted and it was announced that someone had fainted. He was lying in the middle and blocking the way. There was no way to advance, but a chance to rest. People got angry. But we started to move again. They moved the person aside. Pushed him into a side tributary pipe—the people at the end of the line would take him out. I lost sense of time, and for moments I did not remember where we were going. From the head of the line came the order: "Prepare for exit—those in front are already out."

Even after the end of the "action," which lasted from September 1 to September 4, the ghetto did not regain its calm. Gens was executed, and kidnapping and expulsions continued. On September 23 the Germans began the final destruction of the ghetto, in which there were still about 10,000 Jews. Eight thousand Jews were deported, half of them to forced labor camps and half to immediate death. Two thousand Jews remained holed up in hiding places, and only a few managed to find their way to the forests.

We ask again: Why was there no revolt in the Vilna Ghetto?

It is reasonable to suppose that the Germans knew of the existence of an armed resistance force in the ghetto, and in light of their experience with the Warsaw Ghetto, tried to get the Jews out of the ghetto without a battle. Gens and the Jewish police aided them, assuming that this time the deportations would not lead to the extermination camps, or fearing that revolt would bring about the destruction of the ghetto and *all* its inhabitants. Abba Kovner argued years later that "The Germans succeeded in creating illusions among the Jews of the Vilna Ghetto that they were in a situation of choice—of life or death. . . ." There were, however, also serious internal doubts among the fighters themselves. Abba Kovner acknowledges that the fighters had doubts: "Were we permitted to lead people into fire? Most of the people were unarmed—what would happen to them? And if it turned out in the meantime that the ghetto was not being destroyed?" The decision of the fighters and the circumstances which brought them to the decision to refrain from a planned revolt in the ghetto meant that all means and efforts had to be concentrated on getting out. The organization of the flight from the ghetto, caught up in deportations, created tension between the fighters and the despairing masses of the ghetto, especially when it was not possible to take many people, and not unarmed ones, by way of the canals to the forests.

Rozka Korczak summarized the organization's actions and doubts with regard to the decision to flee to the forest:

> This decision was made after much agonizing, and in effect contradicted the declared policy of the organization. The central mission—mass armed insurrection—was not carried out. The difficult question of the correctness of the PPA's assumptions over the course of its existence bothered the fighters and demanded an answer. Seeing the PPA in terms of its final failure—that is, the non-

realization of the central mission for which it was founded—is not necessarily an inclusive view, based on objective evaluation, but at that time it expressed the feelings and disappointments of many fighters. But sentences should not be passed against those who stood in the center of events and who to a certain extent directed them. They were not meant to make historical judgments. But whoever surveys the events today, far from that time, is not free of the obligation of seeing the entire picture.

Chapter 5

Revolt in the Camps

The Nazis built more than one thousand concentration, death, labor and transfer camps on German territory, in the countries it conquered, and in the areas it annexed. Nazi Germany operated this system of camps for three reasons:

1. to isolate, punish, and frighten their opponents, in particular those from the left, in order to repress all dissent;

2. to exploit the work of German prisoners defined by the Nazis as "asocial" elements (criminals, people who refused to work, homosexuals, prostitutes, Jehovah's Witnesses), kept in the camps under conditions of slavery. Later, during the war, the Germans used such camps for massive exploitation of the labor of subject peoples;

3. to physically destroy masses of people, in particular Jews, in the framework of the Nazi plan for "the Final Solution of the Jewish Question."

Tens of millions of people passed through the camps (including prisoner-of-war and foreign-worker camps in Germany) and millions were murdered in them. Few Jews were in the prisoner-of-war camps which held Soviet soldiers, since prisoners identified as Jews were murdered immediately or within a short period of time. There were no Jews among the foreign laborers brought to Germany with the exception of tiny groups of migrant workers and individuals who entered Germany illegally, disguised as non-Jews.

FORCED LABOR CAMPS

Tens of thousands of Jews were taken to forced labor camps within the bounds of the *General gouvernement* and in the annexed territories. The slave laborers in these camps worked at paving roads, excavation, construction, swamp-draining, seasonal agricultural work, and so on. The conditions in the camps were inhuman: The workers did not receive the minimal nourishment required for their tasks, and suffered from poor housing and sanitation, which encouraged the spread of disease. Sick prisoners were not given any real medical care, only limited rest days. Any deed seen as contrary to the camp regulations, including carelessness, led to harsh physical punishment. Poles and Ukrainians, noted for their hatred of Jews, were made guards and officers in these camps. They were helped by Jewish hooligans, or by Jews willing to do anything in order to stay alive. Human life had no value in the camps, since other prisoners could always be brought in to replace those who died or were murdered. Most of the camps were temporary, set up in order to work on a particular project.

We know of no uprisings in the labor camps, with the exception of a handful of attacks on guards or particularly cruel foremen. These were acts of desperation rather than planned operations with specific goals. There were people who escaped, but even after passing through the dangers of getting back to the ghetto, the escapees were still not free from the threat of persecution and punishment.

In some ghettos the transport of the population to the camps aroused opposition and resistance. This resistance was not at first directed at the Nazi authorities, but rather against the *Judenraten*. It was the *Judenraten* and the Jewish police in the ghettos that would send the weak and unprotected, as well as refugees from small towns, to forced labor camps. The transfers to the camps were a source of corruption among the police. People paid ransom, in different ways, in order to protect themselves from being sent away. In some ghettos— the Lodz Ghetto, for instance—the practice was to include people who were "inconvenient" in the transfers. The transfers were one of the major reasons for the hostility of the public towards the police in the ghettos. (It was only later, when the great deportations took Jews by the thousands to the death camps, that the resistance struck out against the Nazi oppressors directly. See chapter 4.)

The underground organizations in the Warsaw Ghetto refused to be sent to forced labor camps and in some cases clashed with the Jewish police over this issue. At first people went to the camps of their own volition, believing that in exchange for work in the camps they would be allowed tolerable living conditions. When the truth about the camps became known, the flow of volunteers stopped and it was difficult to find people to send. The *Judenraten* tried to organize aid for camp laborers and their families who had remained in the ghetto, but this aid was not enough to provide for the needs of those in the camps. The *Judenrat* of Warsaw, which visited a labor camp, was greeted there with much hatred. There were places, such as in the ghettos of Zaglembia, which kept up regular contact with those who went to the work camps, something which helped to ease the lives of those in the camps.

CONCENTRATION CAMPS

When Hitler gained power, the Nazis set up improvised camps in which they imprisoned people considered to be opponents of or inconvenient to the regime. These camps were used to circumvent formal judicial and legal procedures, to suppress political opponents, take revenge upon them, break the resistance of those who refused to obey the Nazis, and get rid of elements dangerous to the regime. These camps, organized and commanded by the SA, had a temporary character, but the news and rumors about what was being done in them created fear and terror among many.

Dachau

In March, 1933, the SS set up the Dachau concentration camp, near Munich. The camp was under the supervision of Heinrich Himmler, the head of the SS, who was appointed at that time to head the Bavarian police as well. Dachau held mostly political activists and officials, many of them Communists. Dachau was made into a model for other concentration camps. It was based on the principle of preventative detention, that is, the Nazis took advantage of a loophole in the law in order to carry out widespread arrests based on political accounts, without needing to go through the regular judicial framework.

It was not only the method of imprisonment that circumvented the law—more importantly, it was the regime imposed in the camps. The concentration camps were under the exclusive control of the SS, which did not give any other body right of entry or of interference. In 1933–1934, a set of regulations was drafted in Dachau, organizing the prisoners' lives and setting out the rules of discipline and punishment by the SS. These regulations dictated the rule of terror behind the barbed wire fences and guard towers of the Nazi concentration camps. The author of the regulations and of their method was Theodore Eicke, a senior officer in the SS. He was a zealous Nazi, commander of the Dachau concentration camp and the first director of the entire system of concentration camps. According to Eicke, each prisoner was "an enemy of the people." Contact between prisoners and SS men was totally forbidden. The attitude of the concentration camp official to the prisoners (and in this case the prisoners were German) was expressed by the emphasis on superiority, severity, and hate. The daily schedule of the prisoner was set out precisely, from morning to night. Any deviation from the established order was met with public physical punishment. At any sign of opposition or resistance by a prisoner, including the expression of an outlawed political idea, an SS man could shoot the prisoner. In time, the SS unit comprising the camp guards became an independent unit, called the *SS Totenkopf* (skull).

"Re-education" in the Camps

At first the Nazi authorities pondered the question of whether the concentration camps should be a temporary means of establishing the regime and eliminating opposition, or a fixed element in the structure of Nazi society. Hitler was the one who decided that the concentration camps were an integral part of the system. During the years 1936–1939 the following camps were established: Sachsenhausen (1936), Buchenwald (1937), Mauthausen in Austria (1938), and Flossenburg (1938), as well as the women's camp in Ravensbruck (1939). In the years 1936–1937 the number of prisoners in the concentration camps at any one time varied from 7,000 to 7,500, while at the outbreak of the war their number approached 25,000. All in all, from their establishment until the outbreak of war in September, 1939, some 165,000–170,000 prisoners had passed through the camps. The greater part of them were released from the camps after "re-education" and after they bound themselves to keep secret what they had seen and experienced behind the barbed wire fences. Many of them were physically or mentally unfit, and the fear that they would be sent back never left them. The number of people killed in the camps in the period before the war was, however, small compared to what happened during the war.

Until the outbreak of World War II, the concentration camps held primarily political opponents of the regime. From 1937 on, repeat criminal offenders and "asocial" elements were also imprisoned there. Only a few of these were sentenced to unlimited imprisonment, and remained there until they died, or in some cases, until their liberation at the end of the war. In the early years, Jews were brought to concentration camps because of political activity rather than because of their Jewish origin. The fate of the Jewish prisoners, though, even if not imprisoned for being Jewish, was worse than that of other prisoners. In November, 1938, 30,000 Jews from within the borders of the Reich were arrested and sent to concentration camps. In the cold fall and winter, the Jews were packed into dilapidated shacks and tortured more cruelly than were other prisoners. However, the tens of thousands of Jews imprisoned in 1938 could at that point still hope to win their freedom if they possessed an exit permit and could arrange to leave the Reich permanently.

With the war came a change in the role and extent of the concentration camps.

Expansion of the Camp System

At the outbreak of the war there were about 25,000 prisoners in the camps. (In 1944 their number reached 525,000, and close to the end of the war it exceeded 700,000.) In September, 1939, the Stutthof Camp was established, in June, 1940, Auschwitz was founded, and in August, 1940, Gross Rosen was created; others followed as the "need" increased. During the war the Nazis used the camps to liquidate resistance groups and people suspected of underground activity in the occupied countries. Masses of people caught committing crimes or disobeying orders, like smuggling food, absenting themselves from work, or refusing to report for forced labor in Germany were sent to the camps. Many were caught during punitive retaliation operations carried out by the Germans in response to attacks on German officials, military personnel and policy, or sabotage and revolutionary activity. The camps operated for a time, and some camps did so as a matter of course, a process of "execution by labor." The work had little value or purpose, but the prisoners were forced to engage in hard labor under conditions of starvation and oppression which led to death. At the beginning of 1942 there was a change, and the Nazis tried to make good use of the work of the prisoners, especially in military industries, because the work force in the Nazi Reich was shrinking as a result of the war. The effort to harness this labor force to the war effort somewhat softened the regimen in the camps and brought about a certain improvement in the conditions of life. There was now a possibility of surviving there for a longer period of time.

In 1942 significant numbers of Jews began arriving at the camps. The few Jews already imprisoned in Dachau, Sachsenhausen, and Buchenwald had endured a period of tortures and survived them, and were not much different from the other prisoners in the camps. But in other camps, such as Mauthhausen, Auschwitz, and Majdanek, the Jews who arrived before 1942 had almost no hope of remaining alive. In these camps the Jews were handed over to special torture units, and they could hope to cling to their lives for only a few weeks, or at most a few months. In 1942 the concentration camps, and especially Auschwitz-Birkenau, became the destination of massive transports of Jews. Even the few Jews who remained in the concentration camps within the Reich were removed and sent to Auschwitz-Birkenau.

As noted, a certain improvement in the conditions at the camps began in 1942. Large factories were built close to them, all of them belonging to huge companies like Krupp and I.G. Farbenindustrie, and the major part of their work force was comprised of prisoners in the camps. It is well-known that the missiles Germany manufactured as the weapon designed to bring them victory were made in factories set up near camps. The Buna-Monowitz camp next to Auschwitz contained a large factory for the production of rubber and synthetic fuel. The Jews concentrated in the many camps established to support the industries benefitted indirectly from the improvement in the conditions, meant to make the prisoners into effective workers.

Even so, the fate of Jewish prisoners was worse than that of others, even at this juncture. For instance, when the practice of killing sick prisoners of all nationalities by injection ceased, dying and sick Jews continued to be subject to "selection" and death. They were forbidden to send or receive letters and food packages from outside. Most of the Jews really did not have anyone to write to, because their relatives and friends from their home communities had also been transported.

The Jews also suffered from anti-Semitism within the camps. This hatred, characteristic of the SS soldiers and officials, was an important factor in the relations among prisoners. Especially notable were the attacks on Jews by prisoner-overseers. The Jews sensed that they had no chance of remaining alive until the war ended, that as the war neared its end, the Nazis, facing defeat, would murder the last of the Jews, who were the last witnesses to their great crime.

DUAL-PURPOSE CAMPS

The number of Jews who were interned in the concentration camps (estimated at more than a quarter million) was a small minority of the Jews expelled and uprooted from their communities. Most were "exterminated" without even being admitted to a camp. In order to understand the connection between the concentration camps, particularly Auschwitz-Birkenau, and the effort to wipe out the Jews, it is best to quote Rudolf Ferdinand Hoss, a commander of Auschwitz, who wrote the following in his autobiography a short time before he was executed at the order of a Polish court in 1947:

> In the summer of 1941 (I cannot recall the exact date), I was suddenly summoned by the SS Reichsführer to Berlin, directly through his adjutant. Contrary to his normal practice, that is, without his adjutant being present, [Himmler] said approximately the following: The Führer has ordered a final solution to the Jewish question, and we of the SS are to carry out that order. The existing extermination camps in the East do not have the ability to carry out the major operations which we conceive. I have therefore assigned the task to Auschwitz. First because of the convenient transport connections, and second because the area to be assigned for this purpose can be easily sealed off and camouflaged. . .

In this way Auschwitz became not only the largest concentration camp of the war years, but also the central slaughterhouse or, as it has sometimes been called, "the death factory." The horror of a concentration camp through which millions of people passed and in which

masses of Jews were exterminated (we cannot establish the exact
number, but it is estimated to be in the area of two million) made
Auschwitz the ultimate symbol of Nazi atrocity.

The "Selection" Process

Two camps served double purposes for the Nazis, that is, both as
"conventional" concentration camps and as extermination camps carrying out mass murder in gas chambers and the subsequent incinera-
tion of the bodies. The first and largest was Auschwitz-Birkenau, in
Upper Silesia, near the town of Oswiecim, once part of Poland and
annexed to the Reich during the war. The second was Majdanek, near
Lublin. The transports of Jews came to Auschwitz from all over
German-occupied Europe. The infamous "selection" took place at the
gates of the camp. A certain percentage of young people who could
still work were left in the camp, and the rest (the majority), including
children, old people, and many of the men and women, were taken
immediately to be killed. No registration of accounting was made of
those murdered in this way. Only their possessions were appraised
and stored. These included the hair and gold teeth of the victims.

The number of people kept alive to work in the camp was arbitrary,
and dependent on the need for additional labor and the frequency
with which the transports arrived. Between March and August of
1943, when huge loads of Greek Jews arrived at Auschwitz, 41,776 of
the 54,533 Jews who arrived were sent to the gas chambers. An even
greater slaughter took place in the period from May to July, 1944,
when, during a period of 56 days, 434,351 Hungarian Jews arrived at
Auschwitz. The majority were sent immediately to death.

Of the people "selected" for the camps, most died of cold, hunger,
and exhaustion, or were murdered on the eve of the liberation, during the evacuations and death marches of fall, 1944, to May, 1945.

It is often asked why the Jews brought in this way to Auschwitz did
not fight back or defend themselves, or even try to flee from the horrible death that awaited them. There is no easy answer. A larger number of these arrivals, including Greek Jewry in its entirety, and,
apparently, the majority of the Hungarian community, had no idea of
their destination, and may have remained ignorant to the very end.
Those who knew or guessed what their fate would be were often occupied during their last moments comforting their children and families, trying to ease their suffering and pain. The "selection" also added

an element of confusion and uncertainty. But more than anything else, the determining factor was that the Jews had no place to which to flee. All directions were closed to them. Furthermore, the Nazis' inhuman methods of terror and oppression seems to have had the power to paralyze the Jews. Even so, there were from time to time uprisings at the doorways to the houses of death and attempts to escape from the camps. One SS man later brought to justice, Franz Hoffmann, had often been on the scene when the transports arrived at Auschwitz. He testified that "there were riots among the prisoners chosen for death." The Auschwitz underground reported that it managed, between the 25th and the 28th of May, 1944, to help a large number of Hungarian Jews escape from the camp. All the escapees were, however, captured and shot on the spot.

One uprising at Auschwitz is well-known. On October 23, 1943, some 1,700 Jews from Warsaw arrived at the camp. They were kept separately because they had certificates of foreign citizenship. They had previously been taken to Bergen-Belsen and promised that they would be freed. Instead of being given their freedom, they were sent to Auschwitz. These Jews knew very well what awaited them. They had deluded themselves with hope for a long time, and they were apparently in relatively good physical and mental condition. A riot began among a group of men sent into the gas chamber and told to undress. Three or four armed SS men arrived on the spot in order to reestablish order, but the electricity had been cut off and the men attacked the Nazis, wrestled their rifles away from them, and shot them. One SS man was killed and another seriously wounded. The shots caused a commotion among the women, and the prisoners were surrounded on all sides, taken out of the gas chamber, and shot.

EXTERMINATION CAMPS

Apart from the camps which had two functions—Auschwitz-Birkenau and Majdanek—there were camps set up exclusively to carry out the "final solution." The first camp of this type was set up in Chelmno, in the area of of Lodz. The slaughter was carried out in hermetically sealed automobiles into which exhaust fumes were pumped. The people were brought to an abandoned castle, from which they were led directly to the waiting death cars. There were some who succeeded in escaping. Two of them found their way to

Warsaw at the beginning of 1942 and gave testimony recorded in the Ringelblum archives. This was published and distributed by the underground press, and came through the Polish resistance to London.

Gas truck.

Three extermination camps were established near Lublin in the spring of 1942 to carry out the destruction of the Jews of the *General gouvernement*. The Nazis called this "the Reinhardt Operation." The first of these camps was set up in Belzec and became operational in March, 1942. The second was Sobibor, to which Jews from Poland and other countries, including Holland, were brought. The third camp, Treblinka, began working during the last week of July, 1942, its first victims being the Jews of Warsaw.

One of the reasons for the cluster of camps around Lublin was the status and methods of the high commander of the SS in the Lublin district, Odilo Globocnik. Globocnik was known in the SS as a strongman who had defeated the civil authorities of the *General gouvernement* and as an extremist undeterred by any act of cruelty. Himmler sent the "T4" staff and a unit responsible for the mass euthanasia program to aid Globocnik; these groups had carried out the elimination of the mentally and chronically ill within the boundaries of the Reich until that effort was halted, largely because of the opposition from the Church. When the extermination of the Jews began, many members of these units were sent to take part in the operation and make good use of their experience.

There was no selection in the extermination camps. All those who arrived at these camps were sent to the gas chambers. Comforting signs, indicating that this was a transfer camp from which everyone would be sent to work, were placed at the entrances of the camps and within them. But only a few hundred Jews among the hundreds of thousands sent to these camps were kept alive, to service the installations. All these camps were built according to the same plan, and had two divisions. The first, Area A, was used to sort the clothes and belongings of the murdered Jews, and also held the workplaces and dwellings of the Germans, Ukrainians, and their helpers, as well as those Jews kept alive to work in the camps. The second division, Area B, was devoted to the process of extermination, and including the gas chambers, the murder and burial pits, and the barracks of those Jews chosen to take part in the horrible work of the extermination facility.

Why Were There No Mass Revolts?

There were occasional outbreaks of individuals or groups in all the camps, but resistance was quashed as soon as it began. There were no broadly-based uprisings or mass escapes. Only a few individuals succeeded in fleeing Treblinka (and these generally had been employed in Area A in the sorting and arrangement of clothing and belongings). some of these escapees went to Warsaw and revealed what was happening in the camp and what awaited those expelled from the ghetto. Some individuals also escaped from Sobibor, but we know of only one single escape from Belzec.

Some ascribe the absence of resistance in the camps to the lack of knowledge about the purpose of the camps. It is true that many of those brought to the extermination camps knew nothing about them and did not know of the fate of those Jews expelled from Poland's many ghettos, even their own. But as far as we know, there was no significant difference between the reactions and behavior of those who knew where they were going and those who did not. Moreover, the prisoners in the camps, who knew very well about the murder machine operating under their noses, did not rebel or resist when, in the end, they were considered too sick and exhausted to work and were themselves sent to the gas chambers.

This phenomenon has also been seen in other totalitarian countries. Many residents of such states knew that they were to be killed despite their innocence, but nevertheless did not rebel or resist. We have already noted that this is not characteristic of Jews only, since this same phenomenon has exhibited itself among many and varied populations, such as Soviet prisoners of war, non-Jewish concentration camp prisoners, Polish officers, and political prisoners in other dictatorial regimes. Some analysts ascribe this behavior to the paralyzation of body and soul among people who have suffered for long periods under a regime unashamed of committing the cruelest acts, and who are completed severed from the outside world.

According to the figures we possess, 600,000 Jews were murdered in Belzec, 250,000 in Sobibor, and 850,000 in Treblinka. The total for the three camps near Lublin was thus 1,700,000. In 1944, at Himmler's order, the gas chambers at Auschwitz ceased operation, after having taken approximately 2,000,000 lives. This was, apparently, part of a plan Himmler had to carry out separate negotiations with the Western powers, and to create an alibi for himself in the face of the approaching defeat. The Jews were a bargaining chip in the hands of Himmler and his cronies, and the end of the extermination program was meant to be one step in this great plan. The Jews took part in the numerous evacuations and death marches of concentration camp prisoners, and large numbers died in this way. In any case, the Nazis still carried out mass executions at a number of other sites, such as at Gunskirchen near Mauthausen, where the Jews were kept in a separate camp. In the end, there were only 70,000–80,000 survivors among those Jews who had been imprisoned in the camps, as well as close to 100,000 Hungarian Jews who had been sent to the camps during the final stages of the war.

CAMP UPRISINGS

We will now describe three uprisings which did take place in the extermination camps—in Treblinka, Sobibor, and Auschwitz.

Treblinka

When Treblinka was first established, there were several mass attempts to escape from the transports, as well as individual escapes, some of which succeeded. In time, the Nazis tightened the guard and made escape more difficult. The camp was surrounded by three sets of fences and barriers. In addition there were closely-placed guard towers, manned day and night by armed sentries. Any attempt at escape brought severe punishment. In the winter it was possible to see the footprints of escapees on the snow, and they were easily captured. By the winter of 1942 there were no longer any escapes from Treblinka. Individual resistance within the camp was rare. In one instance, during the sorting of prisoners in Area A of the camp, some of them had reason to believe they would be murdered immediately. One of them, a Warsaw Jew named Berliner, broke free and stabbed the Nazi directing the action. Berliner was shot along with 160–170 other prisoners.

At one point, an underground resistance group was organized at Treblinka, which planned a general uprising and escape. This underground movement was made up of two groups. In the first were Polish Jews from Area A, and in the second were Czechoslovakian Jews with military experience, also from Area A. A major factor in the organization and execution of the uprising was the decrease in transports, beginning in the spring of 1943, and their eventual cessation. By mid-1943, the great majority of Jewish communities in the *General gouvernement* had been eliminated.

The Jewish prisoners "employed" in the camp understood very well that the tapering off of the transports and closure of the extermination facility meant that all the Jews there would be destroyed. It should be emphasized that the Jews in Treblinka had been eating well and had succeeded, despite the prohibitions, in stashing away some of the gold and money they found in the clothes of the victims. Under these circumstances, they had more reason to believe that, if they could escape, they would succeed in finding a hiding place or meeting up with the partisans in the forests. The feeling that an opportunity was coming increased with the news of the German defeat at Stalingrad and the reverse which had begun on all fronts in the war.

The Jews' attempts to organize themselves for self-defense suffered many setbacks. An attempt to acquire firearms by bribing Ukrainian guards failed. The rebels managed to smuggle guns out of the SS armory, using a key they had made, but they then noticed that the grenades they had taken were without detonators, and it was necessary to return them. One of the central figures of the underground group at Treblinka, Dr. Chorazycki, who provided medical care to the SS men and moved freely around the camp, had a sum of money for the purchase of weapons. The money was discovered accidentally by an SS guard. Chorazycki fought with him and managed at the last minute to swallow a poison pill he had in his possession. An additional blow to the conspiracy occurred when two of the rebels, Zelo Bloch, the leading figure in the Czech group, and Adolf Friedman were transferred from Area A of the camp, which was the focal point of the underground, to the extermination area. The two turned this to their advantage by helping to organize Area B and establishing a liaison between the two areas. The link was a Jewish carpenter, Jankiel Wiernik, who survived the war.

In the end, it was actually Area B which was the strongest force behind the uprising. It was set for August 2, 1943. There were about 850 Jewish prisoners in Treblinka at that time, about a third of them in Area B. The underground conspirators in Area A numbered about 60. In other words, about ten percent of the prisoners knew of the plan. It was decided that the uprising would be accomplished in stages. The first would be the removal of weapons from the SS armory and their transfer to the points where the uprising would take place. The stationing of different groups near the important points, and the elimination of Germans who would be invited, with various ploys, to come to the work houses was to be done during the daylight hours, with the breakout and escape beginning as evening fell, so that the night could provide cover and make recapture difficult. The second stage included an attack on the SS command post, the severing of the phone lines, opening fire on the sentries in the guard towers, an invasion of the Ukrainians' living quarters, torching and destroying the camp, and flight after joining up with the rebels in Area B.

At first, everything went as planned. Circumstances aided the rebels—on the day chosen for the uprising, a group of SS men and Ukrainians left the camp to go swimming in the Bug River, and the guard was particularly weak. Unfortunately, word of the preparations leaked out to prisoners who were not among the conspirators, which created disquiet and led to last-minute attempts to get hold of clothing and valuables. At 1:00 p.m. there was an inspection of the prisoners, normally a routine matter but this time part of the plan of the rebels. After the inspection, the prisoners gathered near the points where the uprising was to begin. The operation was directed by Galewski and Korland, who were responsible for the prisoners and were therefore allowed to move freely in the camp. At 2:00 p.m., weapons were secretly taken from the SS armory and were distributed to the prisoners at the various starting points.

Soon afterwards, before all the weapons had been handed out, there was a mishap which upset the timetable set by the rebels. An SS man suddenly appeared in the camp and began talking with a prisoner thought by his fellows to be an informer. Then the SS man arrested a young prisoner and discovered money in his pockets. At this point, the leaders of the revolt decided to begin the uprising immediately, despite the fact that the zero hour had still not arrived. The SS man was shot by the rebels. They set fire to the barracks and other buildings and sabotaged vehicles. The rebel commanders lost control of what was happening. The sentries and the rebels exchanged fire. The latter began running out of grenades and ammunition, and, as the fire spread, the prisoners broke through the fences, contrary to the plan. The commanders of the revolt were the last to leave the camp, and most were hit.

The prisoners in the extermination area began their revolt when they heard the gunfire from Area A. They were able to overcome the Ukrainians who guarded them, take control of the guard room, find weapons, and attack the closest guard tower. Guards in a tower farther away opened fire on them and the commanders covering the flight of the prisoners from the area, fell in the exchange of bullets.

When the revolt broke out, there were about 850 prisoners in the two areas of the camp. About 100 prisoners made no attempt to escape. The rest broke out of the camp and about half of them were killed in flight and in the fighting between the fences. Among the fallen were most of the commanders and activists in the revolt. Those who managed to escape headed for the forest some 50 miles from the camp.

Camp commander Franz Stangl called up large forces to pursue the escapees, and they began to close off the area between the camp and the forest. Most of the prisoners were captured and shot on the spot.

The local population did not, for the most part, aid the rebels. The survivors testified that some people in the area stole their money and valuables and turned them in to the Germans. Some of the escapees, however, had the luck to find people who not only refrained from turning them in, but also helped them hide. Between 60 and 70 of the rebels survived the war. Since others no doubt died in the war itself, were captured at a later date, or fell in the ranks of the resistance, it seems reasonable to assume that about 100 people succeeded in fleeing the camp and avoiding their pursuers. the Nazis dismantled Treblinka not long after the revolt.

Paratroopers' monument at Treblinka.

Stanislav Conn, one of the surviving leaders of the Treblinka revolt, wrote in his memoirs that

> the desire for revenge which burned in us—eyewitnesses to Hitler's methods of extermination, methods so carefully designed— matured day by day and began to take on an element of reality, especially when 50-year old Dr. Chorazycki from Warsaw began to play a role. The doctor worked in the camp as a "medical adviser"—a job the Germans thought up as an addition to their wild mistreatment of their miserable victims, before sending them to the gas chambers. He was a quiet, clear-headed man, and at first sight seemed cold-hearted. He would walk around in a white smock, a

Red Cross band on his arm, as he did in his clinic in Warsaw, and it seemed as if nothing touched him. Under the smock, though, beat a warm Jewish heart thirsty for revenge. After the tribulations of the day, tribulations of hellfire, the four initiators of the rebellion would meet at night, on wooden sleeping platforms, and discuss our plan. The four were Dr. Chorazycki, Czech army officer Zelo, Korland from Warsaw and Lubling from Silesia. . .

Dr. Chorazycki took it upon himself to see to the purchase of weapons from outside. He succeeded in making contact with a Ukrainian guard who agreed—for a generous fee, of course—to buy light weapons. A few purchases succeeded, but they came to an end with Dr. Chorazycki's death. . .

If Dr. Chorazycki was the initiator and leader, the title of chief of staff should be given to Captain Zelo. The participation of this military man was of great help in carrying out the mission, which was extremely difficult and complicated. In moments of despair, when some of us lost hope that the uprising would ever taken place, Captain Zelo did not cease to encourage us and call on us to continue. He was the soul and spirit of the uprising. Even when he was transferred to another work detail, all the plans and decisions were passed on to him for approval, despite the danger this involved. Galewski, an engineer from Lodz, was chosen as leader in place of Dr. Chorazycki and he was no less committed in heart and soul and noted for a large measure of calmheadedness and restraint—characteristics very important to our cause, as we discovered later. The date of the operation was pushed back several times, for various reasons. . .

Finally Kalabski gave the signal to rebel. Monday, August 2, 1943, in the afternoon was chosen as the time. The plan was as follows: first we had to trap the top murderers and liquidate them, take weapons from the guards, and cut off the telephones. Then we were to burn and destroy the extermination facilities so that they could never function again, liberate the Polish prison camp at Treblinka, a few kilometers away, and together with them break out into the forests, in order to create a strong resistance force. . .

At exactly 4:00 p.m. messengers were sent to all the groups to tell them to come immediately to the garage to receive weapons. Rodak from Plotsk was in charge of the distribution. Each person who came to receive arms had to give the password: "Death!" The reply was "Life!" There were hurried cries of "Death-Life," "Death-Life," one after the other, as the hands stretched out to take the longed-for rifles, pistols, grenades. At that point the leaders of the murderers were attacked, the telephone lines were cut off, and the guard towers were set aflame with gasoline. . . The gas chambers were also set on fire. The train station went up in flames, including its signs: "Bialystock-Wolkowysk," "Cashier," "Tickets" "Waiting Room." The flames and echoes of gunfire brought Germans from all directions. There were SS men and gendarmes from Kosow, army men from the nearby airport, and even a special SS unit from Warsaw. The order went out to break through the siege in the direction of the nearby forest. Most of our men fell, but so did Germans. Only a handful of us survived.

Sobibor

Few escaped from Sobibor, in comparison with Treblinka. The camp was organized from the first in a way that prevented flight. Even so, individuals managed to escape, and in one instance a group of five prisoners and two Ukrainian guards broke out together (some of them were captured as they fled). Sobibor also saw resistance among the transports arriving at the camp, but these acts of despair accomplished little. The prisoners of Sobibor were divided into two areas, as at Treblinka, and knew that sooner or later they would be killed by the Nazis. The fate that awaited them was made especially real when, in June, 1943, after the closure of the Belzec camp, the last Jews to be used as workers in that camp were brought to Sobibor to be exterminated. A note found in the clothing of one of these victims identified them to the Sobibor prisoners. The note read: "We worked for a year in Belzec, and do not know where they are bringing us now. They say to Germany . . . If this is a lie, know that death awaits you, too. Don't trust the Germans. Avenge our blood." There were several organized attempts to escape in June and July 1943. In June it was a group of prisoners sent to cut wood in the forest, some distance from the camp. The prisoners killed their Ukrainian guard and began fleeing. Ten of them were captured, many were shot, and eight succeeded in escaping.

A secret resistance group crystallized in the camp in July, 1943, and began planning a general uprising. The survivors testified that Leon Feldhendler, formerly head of the *Judenrat* in one of the towns, was the initiator of the group and worked tirelessly to organize the uprising. The group considered several options. According to one plan, Jewish boys and girls who worked as servants in the rooms of the SS men were to kill their masters in their sleep, but the plan was rejected because the organizers thought it unwise to assign the mission to 14–16-year-olds. Another plan was based on torching the camp and escaping in the resulting confusion.

The Sobibor underground was concerned by the ring of land mines which surrounded the camp. Any escape route had to be through an unmined area. Feldhendler, lacking military experience, apparently did not trust his ability to design a plan himself and tried to join forces with prisoners who had such a background. The first such connection he made was with a Jewish former officer in the Dutch army, Joseph Jacob, who organized a group of Dutch Jews to cooperate with Feldhendler's group. Some Ukrainians also agreed to join the rebels. The prisoners planned to enter the armory while the SS men sat in their mess hall, and use the weapons to break out through the main gate and escape into the forest. But one of the Ukrainians informed on Jacob to the Germans. He was arrested and tortured. Despite the torture, he did not give details of the plan or turn in his fellows, and insisted that he had planned the escape by himself. The Germans murdered him together with 72 other Dutch Jews.

An apparently independent escape attempt occurred near the extermination facilities. A tunnel dug from the prisoners' barracks reached under the fence and the mine field. The Germans discovered it close to its completion. They murdered all the Jews in the area—100 to 150 people.

A turning-point in this activity came, it seems, in September 1943, with the addition to the Area A workers of a group of Jewish Soviet POW's from the Minsk camp. Among the newcomers was Alexander Pechersky, a captain in the Red Army, who stood out as the natural leader of the new group. Feldhendler made contact with Pechersky and thus combined the old inmates' expert knowledge of the camp with the military skills of the Russian newcomers.

Pechersky made his plan, taking into account the successes and failures of the previous escape attempts. In his memoirs, published in the Soviet Union, he wrote that he did not agree to a plan meant to save only a small group of activists. He wanted an operation which would give all inmates a chance to escape. At that time, there were some 600 Jewish men and women in the camp, of whom about 40 were members of the underground. The group designed two operational plans, under the assumption that only one would be used. One possibility, on which work was done at night, was the digging of a tunnel. The alternative plan was based on killing SS men in the various camp workshops, followed by general flight. The rebels planned to cut telephone and electrical lines. There were also plans to sabotage vehicles and take weapons from the Ukrainians' guard room. This plan was coordinated with the Jewish kapos in the camp, who asked to join the organization and the revolt. The kapos could announce an inspection of prisoners and lead them all in ordered lines to the camp gate, thus giving the activity the impression that it was being done on orders of the camp command. The weak point of the Sobibor plan, as with the Treblinka revolt, was that only a few prisoners were in on the secret. The operation would come as a surprise to many prisoners and involve them spontaneously, without prior preparation or instruction.

The hard rains which fell at the beginning of October, 1943, washed out and destroyed the tunnel, and the hard labor of many nights came to naught. The only remaining option was an uprising in the camp. October 13 was set as the date, but the visit of a German delegation that day led to its postponement to the next day. Up to a point, everything went according to plan. Eleven SS men were killed without a shot being fired, including Camp Commander Niemann. Other parts of the plan—cutting the telephone and electrical lines and sabotaging vehicles—were also accomplished. The time came for the prisoners to line up for inspection at the orders of the kapos and march together through the gate. At this point a mishap occurred. An SS driver who arrived at the camp saw the body of one of his comrades, and opened fire. Some of the prisoners were already in line when the Ukrainians began shooting at them. Instead of an ordered march there was a spontaneous run for the fence. Many prisoners entered the mine field and were killed. Those who followed them passed through the mines, but many were shot from the guard towers. The armed prisoners returned fire and killed some the Ukrainians. The leaders of the revolt directed the rebels toward the fence near the SS men's quarters, assuming correctly that this area would not be mined. Some 300 of the 600 prisoners succeeded in escaping.

The Sobibor rebellion, and the high price the SS paid, made a great impression. A large force was enlisted in pursuit of the escapees. But the revolt had begun at dawn, and the inmates had time to flee some distance from the camp. Sobibor was close to the forest, and this aided the prisoners. Some of them, mostly Polish Jews, fled to the cities or the Parczew forest, in the north. The Russian group tried to cross the Bug River to the east in order to join the resistance groups there. The Nazis assumed that all the escapees would turn east, and so concentrated their search along the banks of the Bug. The local population did not react in a homogeneous way. Some hindered and some helped the escapees. Estimates are that about 100 prisoners were recaptured during the escape and in the first weeks thereafter. About 200 succeeded in escaping, and most joined resistance groups and fought in their ranks. Some of these fell in battle or were caught later, but at least 50 managed to remain alive. Pechersky crossed the Bug with a group of prisoners and joined the Soviet resistance. He later published a book describing his days in the camp, the organization of the escape, and the flight. Feldhendler was also among the escapees. He was murdered in April, 1945, after liberation, by Polish rioters.

Pechersky wrote the following in his memoirs:

> . . .and now, comrades, I will set out the plan: First we must liquidate the officers of the camp command. Of course, each one must be killed separately, quietly, efficiently, and quickly. I think all this can be done in a single hour. . .
>
> At 3:30 Kapo Brzecki, using some excuse, will lead three people whom I will designate, into the second camp, and these will kill the four Nazis who work there. He will, of course, make sure that each Nazi enters the place in which they are to be murdered separately. . .
>
> At 4:00 those responsible will disconnect the electrical lines between the second camp and the guard room. The wires must be disconnected and hidden so that it will be impossible to repair the telephone lines quickly. At the same time, we will begin the obliteration of the officers in our camp. Each one will be invited individually to the workrooms. In each workroom, two comrades will wait to carry out the execution. . .
>
> Everything must be done by 4:30. At that hour, Brzecki and Geniek will line up all the prisoners as if they were leaving for work, and they will head towards the gate. In the first row will be our Soviet men. These will attack the armory, and the others will continue to march, and in doing so, will protect the attackers. When they get the weapons, they will catch up with the march, walk at its head, and attack the guards. The guards are liable to figure out what is happening earlier than we expect and block the way with machine-gun fire. If we already have weapons, we will begin a face-to-face battle. If we don't succeed in capturing the weapons, we will have to find another way out.

In contrast to the plans, the actual operation went as follows:

Seventy people were chosen to go first, most of them Soviet prisoners, who were to attack the armory. They lined up at the head of the
march. There were many prisoners not party to the plan who could
only guess what was going on. When they understood at the last
minute what had happened, turmoil broke out, with pushing and
shoving. They were afraid to be in back, so they pushed forward.
We arrived at the first gate in disorder. Here we encountered the
commander of the guard, a Volga German.

"Didn't you hear the whistle, you mongrels? Why are you pushing like a heard of sheep? Line up in threes!"

As if by command, the hatchets hidden under the coats were
drawn out and smashed into his head. The line from the second
camp arrived at the same time. A few women who looked like they
were in shock screamed, and some even fainted. Others broke into a
mad run, without thought and without direction. In this situation,
there was no use in talking about organization or restoring order. So
I shouted in a loud voice:

"Forward comrades!"...

"Forward!" someone on my right joined in.

"For the Motherland, for Stalin, forward!"

The rising chant rolled like thunder on a clear day in the death
camp. These slogans united Russians, Polish, Dutch, Czechoslovakian, and German Jews. Six hundred people who had been degraded
and fatigued broke out in cries of "Hora!" to life and freedom.

The attack on the armory failed. Machine-gun fire blocked our
way. Most turned towards the main gate. There, after killing the
guard, and under the cover of the few rifles they had, they threw
stones and sand into the eyes of the Fascists who crossed their path.
They broke through the gate and hurried in the direction of the forest. One group of prisoners turned left. I saw how they cut through
the barbed wire fence. But after overcoming this barrier, they still
had to cross a mine field 15 meters long. Many of them fell there. I
went with a group of prisoners to the officers' quarters, where we
cut the barbed wire. The theory that the area close to the officers'
house would not be mined turned out to be correct. Three of our
comrades, it is true, fell near the fence, but it is not clear whether
they stepped on mines or were hit by bullets, because fire was being
directed at us from different directions.

We were already on the other side of the fence, with the mine
field behind us. We had gone 100 meters, 100 more, fast, faster, to

get to the forest, to get between the trees and find cover—and we were among the trees.

I halted for a minute to get some air and look back. Exhausted, with the last of our strength, running bent over, forward . . . we approached the forest. Where is Loca, where is Shlomo?

. . . It is hard to say for certain how many people fled the camp. At any rate, it is clear that the majority of the prisoners got out. Many fell in the open territory between the camp and the fence. We decided not to stay too long in the forest, but to break into small parties and go in different directions. The Polish Jews went in the direction of Chelm. Their knowledge of the language and the lay of the land is what led them to that decision. We, the Soviets, turned east. Without hope were the Jews from Holland, France, and Germany. In the whole wide area which surrounded the camp, they had no common knowledge with anybody.

Auschwitz-Birkenau

The third place in which there was a large Jewish revolt was in Auschwitz, or more precisely, the revolt of the *Sonderkommando* in Auschwitz. During the last stages of the war Auschwitz was divided into three areas: Auschwitz I, Birkenau, and Buna-Monowice. Birkenau, which included the extermination facilities, was also called Auschwitz II. Those work details who had the misfortune to be forced to work by the extermination facilities were called *Sonderkommando* ("Special Work Details"). The *Sonderkommando* numbered about 1,000 people at the time of the large transports from Hungary in the summer of 1944. After the mass murder of Hungarian Jewry, the size of the *Sonderkommando* was reduced, and its members knew that they would soon be murdered.

An underground group functioned at Auschwitz almost from the time the camp was established. The founders of the group were Polish political prisoners and former officers. It was organized into two divisions. The first was made up of Polish officers and members of the General Underground (AK). This group had strong contacts with the outside world, and functioned within the camp in a separate nationalist framework, without taking in members of other nationalities, or even Polish Jews. The second division—the international one—was founded by the radical wing of the Polish socialist movement. It joined forces with political prisoners of different nationalities, including Jews, and even aided the organization of a separate Jewish group, most of the members of which had Zionist leanings. The two divisions of the Auschwitz underground dealt with mutual aid, sabotage of certain work areas, getting news out to the outside world, and circulating news about political and military developments to the prisoners in the camp. The underground also assisted in an important activity, the organized escape of prisoners, including Jews, from the camp (though dozens of prisoners escaped from Auschwitz without help of the underground). Four Jews escaped in the spring of 1944 and managed to make their way to Slovakia, where they wrote and distributed a detailed report on the camp and its activities. They met with the Papal Nuncio in Slovakia and brought the information to the attention of various authorities. The report made its way to the outside world and served to confirm other reports of mass murder in the gas chambers. A strong link between the Auschwitz underground and Polish military organizations was established in 1944, and plans began for a general uprising and liberation of the camp. For various reasons, these plans were never completed.

The *Sonderkommando* had links with the international division of the underground, and they were party to the plans for a revolt. As part of these plans, a group of Jewish workers in the Union explosives factory was ordered to smuggle gunpowder into the camp. Women prisoners who worked in a different section of this factory and handled the last stage of the assembly of detonators succeeded in smuggling a small amount. This part of the operation was directed by Rosa Robota, a member of the group in Birkenau. The explosive was brought into Auschwitz I and Birkenau in mess tins with double sides, also made in the factory. The *Sonderkommando* used this material to make bombs, under the direction of a Russian named Borodin.

The men of the *Sonderkommando* also succeeded in gaining weapons from other sources, including several pistols. They were in constant communication with the international division of the underground in Auschwitz I. They relayed information about the arriving transports, passed on gold and valuables, and were party to the plan for a general uprising in which they were to play an important part. In a document discovered at Auschwitz, Zalman Lewental, an observant Jew and a member of the *Sonderkommando*, wrote of the horrible suffering they endured during their "work," and of the preparations made for the uprising.

Rosa Robota, member of the Auschwitz underground.

At the beginning of October 1944, the *Sonderkommando* was comprised of 663 men, working alongside the four crematoriums (2, 3, 4, 5) in Birkenau. According to testimony from Greek Jews, the Greek members of the group organized themselves into an underground unit within the *Sonderkommando*. We have no confirmation of the activity of this unit.

The uprising planned for such an extended period of time and such detail went wrong. One explanation given is that news was received from Auschwitz 1 that the *Sonderkommando* was to be dismantled within a few days and its members were to be murdered some distance from Auschwitz. This information was confirmed by an order given to some of the men of the *Sonderkommando* to make preparations for travel. Faced with this information, the leaders of the underground called together their activists on October 7, 1944, in order to decide how to react to this threat. It is said that a German kapo suddenly appeared at the meeting and threatened to tell the SS of the plans. The conspirators stabbed the man with a dagger, threw him into a flaming furnace, and began a spontaneous uprising. Another version has it that the Nazis gathered a group of Greek and Hungarian Jews from the *Sonderkommando*, preparing them to be killed; the Jews refused to obey and began running towards the fences, and their action was taken as the signal for the revolt to begin.

According to the original plan, the uprising was to begin during the evening hours, with the explosion of crematorium number 3 meant to signal the start of the uprising. In the end, it began with fighting in crematoria 2 and 4 between the crematorium workers and the SS men. Crematorium 4 was set on fire and blown up, after which the prisoners began running for the fences, making their way to the nearby woods. All this happened in the middle of the day, and there were thousands of armed SS men in the camp who were immediately activated. They surrounded the area and began firing at the escapees. A group of rebels managed to break through, and distanced themselves from the camp, but large SS forces surrounded them, and almost all the prisoners fell in a hopeless battle with the Nazis. In addition to the kapos killed in the area of the incinerators, three SS men were killed and three more wounded. A small group from among the *Sonderkommando* rebels were taken to the *bunker* (the camp prison) where they were tortured and executed.

The revolt of the *Sonderkommando* made a great impression on the tens of thousands of prisoners in Auschwitz. It was the only attempt at revolt in this huge camp.

A jar containing a Yiddish manuscript written by *Sonderkommando* member Zalman Lewental was unearthed near crematorium 3 in 1962. Lewental was born in Ciechanow and was a *yeshiva* student until the the outbreak of the war. His manuscript was one of three discovered near the crematoria, hidden by Jews of the *Sonderkommando* so that future generations would know what occurred. Lewental's tells the story of those days with great force. The last page in his diary carried the date October 10, 1944—that is, three days after the outbreak of the rebellion:

> We saw what was going on as we worked, and that time was passing without activity. We in the *Kommando* had always argued that the danger awaiting us was greater than that awaiting others, the rest of the Jews in the camp. We knew that the Germans would try, at any price, to wipe out the evidence of their deeds, and that they could not do this without destroying the entire *Kommando*, without leaving one of us alive. So we did not see the approaching front of the war as giving us any chance. On the contrary, we saw it as our responsibility to take action sooner, if we wanted to do anything while we were still alive. At the insistence of the entire *Kommando*, we tried to persuade the camp that this was the final hour, but to my sorrow they rejected us day after day, for many months. But thanks to the efforts and devotion of a few Jewish girls who worked in the

Union armaments factory, we succeeded in obtaining some material which could be useful at the right hour. We had to act. We began pressing our partners to set a date, because our *Kommando* was ready for it, ready for everything. Our Russians coordinated things with those outside the *Sonderkommando* in the camp. Again something went wrong. We couldn't wait any longer, and we decided to act alone. Even with our plans ready, including a plan to carry out the operation late at night and then to escape into the field, we were delayed. We had not succeeded in uniting the two parts of the *Kommando*, that is the *Kommando* of crematoria 1 and 2 with the *Kommando* of 3 and 4. And instead of our *Kommando* carrying out the action and thus exposing those in the other *Kommando*, we decided to wait and carry out a general action, with an equal chance for both groups. Thus we were loyal and comradely. We promised the entire camp that the matter was to happen in the very near future. There were only a few days when we had a chance for the participation of the entire camp, tens of thousands of people. A great disaster brought our entire plan to naught. But no man has the right to denigrate its moral value, the courage and heroism our comrades showed. Even if we failed, there was nothing like our attempt in the history of Auschwitz-Birkenau or in the history of the oppression, persecution, troubles and sorrows that the Nazis brought on the world they conquered. The international underground used us for everything. We gave them all they demanded: gold, money, valuables worth many millions. More important is the fact that we gave them secret documents, information on what happened to us. We gave them the details of events of interest to the world. Everyone is no doubt interested in knowing what happened to us, because without us no one would have known what happened and when. A hundred years hence, no one will believe it. We know this certainly.

The revolt did not end with the pursuit and deaths of the rebels. The Germans conducted an investigation and learned that the explosives the rebels used were taken from the Union factory. A careful examination of the factory led to the identification of three young women who worked there and of Rosa Robota from the women's camp at Birkenau. The latter knew the liaison people from the underground. She was horribly tortured by the Gestapo stationed in the camp in an attempt to force her to reveal the identities of the conspirators, but she did not break. The four women were hanged publicly on January 6, 1945. It was the last execution at Auschwitz-Birkenau.

The uprisings at Treblinka, Sobibor, and Auschwitz-Birkenau disprove the general belief that the Jews did not rebel against the Nazis. We must understand, nevertheless, who the rebels were and in what circumstances they rebelled. It seems that we can point to three factors which were common to all the uprisings in the camps. First, the rebels had been together for some time and had the opportunity to organize, obtain weapons, and make plans. Second, the rebels were relatively well-nourished, were in reasonably good physical condition, and were mostly young and without families. Third, the rebels did not begin their struggle until they were persuaded that they were about to be murdered. No one know better than they what awaited them.

Chapter 6

From Village to Forest

The Nazis accomplished the extermination of the Jews in the territories they conquered in the East—the half of Poland that had been annexed by the Soviet Union in 1939, the Baltic states, Byelorussia, and the Ukraine—in two stages. The first stage began in the second half of 1941 and was carried out by the *Einsatzgruppen*, which shot down rows of people lined up next to burial pits dug close to their homes. The second stage began in the spring of 1942 and continued during the summer and autumn of that year, bringing about the obliteration of the vast majority of the Jewish towns and villages in these areas. During this stage, the greater part of the mass murder was accomplished by firing squads in front of burial pits, by the German police and their assistants from among the local population.

During the first stage, the blow fell on the Jews of Lithuania and the other Baltic states and some of the towns in Byelorussia. The second stage included the communities in the south, the cities of the Polesie, Volhynia, and Podolia districts, which had escaped Nazi "actions" until then. The number of people murdered in these two stages, during which the Jewish communities of these areas were almost completely wiped out, is estimated at one-and-a-half million.

There was almost no organized fighting or defense against the Nazis during the first stage, only local resistance by individuals. There are two reasons for the nearly complete absence of struggle during this period. The first is that the Jews did not know where the prisoners the Nazis captured were being taken, and no one imagined that they would be murdered. Second, the swiftness with which events took place paralyzed any initiative at public organization.

The situation changed during the second stage. While the local population continued to be hesitant, the first groups of the resistance movement had begun to organize themselves in the forests. Furthermore, during the second stage the Jews were no longer completely ignorant of what the Nazis were doing. Individuals who had managed to flee from the mass murder sites told the remaining Jews of the horrible fate of their brothers. This period also saw the creation of links between the Jewish communities in the different ghettos and the exchange of information between them. News was passed from community to community with the help of, among others, local farmers. In these areas, the extermination program was conducted near the homes of the victims. The echoes of the shots were heard in the villages and ghettos. The truth of the extermination became known in detail. The technique of surrounding the villages with German police and local collaborators—Ukrainians and Lithuanians—repeated itself everywhere. The terrible campaign of destruction passed from village to village and left no room for illusions.

Urban vs. Rural Conditions

The character of the Jewish population in the cities and large ghettos was very different from that of the Jews in the small villages near the forest and swamps. The behavior of the mass of Jews in the large cities, as well as the tension between the *Judenraten* and the nuclei of the resistance movements, was similar to that of the Jews of central and western Poland. The East European urban Jew was full of fear of strangers and wild animals and was put off by the difficulties of climate and nature. The Jews of the villages near the forests and swamps did not share these fears. Moreover, many of these villagers took pride in their physical strength and were full of self-confidence. The secrets of nature and forest were well-known to them. They had connections in the non-Jewish villages in the vicinity and knew how to defend themselves. These simple Jews did not submit to the fate the Nazis had planned for them. Their spirit of resistance led to collective rebellion. In many villages there were no social divisions between different groups and strata as in the cities. The *Judenraten* in these villages were generally indistinguishable from the population in general. Important decisions were made communally, in meetings in the synagogues, in an intimate atmosphere of concern for all, mutual trust, and partnership in fate.

This is the background to the phenomenon of self-defense and mass revolt in the villages and towns. Of course, it was only in a small portion of the hundred of towns that there were signs of organizational initiative and general uprising. But the phenomenon is nevertheless worthy of being considered a unique form of resistance, appropriate to local conditions, circumstances, and the character of the population. As in the cities, it was generally members of youth groups or party activists who laid the foundations for revolt. But the *Judenraten* and their leaders were also among the organizers of resistance.

In the large ghettos, most of the fighters came from among the youth groups and the young members of political parties. Their readiness and determination to fight was based on the belief that by taking part in the struggle they were fulfilling a national and human obligation. The ghetto revolts, as we have seen, were not intended to save the fighters or the residents of the ghettos. The fighters knew that their battle was hopeless, no more than a cry of revenge and a call to the future.

This was not the case with the rebellions in the towns and villages and the flight from them into the forest. The motives which guided the villagers in their actions were not national or social motives. what moved them was the desire to live, to survive. The flight into the forest was not an effort to find a framework in which to fight, although many of the escapees did join the resistance movements and made their mark in battle and in deeds of heroism.

Characteristics of Rural Resistance

Similar, indeed almost identical, patterns characterize the organization of groups in the small villages and their escape into the forests. First a group would organize secretly to try to obtain weapons and examine methods of operation. Sometimes such a group would join forces with a group based in the forest, and sometimes it would serve as a warning of the danger on its way.

When the German-led expulsion squads arrived, the Jews would burn the village, open fire or even make use of more primitive weapons. After inflicting casualties on the Nazis, they would escape into the forest. It would not be an organized flight directed by leaders, and the uprising, in almost all cases, was not preceded by preparation and search for an appropriate shelter in the forest.

It is difficult to quote figures of, or even estimate the number of rebellions and escapes from the villages. Dozens of villages and small towns and thousands of people were involved. Tragically, only a small percentage of those who escaped were able to endure. Lacking food and shelter, many of the Jews who made it to the forests—both combatants and non-combatants—then found themselves in conflict with Christian villagers which made the chances of survival in the forest even poorer.

It is reasonable to suppose that the hesitancy of many to choose this option derived from the understanding of what they could expect from it. On the other hand, it is clear that the courageous choice made by the rebels strengthened the resistance in the forests, especially its Jewish factions. The rebellion and flight to the forests and swamps in the east was one of the best defense strategies. The existence of entire Jewish families in the forests, including children and old people, created non-combatant concentrations of people alongside the resistance fighters. These were called "family camps," and these people made up a relatively large portion of all those who survived the Holocaust in those areas.

THE TOWNS OF SOUTHERN POLAND

About the town of Korzec in Volhynia, Dov Levin writes:

> The members of the *Judenrat* in the Kozitz-Korzec ghetto took exception to the call of their former colleague, Moshe Gildenmann, for revenge and flight to the forests, and preferred to continue their policy of persuasion and bribery. But when it became known on September 24, 1942, that "pits were being dug," *Judenrat* member Moshe Krasnostavski set fire to his house while still in it (a planned action), and within a short time the entire ghetto was wrapped in flames, to the point where the Germans and Ukrainians were forced to retreat. *Judenrat* member Yukl Marcus also committed suicide, as did many other residents of the ghetto. Some of them broke out and found temporary shelter in the cemetery and other places. The Germans only succeeded in killing a few people by the pits that

day, and the local farmers were deprived of the property of the Jews, because almost all of it had been burned.

And of another village Don Levin writes:

It seems as if the Lachwa community was one of the few, if not the only one in East Polesie in which not one of its members was executed until the day of its destruction. This was, to a great extent, thanks to the personality and negotiating talent of the chairman of the local *Judenrat*, Berl Lopatyn. At personal risk, Lopatyn saved Jews from other places as well, including Soviet prisoners, and smuggled them into the ghetto. The ghetto organized a night watch to protect the residents from various dangers, mostly from outside. An activist underground group which organized secretly in Lachwa, headed by Yitzhak Rochaczyn, prepared methodically for an uprising and had been promised money from the *Judenrat* for the purchase of weapons. Something went wrong though, and firearms were not obtained, so plans were made to destroy the ghetto with primitive weapons and fire. When, on the night of September 3, 1942, it was learned that the ghetto was surrounded by German soldiers and police and that burial pits had already been dug nearby, the Jews were divided in their opinions. The underground group led by Rochaczyn wanted to use an improvised plan: to overcome the guards at dusk and to flee into the Grycyn forest nearby. Some of the members of the *Judenrat*, led by Lopatyn, proposed suspending the operation for the moment in the hope that, as in the past, they would succeed in putting off fate. After a lengthy debate, it was decided to wait until dawn. In the morning it became clear to Lopatyn that there was no more hope, and he rejected a suggestion that a few families, including those of the *Judenrat*, remain in the ghetto. He set fire to the *Judenrat* headquarters with his own hands. Many Jews died in the attempt to break out of the ghetto, but there were German casualties as well. About 600 Jews succeeded in fleeing to the Pripet marshes, but many of them were caught and cruelly murdered. Only about 120 people, with one rifle and one pistol between them, succeeded in making their way to Grycyn forest where they joined the resistance. Lopatyn was among them. He later fell in action.

Shmuel Spector tells of the progress of the uprising in the Tuczyn ghetto in Volhynia:

In Tuczyn the ghetto was open. Although the local Ukrainian government demanded that it be closed, the *Judenrat* succeeded, with the help of bribes, in delaying the action. Then, in July 1942, the order to erect a fence came from the *Gebietskommisariat* in Rovno. The fence was deliberately put up slowly over the course of a month. The Jews were not ordered to concentrate in the ghetto until September 1942. The destruction of the Jews of the Rovno and other places, and the instruction to set up a ghetto, frightened the Jews. At the beginning of September, the head of the *Judenrat*, Getzel Schwartzman, called a general meeting to discuss the situation. The participants were young activists, including Schwartzman's two sons and eight other people. It was decided to establish fighting units under the command of David Schwartzman, Getzel's son. All those present were assigned to enlist men from among their acquaintances. It was also decided to purchase weapons and flammable materials (kerosene, tar, etc.) with *Judenrat* funds, and to conceal them in the basement of the *Judenrat* building. Five rifles, 25 pistols, and a large number of hand grenades were purchased. The kerosene was ordered on various pretenses from a local Ukrainian cooperative and paid for by the *Judenrat*.

. . . two days before Yom Kippur 5703 (September 22, 1942), the 3,000 Jews of Tuczyn were packed into the fenced ghetto, which included about 60 houses. It seems that the *Judenrat* took advantage of the Yom Kippur services to explain the plan of the uprising to the public. It was said that kerosene would be distributed, and that at a sign to be given by the *Judenrat* the houses would be set on fire with the goal of burning all Jewish property and allowing general flight under cover of the flames. Those with weapons were ordered to open fire at the guards in order to increase the confusion and delay their entry into the ghetto, making escape possible.

On Thursday, September 24, 1942, at 3:30 in the morning, the German and Ukrainian police opened fire and began to approach the ghetto fence. The resistance fighters returned fire and at the same time the house of Sarah the hunchback was set aflame, the signal for all the other houses to be torched. The fire quickly encompassed the ghetto and even spread over the fence. The synagogues outside the fence, which served as granaries, were also set on fire. A few young men began knocking down the fences and *Judenrat* chairman Schwartzman called on the Jews to flee. Because of the fire and the shooting from within the ghetto, the police stopped some distance from the fence and masses of people began fleeing. Most of them headed northeast (to the Postomat forest), and about 2,000 people, two-thirds of the Jews of Tuczyn, succeeded in getting there. The rest died in the flames or from the bullets of the policemen.

Only about 20 members of the Tuczyn community survived the trials of the coming years, fought the Germans, and remained alive after the war.

KOVNO

Kovno was the capital of independent Lithuania in the period between the two world wars. During this period, about 40,000 Jews lived there, making up a third of the city's population. This Jewish community typified the vitality and spiritual richness of Lithuanian Jewry. Jews faithful to the Torah and the traditions of their fathers lived together with those of spiritual and social openness and modern nationalist sentiments. The Jews of Kovno fostered an independent Jewish system of education, and Yiddish and Hebrew flowered there as languages both of everyday speech and of literature.

When the Soviets conquered Lithuania, which became an independent republic of the Soviet Union, the community preserved its character despite the fact that in many things it was forced to act in secret. During the period of Soviet rule before the Nazi invasion, the Kovno Jewish youth movement, *Irgun Brit Tzion*, reemerged and gathered into it young students, recruiting both members of Zionist youth movements and those without any organizational or political affiliation.

This organization continued its activities, and even expanded them, after the Nazis conquered Kovno on July 24, 1941. After the arrival of the Nazis, nationalist Lithuanians began to voice their own anti-Semitism, and this led to attacks on Kovno Jews by bands of armed criminals. They called themselves "partisans" and "freedom fighters," and they were encouraged by the German occupiers. The height of these Lithuanian atrocities was the murder of Jews at the beginning of July, 1941. Eventually the Nazis activated the *Einsatzgruppe*, which pressed Kovno's Jews into a ghetto. Forty days after the establishment of the ghetto, the *Einsatzgruppe* began the methodical murder of the Jews. Soon only 17,412 Jews remained in the Kovno ghetto. The Germans had murdered half of the community in only four months.

From November, 1941, until March, 1944, the Kovno ghetto enjoyed relative quiet. During this "quiet" period an underground group
formed, uniting various political bodies and factions which understood the necessity of coordinating their activities and acting
together.

At various times, the Kovno underground was aided by the
Judenrat and the Jewish police. One man who stood beside the underground, and who won fame as a courageous man dedicated to
the interests of the Jews was Dr. Elchanan Elkes, head of the
Altesterat, the *Judenrat* of Kovno. Dr. Elkes was a well-known doctor
and an active Zionist who had not previously held any senior position in the Jewish community. He consented to head the *Judenrat*
after being pressed to do so by his fellows. Elkes met the challenge
and was able, with the strength of his personality, to restrain and influence the negative forces in the *Judenrat*. The *Judenrat* aided the
fighters in purchasing equipment (although most of the weapons
were obtained by stealing them from German armories and smuggling them into the ghetto) and vital supplies, and helped arrange
the passage from the ghetto to the forest. Members of the underground served in the police. Moshe Levin, a member of the *Betar*,
was simultaneously his movement's representative on the underground command and Chief of Police. Another senior officer in the
police force was Ike Greenberg. Both of them were later arrested
and executed on suspicion of aiding the underground.

The idea of self-defense within the ghetto came to the fore as early
as the murders which ended in October, 1941. The initiative came
from officers in the Jewish police, among them Ike Greenberg, an activist of *Irgun Brit Tzion*. The underground acquired a pistol and organized cells to train people to shoot. In the end, however, the
organization died. It seems reasonable to assume that the lengthy
break in the extermination operation moderated the Jews' enthusiasm for preparing for battle in the ghetto. The call put out to Jewish
centers in Poland by the Vilna underground, for struggle and defense
within the ghettos, did not reach Kovno, and reliable information
about what was happening in Vilna and central Poland did not come
to Kovno until July, 1942.

There were three separate blocs in the Kovno underground, which
came together under a united front: the first was the Zionist bloc,
which included all Zionist factions and pioneer movements, including the *Mizrachi* (religious) Pioneer Movement; the second included

the Revisionist Zionists and their youth movement, *Betar*; and the third was the Communists.

At first the underground groups operated independently; they engaged in cultural activity, and gave material aid to needy members and protected them from being sent to the camps. At the end of December, 1941, the Communists united their ranks. In April, 1941, the Zionist Center, *Matzok*, was established. The small underground groups defined themselves and affiliated with the large political blocs as an awareness grew of the need to create a force to defend the ghetto. At the same time the idea began to spread of organizing an escape to the forests. It was rumored that a resistance movement was forming in the forest, and that representatives of Moscow had appeared in the forests and were guiding the divided resistance groups, helping them unite into disciplined and organized units.

Added to these factors in 1943 was the feeling that the progress of the war had turned with the German defeat at Stalingrad. After tentative contacts between the major underground groups in Kovno, a united organization was established, numbering, at its height, about 600 members. The new organization began functioning with the contact that the ghetto Communists had made with the Soviet paratrooper Gesia Glazer, a Jewish woman from the city of Shavli, whose underground name was Albina. Albina entered the ghetto secretly and spent 20 days there, talking with central figures in the underground. A line of communication was opened between the leader of the Communists in the ghetto, Chaim Yellin, and the command of the Soviet resistance in Lithuania.

One of the boldest ideas of the resistance was the plan to establish a Jewish partisan base in the Augustova forest, about 130 km from Kovno, at the meeting point of the prewar Polish, Lithuanian, and German borders. The Jews were promised that a Soviet unit would be parachuted into the forest and would establish itself together with the Jewish fighters in the area. The Augustova plan was the subject of much debate. Some Zionist organizations, especially *Irgun Brit Tzion*, opposed it as being a badly planned project. Despite this, fighters began leaving for the forest, most of them from the Communist and *HaShomer HaTzair* groups. There were many obstacles which hampered the attempts to leave the ghetto for the forest. Of the approximately 100 people who left for Augustova, ten were killed in clashes with the German and Lithuanian police. Forty-three fell into the hands of the Gestapo. Some of these were imprisoned and murdered while in jail, and only a few returned to the ghetto. Only two out of the 100 succeeded in arriving at their destination. These two returned to Kovno and reported that there were no partisans in Augustova, and that the relatively sparse forest did not seem appropriate for a resistance base.

Chaim Yellin, commander of the underground in the Kovno Ghetto.

The failure of the Augustova operation, which cost the lives and freedom of the best fighters of the ghetto and endangered the entire underground movement, led to frustration and disappointment but not to inaction. It pushed the underground, and especially its Zionist faction, to search for hideouts and safe houses among trustworthy Lithuanians. This initiative saved dozens of women and children (the partisan command prevented them from coming to the forests, preferring men who could fight). Furthermore some groups, notably the Communists, kept alive their belief in the possibility of breaking through to the forests.

In the middle of November, 1943, there can an opportunity for the Jewish underground in Kovno to join the resistance movement in the Rudniki Forest, in which strong partisan units had already established themselves, including the Lithuania partisans. It was proposed that the fighters be taken from the ghetto to the edge of the forest by truck. The attempt was successful, and between December 17, 1943, and April 14, 1944, nine groups totalling 180 fighters succeeded in reaching the forest this way.

The underground suffered heavy blows, which seriously affected its ability to maneuver and carry out operations. Chaim Yellin, the force behind the move from the ghetto to the forest, was caught and murdered, as were Moshe Levin and some of his comrades. The members of the *Judenrat* were arrested and warned to end all secret operations. A total of about 200 Kovno fighters made it to the forest. They took part in many battles, and forged strong friendships among themselves and with members of other units in the forest. The feeling of being part of a fighting unit, which first emerged and took form in the ghetto, continued among the partisans.

THE TOWNS OF BYELORUSSIA

The witness Moshe Demszek, who was one of the partisans in the town of Nieswiez in Byelorussia, told of the resistance of the Jews of this town:

> . . .on the last night before the destruction of the ghetto (July 21, 1942), we gathered in the synagogue. We had heard from certain sources that the destruction would take place the next morning. Some of those gathered in the synagogue advised flight. Others thought we should defend ourselves. Our group went straight to work. Assignments were given out. Those without guns were to pour flammable liquids on the Germans, and others were to set the houses in the ghetto on fire. We sent five men out of the ghetto that night to set fire to the rest of the city. Among the five was Benny Shabis. At 1 a.m. we took the machine gun up to the attic of the synagogue. At 6 a.m. the Germans arrived with their vehicles at the ghetto. They ordered us to board the trucks. We began shouting: "No one get on the trucks!" Then the Germans began breaking down the gate and the struggle began. The machine gun began shooting from the synagogue. Aharon Gach and others had two grenades. My friend, Flit, began setting the houses on fire. The five men outside began torching other parts of the city and the flames took hold in the ghetto and in the city. People began cutting the veins in their arms. I ran to the place where I was to cut the barbed wire fence. I saw we would not be able to hold out for very long, be-

cause I had only one grenade and one bullet in my pistol. The Germans opened heavy fire, from all sides. The ghetto was filled with dead and wounded. I went to the hiding place where my brother and sister were. Late at night we escaped to the forest.

Shalom Cholawski wrote of the town of Kleck in Byelorussia:

The Germans entered Kleck on June 26, 1941. On October 31, 1941, came the first "action," in which about 4,000 Jews were executed. Dov Banascik, a man of strong body, fought fiercely with the murderers, refusing to hand over his child. Yeshayahu Kaszecki brought the ghetto news of a resistance group in the forest, but was warned by the *Judenrat* to stop this "propaganda."

We have no knowledge of the existence of an organized underground after the first "action." There were, apparently, groups of active young people which organized in the summer of 1942 to plan flight into the forests. On July 21, 1942, evil rumors came to the ghetto. About 200 young people gathered in order to leave. *Judenrat* chairman Cerkowicz appeared before the gathering and asked them not to carry out their plan, because it would bring destruction on everyone. But he concluded his speech weeping: "Maybe it is too early: maybe it is too late—do what you think best." The gathering dispersed. within a few hours the ghetto had been surrounded by German police. This was on the night before July 22, 1942. The Jews of the ghetto poured kerosene on the houses and set them on fire: among those who did this were some members of the *Judenrat*. Jews took up positions and threw stones on the Germans. The latter opened fire. It is said that Yitzhak Finkel and Avraham Pozarik threw a few hand grenades on the Germans.

Many Jews were killed and wounded in the ghetto. Jews broke through the fences, cut the barbed wire, and ran in all directions, but many fell as they fled. Some tried to find cover in basements and bunkers. Many were burned in their houses, and there were those who committed suicide by swallowing poison. Many suffocated from the smoke.

Meirowicz fled together with a group of 23 people. Most of them were shot on the way, and only five escaped. A small number of Jews escaped into the nearby forests, most of them to the Kopel Forest, to the embryonic Zhukov Jewish resistance unit. Sixteen men survived the battles of the resistance.

Mir

Especially fascinating is the story of the Jews of the Byelorussian town of Mir. Like many towns in Byelorussia, Mir also suffered from an expulsion "action" during the first stage of the extermination operation by the *Einsatzgruppen*, on November 9, 1941. An underground group arose in Mir, including members of the youth movements, and it put together a plan for the day of destruction. Oswald Rufajzen played a decisive role in the history of this underground and the escape from the Mir ghetto.

Oswald Rufajzen had been born in western Galicia. In his youth he had joined the pioneer Zionist *Akiva* youth movement. At the outbreak of the war, he fled westward with his brother and arrived in Vilna, a center of Zionist activity. His brother emigrated to Israel, while Oswald found himself caught under the Nazi occupation. While in Vilna, Oswald learned to be a cobbler, and thanks to this profession he was able to get out of Vilna's Lukishki Prison alive. He tried to return to his home town and his parents, but failed. His parents were later sent to Auschwitz. He disguised himself as a Pole and was appointed interpreter to the German police in the Mir area. Owing to his good knowledge of German he received the privileged status granted to those of German origin. Oswald wore a uniform, became friendly with the chief of the local German police, and was soon allowed access to classified and secret documents. Rufajzen made contact with the members of the Jewish underground in Mir. Among the leaders of this underground group were Shlomo Charchas and Berl Reznik, who had also been in Vilna. Oswald helped the underground obtain considerable quantities of weapons, supplied intelligence on a regular basis, and participated in the activities of the underground in the town. He did not encourage the conspirators to begin a revolt in the ghetto, but supported the idea of a mass escape. There was tension in Mir between the *Judenrat* and the underground. The *Judenrat* believed in the efficacy of the bribery and connections which they had made with the Germans. The *Judenrat* asked for information on the strength, weapons, and plans of the underground, but the latter did its best to keep these things secret. When Oswald learned of the date set for the destruction of the Mir ghetto and the plans to murder the Jews on site, he not only warned the ghetto of what was about to happen, but also planned an operation meant to make it possible to evacuate the Jews and allow them to escape into the forest. He told the people of the ghetto of a date the Germans would be out of the area pursuing resistance fighters in the forest, and suggested taking advantage of their absence for mass flight. But in spite of the advance warning and even though there was a plan of escape, only 182 of the 850 Jews in the ghetto took flight on August 9, 1942. The Jews of the Mir ghetto, even though they knew that the coming expulsion really meant the destruction of the ghetto and the murder of all its residents, hesitated to abandon the ghetto and escape, and made it the subject of debate. These doubts were expressed even among members of the ghetto underground.

How can such a phenomenon be understood? Does it indicate that even in the most favorable of circumstances, when there was advance knowledge of what was to happen and a way out, only a certain portion of the public, including those of the towns and villages, were prepared to take the risks and endure the severity of hiding and fighting in the forests? It may be that the hesitation of the Jews of Mir derived from the stories of escapees from other ghettos who had lived for a time in the forests and in the end made their way to Jewish towns exhausted and disappointed. In any case, only about 20 percent of the population of Mir took advantage of the opportunity to flee the ghetto without a fight.

The rest of Shmuel-Oswald Rufajzen's story deserves to be told. The German police chief learned of the mass escape of Jews from the ghetto on a day when the Germans were not in the vicinity, and ordered an investigation into how this information was obtained by the Jews. During the course of this inquiry, someone informed on Oswald. The German commander tried to get him to say whether or not he had really been responsible and what had motivated him to do so. Rufajzen confessed in the end that he was Jewish and had acted as he did in order to save his fellow Jews. Surprisingly, Rufajzen was neither imprisoned nor executed (his patron apparently had mercy on him and may have wanted to keep the whole embarrassing matter quiet), and when he fled, no one pursued him. He wandered for a time and then found shelter in a monastery. Rufajzen later converted to Christianity and became a Carmelite monk. Some years after the war he was sent by the Monastery to Israel, where he conducted a legal battle to be recognized as a Christian of Jewish nationality. His request was not granted, but Rufajzen remained in Israel (where his brother lived in an agricultural settlement in the Galilee.) He now serves as a tour guide and tries, it is reported, to infuse his charges (or pilgrims) with a love of Israel and its people.

Minsk

Minsk, the capital of Soviet Byelorussia, had a large Jewish community on the eve of the Second World War. The Russian revolution had led to cultural and economic changes in the city, which in turn contributed to the crumbling of the structure of the Jewish community, the dismemberment of Jewish political parties and organizations, and the gradual elimination of cultural and educational institutions. Despite this, there were still signs of Jewish tradition and strong links among Jews, more so than in other cities in the Soviet Union.

A number of ghettos were established in those areas of the Soviet Union conquered by the Germans at the beginning of the war. The Minsk ghetto was the largest of them, and existed until September, 1943. There were close to 80,000 Jews in the ghetto, and together with Jews from nearby towns, there number reached 100,000.

In November 1941, the Germans brought some 7,000 Jews from Germany and Austria to Minsk and settled them in a small separate ghetto. Among these were Jews who had fought in the German army in the First World War and Jews who had converted to Christianity.

By August 1941 there was already a Jewish underground in Minsk. It was made up of two groups: the first consisted of "western" Jews—that is, refugees from Poland, many of whom once belonged to Communist movements; the second consisted of "eastern" or local Jews. The major difference between them was that the "western" refugees had experience in undercover activity, while the locals were acquainted with the methods used by the Soviet Union, and expected that the Red Army would be coming to back them up. They thus hesitated to take any independent initiative.

The idea of fighting within the ghetto was not brought up in Minsk. The Jews of Minsk, who saw themselves as part of the Soviet nation, could not conceive of acting separately as Jews, but rather aimed at integrating themselves into the general struggle against the Nazis, guided and led by the Communist underground. Probably the fact that the Byelorussians had generally had good relations with the Jews, in contrast with the Lithuanians and Ukrainians, made cooperation between Jews and non-Jews in the resistance groups in the forests easier.

In September 1941, a representative of one of the partisan groups in the area arrived at the Minsk ghetto in order to establish links with it. There were also strong links between the ghetto and the municipal council of Minsk, which was headed by a man named Isai Pavlowicz Kuziniec, assumed to have been a Jew, who helped the underground in the Minsk ghetto as much as he could.

Just as the Jews of the ghetto received help from the Byelorussian municipal council, the ghetto assisted the Byelorussian underground of Minsk and the Byelorussian partisans in the area. Eliyahu Mushkin, first head of the *Judenrat* in the Minsk ghetto, played an important role in this. Mushkin and the rest of the members of the *Judenrat* were not elected by the Jews and had not even been active previously in Jewish public bodies. Mushkin nevertheless accepted the offer of the underground, and proved his loyalty to his brothers by supporting them in secret. The Minsk police also contained members of the Jewish underground. The director of the municipal hospital allowed the hospital to be used as a hideout for members of the underground during times of danger or escape. It can be said in praise of the doctors of Minsk that they fulfilled their obligations as doctors, with loyalty and devotion. Children also took on special responsibilities. They guided groups from the ghetto to the forest and from the forest to the ghetto, helping them along hidden paths.

Hirsch Smolar, a veteran Communist from Poland, and among the activists of the underground in the Minsk ghetto and of the partisans in the area, wrote in his book *Soviet Jews Behind Barbed Wire* about the children of the Minsk ghetto:

> Wilik Rubajin was 12 years old. In the confusion of the first days of the war, his parents were lost. He remained alone until he was adopted in the ghetto by Sarah Goland, an activist in the underground . . . Wilik quickly understood the meaning of the secret conversations he heard in Sarah Goland's house, which was often visited by messengers from the forest. Wilik Robajin wanted to be one of them, and was successful in bringing many Jews from the ghetto to the forest, until there were indications that he was no longer safe in the city.
>
> He was then admitted, despite his youth, to one of the partisan units, receiving full rights. He was considered one of the best saboteurs of the unit. By his thirteenth birthday Wilik could already take

credit for the sabotage of seven German convoys and of stores of weapons and ammunition. . .

In the ghetto, a new word passed from mouth to mouth which rang like a slogan: *dardakim*. It was known that those who guided people to and from the forest were children. Only a select few, central activists in the underground, knew who they were.

Bunka Hamer, also twelve years old, knew the dangerous paths to the forest so well that it seemed as if every bush which grew along the paths was meant for him alone, to help him keep from falling into a German ambush. This child succeeded in bringing more than one hundred Jews to the forest. Davidka Klivanski made the trip from ghetto to forest 12 times, leading organized groups of 25–30 people. Little Fania Gimpel had a special job. She was responsible for getting our doctors, for whom many partisan units were impatiently waiting, out of the ghetto. I met Simla Peterson when they began sending people to the area in which Lapidot's partisan unit operated. I wanted to be sure it was right to put the lives of organized fighting units in such young hands. I saw before me a short girl with the face of an adult woman, a face that knew suffering, wrinkles cut into her brow, her bright eyes expressing deep sadness. She heard me out with an expression of near-apathy and responded with a single Russian password which was then in daily use: "*Poriadok,*" that is, "it will be all right." While in action, she walked with gun drawn, and an expression of pride appeared on her face. I had heard praises of Simla in my days of hiding. Mira the "operator" watched her carefully after she returned from leading a group of Jews to the forest. One night, the Gestapo broke into her apartment. Simla succeeded in hiding herself in a previously prepared safe place. They took her mother and younger siblings. Simla became even quieter than she had been before, and stubbornly continued her work, helping Jews to leave the ghetto.

The underground saw getting as many Jews as possible to the forest as its major task, but was not unconcerned with what went on in the ghetto. For instance, when policemen wanted to use the ghetto market which dealt in smuggled merchandise as a source of personal income, and demanded protection money from the Jews, they were warned off by the underground. Dr. Lieb Kulik was asked by the underground not to reveal who was hospitalized with typhus, and he consented. The underground forged documents and so interfered to no small measure with the Germans' intentions to divided the Jews into "useful" and "useless" categories.

The passage to the forest began in 1942, after the second visit of the partisan Siedlecki, who said that his commander, Bistrov, was willing to accept people from the ghetto into his unit on the condition that they come already armed.

The Minsk ghetto underground assigned Boris Chaimowicz, who had military training, to prepare the first group for transfer to the forest. Hirsch Smolar described the first trip to the forest as follows:

> The first partisans' exit from the ghetto was accomplished in viola-
> tion of all the rules of conspiracy. First, they confiscated two wagons
> in the ghetto itself, installed double floors in them, obtained horses,
> and left the ghetto in this manner at 4 a.m., supplied with forged
> documents identifying them as heating workers. They traveled to
> Kalwaria, where Kordiakov waited for them. He helped them un-
> earth 13 rifles and 4,000 bullets buried there. They threw the yellow
> stars from their clothes into the same hole, and went through the
> middle of the city in the direction of the Bobrowich Forest (some 30
> km from Minsk).

Group after group left the ghetto for the forest, and many Jews, including those who were not members of the organization, took an interest in the possibility of leaving the ghetto to join the partisans and learned that the "passport" was a gun. Even so, the road to the forest for the Jews of Minsk was not without its obstacles. The Germans fought the Byelorussian underground and tracked down the Jewish underground in the ghetto itself, as well as making use of Jewish informers. We do not know the exact number of Jews who left the Minsk ghetto for the forest—some put it at between 8,000 and 10,000 people. In any case, it was a very large number compared to all the other urban centers from which Jews tried to escape. It is estimated that about half of those who left the ghetto—combatants and non-combatants—were still alive at the end of the war.

FAMILY CAMPS

Not only armed men and women left the Minsk ghetto for the forest. There were also entire families. These families formed a family camp built around a nucleus of fighters under the command of

Shlomo Zorin. This family camp, called "Zorin Camp" or "Unit 106," numbered about 600 people and was the largest family camp outside the well-known one led by the Bielski brothers, which contained 1,200 people. Both of these family camps were located in the large forested area of Nalivoki.

The "family camp" of the Bielski brothers in the Nalivoki Forest.

What was the character of the family camps and how did they come into being?

For the most part, they were made up of whole families of Jews from the villages close to the forest, who were well acquainted with the paths and life of the area. At the head of the Jewish families who fled into the forest for shelter were hard and strong men. Unlike the members of the underground groups in the ghetto, who set out with guns in hand to join up with partisan groups and fight the Germans, these families were seeking shelter and cover from the murderous enemy and from nature. Over time, a nucleus of armed men came together in the family camps, especially in the largest of them. These men defended the camp from enemies, led it in flight from the nearly daily German searches, and enforced rules of behavior and discipline.

In time, the family camps became a fixed feature of the forests, and they even cooperated with the partisan units. The family camps provided the partisans services such as sewing, shoe repair, medical care, laundry, cooking, and so on, and in exchange the partisans protected the camp.

The family camps came into being during the extermination operation the Nazis carried out in 1942, before the partisans had established themselves in the forest. When the Soviet command began organizing partisan camps in the forest, they found the family camps already there. Even though the Soviets did not encourage massive flight of Jews to the forest, they did not interfere with them, and there were even Soviet commanders who, out of sympathy, helped the residents of these camps. Jewish partisans did all they could to make the conditions of life for the family camps easier.

The family camps were concentrated in the large forests of Byelorussia and the northern Ukraine. There was a dispute as to what was preferable—to divided into small groups of one or two families, or to establish a large and heavily populated camp. There were important arguments for each.

Tuvia Bielski.

The small group had the advantage of mobility and the ability to hide when being chased, but, on the other hand, such a group was vulnerable to attacks by local farmers and robbers. A large camp was safer from such attacks, but hard to move if pursued, and was thus dependent on the protection of the partisans.

We do not know the total number of Jews from the cities and towns who lived in family camps, but is is estimated as being in the tens of thousands. It is estimated that 10,000 Jews survived the war in family camps.

Below are descriptions of Jewish life in the forests, the campers' relations with the partisans, and their clashes with the Germans. The book, *Jews of the Forest* by Tuvia and Zusia Bielski tells of the Bielski group:

> Before much time had passed, eight young men from the Nowogrodek ghetto appeared. Zusia and Ashael took them to the main point. The arrivals were greeted with bread, meat, and vodka. They rejoiced in the welcome and told of troubles. They told of life in Nowogrodek and of the terrible murders. They began to think about saving another group. They did not sit with their arms folded. The group was made up of 18 armed men. In the meantime, rifles had been obtained from farmers. Those who came from Nowogrodek were Yehuda Bielski and his wife Ida, Ya'akov and Yisrael Yankelowicz, Pesach Friedberg, Eliahu Ostacinski, Aharon Lubczanski, and others.
>
> The farmers knew that the Bielski group was armed, and that it was dangerous to provoke them. Some of the farmers became more friendly, and others tried to find ways to get rid of the Jewish band. But the group had already gotten its bearings and was beginning to think of how to get rid of informers.
>
> Martinavski, a policeman in Greater Izwa, was the first target. He had turned a group of five Jews he found hiding on one of his farms over to the Germans. His brother-in-law, the woodsman, said that he could recognize the individual footsteps of each of us, and could identify the footsteps of Tuvia and Zusia and of "Little Ahrale." Their family had known our family. My father brought up Martinavski Senior and had employed him. Now his son was acting against us.
>
> The Bielski group grew. The first group from Lida was added: Sonia, Tuvia's wife; her brother-in-law Alter Tiktin, a well-off wholesaler; his wife Regina; their 20-year old son Grisha; and their daughter Lilia. Sonia, Tuvia's wife, was immediately accepted as a

fighter. She learned to shoot all the weapons, and later manned the machine gun. Her brother-in-law the merchant also took part, just like the young people. Together with his son, these people strengthened us.

The group continued to grow all summer. Representatives were sent to the nearby ghettos. Jews heard of us and came. Farmers advised individual Jews hiding with them to join the Bielski band, where they would lack nothing. At the beginning of the winter, the force numbered more than 100, among them children.

In the summer of 1942, the Jews of the group ceased to speak to each other in whispers. They stood tall. They attacked a German company and obtained all they needed. There were wagons for hauling and travel, and horses to ride. Their armed calvary crossed the surrounding territory by its length and breadth. There were those who entered villages in force, called out the farmers and explained their mission. They were partisans, fighting the Germans, not simple Jews. Everyone was obligated to help them with information, food, and everything else they needed. "Don't believe that Stalin fled and that the Germans will win. The Germans will never win. The Red Army will return, and in the meantime, the partisans will do their job. The Germans may have control, but the partisans reign." In such a speech in a village they would first announce: "The village is surrounded, machine guns on all sides." The first such speech was in the village of Kaminka.

There was already a sort of government of the unit. Tuvia Bielski was chosen commander. It was given a name: the Marshal Zhukov Regiment. It was Tuvia's suggestion. He had heard that Marshal Zhukov was the commander of the Byelorussian front. The unit was part of the Soviet partisan movement, even though it had still not met up with any real Soviet authority. Discipline was imposed. It was forbidden to take more than ordered. Orders covered food, transport vehicles, and work tools. It was forbidden to take clothing without permission, including from prisoners. When the commander learned that an order had been violated, he would force the offender to return what he had stolen. Sometimes there was punishment. Once a mother came and complained that her son had taken something illegally from a village. The old people understood the importance of good relations with the non-Jewish villages.

The group was usually disciplined. The Bielski brothers were the founders and the nucleus of the fighting force. Zusia and Ashael were commanders of squads. The fourth brother was an excellent scout, and captured arms as well. Most members of the group were relatives, related by marriage, with everyone recognizing the authority of the commanders. And the commanders listened, of their own accord, to the advice of the older relatives.

The brothers sometimes made things difficult for complainers. When the size of the group reached 50–60 people, there were older people who advised not bringing more people in from the ghettos, because "there wouldn't be enough food," because "a large camp would be easier to capture," because "they will kill us all," but they were silenced with reminders of their duty: "What are we here for, to save only ourselves? As long as it is possible to save another Jew from the claws of the Nazis, we will do so," said Commander Tuvia. "Would that we had tens of thousands of Jews. The food we can find."

The group actually had to grow because everyone who joined it wanted to bring his relatives as well.

The attraction of the group grew. The local farmers and policemen passed on the word to the ghettos, but with exaggerations: "The Bielski group wanders like angels of sabotage armed from head to foot. They bring the Christians to justice, killing and plundering them. It is not only the men who fight. Teible Bielski (the sister, wife of Avraham Zintalski), dresses in pants and has pistols in her belt. She fights and shoots like a man."

The legend of the Bielskis spread through the ghettos, and Jews dreamed of escaping to them, either to save themselves or to join their forces. There were Jews who broke through the ghetto fences at night, wandering and looking for the Jewish partisans. Some were captured by the Germans and the police, some were turned in by informers, and some were robbed or killed by Russian partisans. There were Jews who thought that if things were well with the Jewish band, they must certainly be better with the Russian bands which were springing up. Jewish youths went to the Russian bands, and when the Polish resistance fighters appeared, they went to the Poles as well, doctors, engineers, secretaries, artisans, and simple fighters. Not all had the same fate. Some were taken in and lived with the Russians in relative equality. . . . When the fair-minded Russians learned of the existence of the Bielski band, they tried to send Jews to them.

The heads of the Russian groups turned to the Bielskis for artisans, doctors, and clerical help. The Russian partisan movement was much assisted by Jewish professionals, both men and women. It had no interest, however, in Jewish children or old people. These were nothing but an unneeded burden, interfering with the war. The Jewish partisan group could not obtain the help of the Russian partisans in surrounding a town and liberating the residents of its ghetto, in order to allow them to flee into the forest. The partisan commands did not find this in their plans. What the Jewish partisans could not do on their own could not be done at all. There was no one to fight for the Jews.

The opposite was also true. The Jewish partisans had, from the start, problems with their comrades-in-arms. Russian partisans decided during that early period to shoot the Jewish "robbers" who appeared, in response to complaints by the non-Jewish population. When the Jewish group developed, they tried to divide the combatants from those who did not fight, because the non-combatants seemed unimportant to the Soviet partisan campaign. The Bielski brothers often had to take on the high officers of the partisans in order to repeal anti-Jewish decrees, deny accusations, and counter those who plotted against them. In fact, they were sometimes aided by the chief commanders. With their heroism, daring, and the clear usefulness of their service, the commanders of the Jewish group succeeded from time to time in overcoming the attacks on the existence of their unit and its members.

This is the story of the young Jewish man Pinhas Zajonc, who with his family hid in a bunker in the forest (see the memoirs "Two Weeks from Among Many" in *Yilkutei Moreshet*):

The next day, February 24, we woke as usual in the morning. It was a pale, pleasant day. The sun shined and warmed our bodies a little, snow did not fall, and the footprints we left five days previously remained uncovered.

We made ready to prepare something to eat. Yehuda suggested: "Maybe we could make potato pancakes?"

The idea was accepted by everyone. While we had no oil, we still had some firewood left, and we had a grater (father had managed to make one from a sheet of metal in which he made holes with a nail, before he was killed). We began to peel the potatoes and Mother went out to bring water from the spring. She soon returned with a full pail.

We suddenly heard the sound of heavy steps, coming closer. We all began to tremble. We felt that disaster was approaching. It is important to know that in a bunker you hear the steps sooner, and can tell whether they are familiar or not. These footsteps were not known to us at all. They sounded very heavy, like the steps of German soldiers.

We were not mistaken. They were Germans who had come across our footprints in the snow.

At this point, everything happened with dizzying speed.

My mother was the first to approach the door and open it. She made out two Germans at a distance of a few paces from the bunker. At that same moment there was a shot. A bullet hit her hand and wounded her. She screamed in Yiddish:

"*Ratevet zich, di doitchn zenen da!*" (Save yourselves, the Germans have come!)

She began running. The Germans retreated. They were apparently afraid that we might be armed. They called for help and the bunker was soon surrounded by dozens of Germans.

We managed to get out of the bunker before the reinforcements arrived. The first were Zanko Yehuda and his son, then my little brother and my Aunt Rachel, then my other aunt, and I was last.

As I left the bunker I threw my heavy coat on myself and I began running swiftly. I heard the sounds of rifle and machine gunshots behind me. The bullets whistled around me. I turned my head and saw dozens of Germans and Ukrainians running after me. I made out Mother, also running among the trees, blood streaming from her hand, calling and crying: "Where is my son?"

I kept running until I came to a little clearing. I speeded up in order to cross the bare patch quickly. I knew I was exposed to scores of death bullets, flying in all directions. The Germans ran after me and called out to encourage one another, and it sounded like thousands of Germans had conquered the forest. I heard grenades exploding and I ran and ran. I was already close to the end of the clearing and I suddenly fell. My right foot had slipped. I did not know at that moment that it had been hit by a bullet. I felt no pain, it only seemed as if my leg had become heavier, as if someone had tied a heavy stone to it.

The distance between the place I fell and the first trees was less than five meters.

I had fallen on my stomach, and when I turned over there were already many Germans standing over me, pistols drawn, and I lay in the snow and cried.

"Get up, you damn pig!"

I shouted in Polish, without reason or logic: "*Ratujcie, ja iestem raniony!*" (Help, I'm wounded!).

Sadness overcame me. I counted the last seconds of my young life. I was sure that they would soon shoot me and would thus conclude my life. I cried bitterly. I cried quietly. It was sort of eulogy to myself.

One of the Germans, apparently the commander, ordered: "He'll die anyway. Hurry up and catch the rest of the Jewish dogs!"

In an instant the German had dispersed. I remained laying alone on the snow. I tried to crawl without success. My foot was so heavy that I could not drag it. I tried again, and cold sweat covered me, but I did not succeed in moving from my place. I began crying out loud, but with all the noise I did not hear myself. I tried again and again, until I succeeded in moving a little. I advanced slowly, dragging my wounded foot. I was not afraid of leaving footprints, because the entire area around me was trampled with the boots of the German murderers. After a great effort, I arrived at the first bush, which grew on a little mound. I pulled myself under the bush and sat up inside it. I put my hand in my pants and took it out covered with blood mixed with a multitude of lice. I understood then that I was wounded.

Only a few minutes passed and the Germans returned, shouting and cursing. They searched around them. I saw them through the leaves of the bush. They passed me, at a distance of a meter, but did not discover me. I was afraid they would search the area carefully and then find and kill me.

I sat and cried quietly. Shots and grenades echoed in the air. I thought of my bitter fate, of my father who had fallen and the rest of my family, and suddenly I heard voices, words in Yiddish. It was my mother, who had been captured by a German. I peeked through the leaves and saw her crying, her hand dripping blood as she murmured:

"*Vu zenen meine kinder . . . S'eiz mir kalt . . . Vu zenen mein kinder . . .?*" (where are my children . . . I'm cold).

I shut my eyes so as not to see her. I could not look. I started crying again. I knew there was no point in living without Father and Mother.

At that moment, I heard a dull thump very close to the bush in which I sat, as if someone had hit it with a blunt instrument. Immediately after the thump I heard a shot in the air. I glanced through the leaves of the bush and I saw Mother sprawled on the snow, in a pool of her blood.

The German walked away after "winning" his battle with this poor, defenseless woman. It was a waste to kill her with a bullet. That was too easy a death for a Jew. He had murdered her with the butt of his rifle and afterwards shot in the air as a sign of victory.

The sight shocked me to the depths of my soul. I cried loudly, without caring whether they heard me. I decided to turn myself in to the Germans. The snow was melting around me and mixed with the blood flowing from my wounded leg. If I could have, I would have run, so that a stray bullet would hit and kill me. I was afraid that a death like Mother's awaited me. I tried to get on my legs. There were still shots around me. I succeeded in standing without feeling pain. I walked a few steps away from the bush and then started to run, and to my amazement, it was not particularly difficult. I ran swiftly, as I have never run before. Along the way I came across mounds of sand, and I ran up them on purpose, in order to be a better target for the bullets, being afraid to fall into the hands of the Germans alive. My running brought me to a dirt road which crossed the forest. I stood for a short moment. My foot began to hurt. I felt the blood dripping and filling up my boot. I suddenly made out a wagon traveling in the direction of the village of Pognov. The wagon was full of wood and an old farmer sat on top. I knew all the farmers in the vicinity, but the face of this farmer was unknown. I asked him to take me past the village. He agreed. I got up on the wagon and sat, and then I felt how tired I was. I felt hunger and cold. But I no longer heard shots. Quiet prevailed.

The Farmer asked me questions, and I answered, but I saw that he was hard of hearing. When we approached the village I saw the farmers fleeing and hiding behind the houses. I shouted to the farmer, right into his ear, to halt. I understood very well the meaning of the farmers' flight. Four carriages harnessed to handsome horses passed by, with armed Germans riding in them.

These were the murderers of my family. They had finished their "work" and were returning to the city. An urge for revenge flooded my entire being. If I could only take revenge upon them, cut them into pieces, I would do it. . . .

The Germans passed and we continued on our way. I got off the wagon. Limping on my wounded leg, I approached a farmer for whom I had grazed cows a year ago. He knew my father. I told him that I was wounded. He tore his filthy shirt off and bandaged the wound. The bullet had gone straight through my leg, and the hole was relatively small. Lice swarmed around the wound. I asked the good farmer to walk with me to the forest. I wanted to see my family for the last time. I told him, among other things, that in the forest, inside the bunker, were hidden a few gold coins, and promised him that if I could find them I would give him one. He consented to my request.

My foot began to hurt me more and more. I was hungry and frozen. I cried the whole way. After about half an hour I arrived at the bunker. Many farmers stood around it. I knew many of them and they knew me, because the year before I had worked as a cowherd for them. Only a handful knew I was Jewish. Now everyone knew.

Heavy smoke spiraled up out of the bunker. Everything was on fire from the grenades the Germans had thrown inside. A few of our cooking utensils were scattered about. I saw the farmers surround the forest guard who told them, among other things, about my father, how he had been caught by the Germans. He related that the Germans brought my father back to the forest in which he had been captured, two weeks ago, and put him in the forest guard's hut. They tortured him and dealt him heavy blows, and tried to get out of him where the rest of the Jews were who were hiding in the forest. The guard saw all this with his own eyes. After the Germans failed to get anything out of him, they took a dagger and cut a deep gash in his chest. They asked the guard for salt, and sprinkled it into the open wound. Even after this, my father did not let a word cross his lips. So then the Germans decided to take Father to the place where he had been captured, and there they discovered the footprints that led to the bunker.

Chapter 7

Guerrilla Warfare, Jews in the Partisan Movements, and the Jewish Struggle in Occupied Europe

Before discussing the role and dimensions of the Jewish component of the general partisan movement in Eastern Europe and in the various guerrilla movements in occupied Europe, it would be best to try to characterize the different national resistance movements.

There is today a great European literature which glorifies the strength and achievements of the resistance to the Nazis during the Second World War. The nations which were under German occupation want to give an important place to their resistance movements and pass on to future generations a tradition of disobedience and struggle against the Nazi conqueror. Germans and Austrians also write much of and glorify the role of the resistance movements in those countries. The number of books, publications of various kinds, and memorials meant to publicize the resistance to Nazism and Nazi rule is impressive, but unfortunately does not correspond to the actual significance of the movement in its time, to the motives of its central components, and to its limited achievements.

It is impossible to speak of a uniform resistance movement covering all countries in Europe. Some countries made alliances, whether by choice or under duress, with Nazi Germany (Hungary, Slovakia, Croatia, Romania, Bulgaria, Finland).

These countries had to accept Nazi dictation of their foreign policy, and most of them fought actively on Germany's side in the war and provided the Reich with economic aid while preserving a certain

215

autonomy over their internal affairs. In these countries, the resistance to the government and the struggle against the Nazis was small, almost unnoticeable. Large-scale revolt did not break out in Slovakia until 1944, close to the end of the war, when Soviet forces were approaching.

It is important to note that these countries did not follow a single policy with regard to turning in their Jewish citizens. Some countries aided the Nazis in their project almost without reservation (Hungary) or even initiated and carried out the program on their own (Croatia and, for a time, Romania). On the other hand, there were countries which refused to hand their Jews over, such as Bulgaria (with the exception of the Jews in the territories annexed to Bulgaria during the war) and Romania during the latter part of the war. Finland took an uncompromising stand in protecting its few Jews.

In a quick survey of our subject in the occupied countries, it is difficult to point to common, consistent lines of development. Political parties and movements with Fascist and Nazi sympathies were active in all European countries. These parties supported the ideology and territorial ambitions of the Nazis and wished to join, while preserving a separate national identity, the "new order" the Nazis promised to inaugurate. While these parties were not mass movements, and in most of the countries did not grow much during the occupation, the support they received from the Nazi conquerors and their knowledge of the internal workings of their countries allowed them to inflict significant damage. Large parts of the populations of the occupied countries, such as France, had no ideological sympathy with racism and Nazism and saw the Germans as historical enemies. Their leaders concluded, however, that the existing balance of power would ensure a German victory and that common sense and the desire to survive required looking for a way of reasoning with the Nazis and adjusting to the reality of German-Nazi control.

The attitudes of the local populations to the Jews in different countries were extremely complex. Many Lithuanians, Latvians, Estonians, and Ukrainians believed that the Germans would help them win partial or complete independence from the Soviet Union. This belief was often accompanied by a fierce and cruel anti-Semitism, which they expressed by aiding the Nazi death campaign, and in pogroms and massacres they organized on their own. Only a few people distinguished between the nationalist motives which led to support of the German cause and the murder of the Jews. The Poles were unified in their opposition to the German-Nazi occupation, but their resistance did not include, at least not always or consistently, opposition to Nazi policy toward the Jews. In France, the Vichy government, led by Marshal Petain, passed anti-Jewish laws without German pressure. In other countries, such as Belgium and Holland, most of the population was sensitive to the Jewish tragedy, but the officials of these nations, who claimed to represent the national will of their peoples, followed the Nazi occupiers' anti-Jewish policy. In some countries, including Poland, there were organizations and individuals who, for various reasons, worked to save Jews.

It was rare for entire nations, or large parts of them, to refuse to turn Jews over to the Nazis and to try to save them. Denmark was an exception to this rule. The Danes put up no real military resistance when Nazi Germany attacked their country in April, 1940. The Germans treated the Danes with an intentionally easy hand, and after the Danes accepted economic dependence on Germany, they were allowed relatively wide freedom in their internal affairs. But Denmark absolutely refused to adopt an anti-Jewish policy, despite encouragement and pressure from various German authorities, and would not have any part in the expulsion of its Jewish community. In the end, in September, 1943, when the Germans tried to deport Danish Jewry without the consent of the Danes, the local population, led by political groups of the left and members of the underground, organized a huge rescue operation, which transferred some 7,200 Jews to neutral Sweden. The 425 Danish Jews who were sent to the Theresienstadt ghetto-camp were saved thanks to the concern and intervention of the Danes.

Danish Jewry was saved because of the courageous and consistent stand of the Danish people and their king. There was another European nation which played a great role in saving its Jews — Italy and the Italian people. Italian Fascism was not, at the start, anti-Semitic. Anti-Semitism was not an integral part of its philosophy; in fact, there were many Jews among the members of the Fascist Party and many more supported it. Political developments, the spread of Fascism and, most of all, the alliance with Nazi Germany, led Mussolini and the Fascist regime to adopt racism and legislate anti-Semitic laws in 1938. While the anti-Jewish regime in Italy did not have the same dimensions and severity as in Germany, foreign Jews were placed in prison camps and the status and rights of Italian Jews were restricted. Even so, during the war, and particularly when the

Germans demanded the extradition of Italian Jewry, the Italians refused. The resistance included various levels of the government and the public and frustrated the German plans. Jews were also protected from the Germans by the Italians in areas conquered by Italy, in parts of Yugoslavia and Greece and in southern France. There were many motives behind this refusal to hand Jews over to the Nazis, one of which was the desire not to appear as if Italy was accepting orders from Germany. But in all the many instances of Italian opposition to the German policy, we find justifications based on human concern for the Jews. During the last stage of the war, however, the Fascist Republic in northern Italy deprived the Jews of their property and their freedom and finally handed them over to the Germans. When, in the middle of September, 1943, the Germans overran Italy, they immediately began hunting down Italian Jews and sending them to camps in the east. Some 8,630 Italian Jews were sent to Auschwitz during this "action." But even at this point, there was much willingness to hide Jews, including foreign Jews. It is difficult to say exactly how many Jews were saved by the Italians' refusal to accept the Nazis' anti-semitic policy, but it clearly played an important role in the survival of the majority of Italian Jewry.

Gradual Development of Resistance Operations

There is a general tendency to exaggerate the dimensions of the resistance. Most books which deal with the story of the resistance to the Nazis see the resistance as a battle strategy taken up by conquered nations after being defeated on the front. In other words, once the peoples of Europe could no longer fight the Germans in pitched battle, they began fighting in unconventional ways.

However, when we examine the activities of the resistance and guerrilla movements in different countries, it becomes clear that there is no firm foundation to this argument for the continuous and general nature of the resistance in Europe. This image fits only the Serbs of Yugoslavia. Soon after Yugoslavia was defeated at the front by superior German forces, the Serbs began a stubborn guerrilla operation in the mountains, a war which continued and broadened to become a general popular resistance movement.

In all other countries the process was gradual and limited. The struggle generally began with individual, sporadic acts of resistance, which in time broadened and became stronger. There were countries in which small-scale military activities continued for a while after surrender, such as in Poland, but these ceased within a short period of time. The starting point for the resistance during the war was the tension between obedience and collaboration on the one hand, and refusal and lack of acceptance on the other. Collaboration of the sort in which individuals were forced to obey German orders, work for them, and give them crops or property was a general and inevitable phenomenon. It was only gradually that individuals felt the urge to frustrate the plans of the enemy. This was expressed by avoiding the performance of obligations, in sabotage at work, in refusal to fill production or crop quotas, or refusal to be taken for slave labor in Germany. Objection to racism, violence, and Nazi ideology and government was certainly a motive for many.

Individual resistance developed into organized political, national, or religious resistance. It began with public acts of resistance, and when these were forbidden and led to imprisonment and death, the groups went underground. Some parties, especially the Communists, who had taken a strong and uncompromising anti-Nazi line, were hesitant and confused at the beginning of the war, seeing the war as a fight between two "imperialisms." Political parties in the resistance movement began propaganda activities, put out underground newspapers, and organized strikes and sabotage. At this stage, there was already division, lack of coordination, and even conflict between different political tendencies. These conflicts sometimes led to violence and civil war during the last stage of the resistance, the stage of guerrilla war and armed struggle.

The armed struggle began on a significant scale after the turning point of the war in 1942-1943, after the Nazi defeat at Stalingrad and the British victories in the Near East. At this point, the national political movements began organizing themselves for the end of the war.

This organization involved taking account of the status and political character each country would have when peace came under the protection of the Allies. Against this background, the fighting against the Nazis grew along with the struggle between internal forces. Not even Yugoslavia was spared this kind of conflict. In Poland, an underground military organization was established and headed by members of the Polish regular army immediately after independence was lost, but as we have noted, this organization was hesitant to act until the end of the war. In Poland, there was fierce conflict between this central body and the Communists, who began organizing at the beginning of 1942. From the point of view of the Poles, there were two enemies — the Germans and the Soviets. Such conflicts developed in almost all countries, to different degrees. There were countries in which the resistance to the Nazis became limited to irregular skirmishes with especially cruel and hated officials, and to individual operations of great military sensitivity, such as the sabotage of the heavy water factory in Norway. But the resistance in these countries did not use trained combat units or guerrilla tactics. In many countries, such as the Czech Protectorate, the resistance refrained from guerrilla actions which were likely to bring about retaliation and great loss of life.

Nor could the resistance leaders expect aid from the Western Allies. In fact, the expectations of the great powers — England the United States on one side and the Soviet Union on the other — were very different.

Great Britain, and later the United States, were mostly interested in intelligence from the occupied areas, in aid for escaped Allied prisoners (especially pilots), and in sporadic operations. The opposite was true of the Soviet Union. It demanded that its supporters fight the enemy from the rear, and sabotage transportation arteries, factories, and the enemy's mobility.

This explains, at least in part, the great differences in the evaluation of the contribution of the guerrilla campaigns by the two sides. Soviet historians give much praise to the partisan war and its achievements, while some western historians, especially the British military historian B.H. Liddel-Hart, cast doubt on the value of the guerrilla campaign. Liddel-Hart argues that the guerrilla war did not affect the great campaigns in any noticeable way, and sometimes brought about serious negative consequences, and that its influence on the character of the regimes which took hold in some of these countries was undesirable. Without entering the political debate inherent in some of these arguments, we must acknowledge that, more than once, military resistance movements and guerrilla forces abstained from a given action out of fear that the price of the Nazi retaliation would be too high.

Guerrilla warfare is a struggle of the weak against the strong, against heavier and more sophisticated weapons. In general, guerrilla fighters have the advantages of knowing the territory, support of the local population, and the use of hit-and-run tactics. Polish partisans operated at times as units enlisted to carry out specific operations, or for a period of training, after which they returned to their homes and work. They would disappear in the same manner when the Germans conducted searches for partisans in the forests.

Barriers to Development of Jewish Guerrilla Movements

It has often been asked why Jews did not set up a guerrilla movement of their own, similar to many of the other national partisan movements. There are various answers to that question, and some were presented in the chapters which dealt with the organization of the ghetto undergrounds and the flight to the forests. The Jew who fled to the forests, as we noted, was not a fighter who left his parents and relatives in a secure house and whose decision touched on himself alone. The Jew abandoned his loved ones and community with a feeling of fear, knowing full well that the farewell was final. The non-Jew went off to fulfill his national obligation knowing that he had the support of the allies, a great power, or a government-in-exile in whose name he acted. The partisan could present himself to a village farmer and ask for food and intelligence as a fellow-countryman, with whom he could settle accounts in the future if he were let down or betrayed. The Jew was foreign, persecuted, abandoned. Jewish survival in the forest depended on affiliation with large groups, as a fighter in a general unit, or in a Jewish unit integrated into a larger partisan base. Furthermore, the individual Jew or group of Jews who wanted to be part of an existing partisan framework in Eastern Europe found the way blocked by many barriers, beginning with the fences around the ghetto, and including the difficult search for a base in the forest and if they made it, assignment to inferior positions in the fighting units.

The Jews who wanted to join guerrilla forces outside Eastern Europe fared better. In the Balkans — Yugoslavia, Bulgaria, and Greece — Jews were accepted into the fighting units and organizations with full equality. In Western Europe — France or Italy — there were many Jews who joined the resistance not as Jews but as Frenchmen or Italians motivated by patriotic or political obligation or loyalty. It is reasonable to assume that their Judaism was also an important motive in their decision. Moreover, many Jews in the western countries, concerned with the sufferings of their people, did not enlist in a fighting unit, but preferred to engage in the rescue of other Jews, which they saw as an important cause with a chance of success.

This was the pattern in Hungary, for instance, where members of youth groups did not engage in obtaining weapons and armed defense, but rather devoted their efforts to producing false papers, finding hiding places, storing food, and stationing defense forces in front of houses, families, and children. The wide-based rescue movement in Budapest created by the youth movement was aided by the large-scale activity and devotion of non-Jews such as the Swede Raoul Wallenberg and the Swiss Charles Lutz. These youths were the unsung soldiers of this great rescue movement. The members of these youth movements, who had spent day and night in a stubborn, constant struggle to save lives, were asked after the war why they had not fought or rebelled. In hindsight, we have to admit that their judgment was correct. In the circumstances which existed in the summer and autumn of 1944, when escaping the expulsion orders for days or weeks could and did save many, the choice to struggle for life was without a doubt the best and most promising decision.

PARTISANS IN THE SOVIET UNION AND EASTERN POLAND

In the Baltic countries, in the Vilna area, in Byelorussia, in the western Ukraine, and in all parts of the Polish state during the period between the two wars, Jewish partisan activity was well-established. According to estimates, there were more than 20,000 Jews in the partisan units in the forests. As we noted, several factors made survival possible for the large concentration of Jews in the forests. The geographical area was heavily forested and had large swamps, and was thus favorable to the establishment of partisan groups. Most of the partisan units in the area during the last stage of the war were under Soviet command and for various reasons accepted Jews into their ranks (with the exception of some Polish and Ukrainian units, which operated independently and at times displayed enmity towards the Jews). Many Jews in these areas, from towns and villages, were acquainted with the countryside and forest and were willing and able to adjust to life in the forest.

There were three stages in the development of the partisan movement in the forests:

In the first period, from the middle of 1941 to the end of 1942, Soviet soldiers and escaped POWs, Communists officials in danger of being killed by the German invaders, and common outlaws concentrated in the forests.

In the second period, from the end of 1942 to the end of 1943, Soviet representatives and paratroopers came to the forests and took command of the partisan forces. The number of partisans grew considerably, and the groups cooperated with one another. In time, the partisans excelled in having a high level of organization and discipline, efficient equipment and communication in their operations. They took part in many battles, and were able to keep from being captured by the enemy. At this point, the partisans became a problem for the Nazis, cutting off lines of communication, attacking groups of soldiers, punishing collaborators, and most important, instilling fear in German soldiers and making them feel as if they were surrounded by hostility.

In the final stage, in 1944, the partisans in the east functioned as a support group for military actions at the front, or aided in the liberation operations which increased with the approach of the Red Army.

Recently published research data indicate that, of all the Jews imprisoned in ghettos, about 12 percent escaped to the forests in western Byelorussia, and some 14 percent in Volhynia. According to this data, there were 63 underground organizations in 110 western Byelorussian ghettos helping Jews escape to the forests, and 30 groups in Volhynia.

More than 600 underground members escaped from the Vilna ghetto into the forests. In July, 1943, a group of FPO men left the ghetto under the command of Yosef Glazman, heading for the Naroch forest some 120 kilometers to the east. At that time, the forest was sheltering a number of Jewish groups and family camps. About 150 FPO men arrived at the forest at the beginning of September 1943, and aided the establishment of a Jewish regiment called *Nekama* ("Revenge"), which numbered about 250 fighters. The conditions in the Naroch Forest were harsh, and the fighters lacked arms and food. A decision was made to disband the Jewish regiment. Glazman tried to preserve the framework of a Jewish unit by obtaining permission to transfer his men to the Rudniki Forest, where the survivors of the Vilna underground were gathering after the destruction of the ghetto. But the Soviet commanders did not agree to the transfer. German forces cut down the partisans in the Naroch Forest. More than 100 Jews fell, including Yosef Glazman.

Jews were the first to arrive in the forests near Bialystok and lay the foundations of partisan activity there. They came from towns nearby, including Sufrasal, Bialystok, Krynki, and Slonim. The various component groups of the Bialystok underground debated whether it would be best to concentrate only on fighting in the ghetto, or to simultaneously fight in the ghetto and smuggle people out to the forest. In the spring of 1943, the ghetto underground made its first contact with a group that had established itself in the forest. At the time of the revolt in the ghetto in August, 1943, there were already several dozen Jewish fighters in the forest. They had a few rifles, a machine gun, grenades, and a pistol.

After the revolt, refugees and groups of fighters began coming to the forest, strengthening the ranks of the Jewish unit. There were female members of the underground who lived in Bialystok disguised as Poles and who maintained contact with and aided the underground and the partisans in the forest. It was not until the spring of 1944 that Soviet partisans appeared in the forests in the Bialystok area and the Jewish unit was integrated into the larger partisan fighting force.

CENTRAL POLAND — THE GENERAL GOUVERNEMENT

A large-scale underground movement functioned within the Jewish communities and ghettos of Poland. While this movement exhibited initiative and daring in many areas, it did not have great success in guerrilla warfare or in the partisan struggle outside the city. In the Cracow ghetto, the sabotage and fighting were concentrated within the city limits. These operations, the product of a decision to attack the Germans outside the ghetto in order to lessen German retaliation on the Jews, should be seen as urban guerrilla activity.

Why did the Jewish partisan struggle in Poland fail to reach large dimensions? The answers to the question are complex. First, central Poland is thinly wooded in comparison with the great forests of the east. Second, the strong military resistance under the sponsorship of the Polish government in exile (the *Armie Kriova* or AK) did not make use of guerrilla tactics at the start and saved most of its strength for military operations during the final stages of the war. In 1942, there was very little AK partisan activity in the forests. The AK did not encourage Jews to escape into the forests, and in most cases the unit commanders were not willing to accept Jews into their ranks. The

Fascist faction, NSZ, which remained, for most of the period, outside the framework of the AK, was extremely anti-Semitic and even murdered Jews who escaped to the forests. There were AK men who were sincerely concerned about the fate of the Jews and who tried to defend them in the forests, but their numbers were small and their power limited.

The Polish Communists were friendlier to the Jews, for two reasons. First, unlike the AK, the Communists wanted to begin an immediate struggle with the Nazis, and the Jews were a natural ally in this aspiration. Second, the Communists and the political left in general were somewhat more sensitive to the fate of the Jews.

In the period between the two world wars, there were many Jewish activists in the Polish Communist Party. Communist partisan activity did not begin, however, until mid-1942, and was not fully organized until 1943. The Communists, who had been rejected by the great majority of the Polish people, invested much effort in winning the sympathy of their countrymen. Even though they were willing to accept Jews into their ranks, they made sure that the percentage of Jews was not too high, so that theirs would not be accused of being a Jewish organization. The *Armie Ludowa* (AL) was a Communist guerrilla unit which did not become a force to be reckoned until the end of 1943. By that time, most of the ghettos had been destroyed and their inhabitants deported. Only the few Jews who had managed to enter the forests and survive in them before that time were able to benefit from this change.

This illustrates the importance of the third factor — timing. While the extermination campaign was at its height (spring 1942-spring 1943), the partisan movement in the *General gouvernement* was still weak. When the partisan movement gained in size and strength, and there were elements within it friendly to the Jews, there were very few Jews left; those still alive were imprisoned in labor and concentration camps.

According to data published by the Poles, about 25,000 people took part in the partisan movement in the *General gouvernement*, both in the Communist-associated AL and in the AK. The number of Jews who succeeded in escaping and finding shelter in villages, forests, and mountains was apparently in the tens of thousands. But of those, only 2,000 ended up as armed fighters in the forests, and 3,000 wandered the forests and villages. The rest were caught, murdered, or died in the wild.

Jews played a major role in the crystallization of the partisan force organized by the Communists. Among the Communist partisan commanders were many Jews, though most of them hid their origins. There were 40 Jews among the paratroopers who came from the Soviet Union in order to organize guerrilla warfare in Poland.

The years 1942-1944 saw the organization of 27 Jewish partisan units, and these carried out combat operations over a period of a few months. The most notable were the unit commanded by Yekhiel Grynszpan, which numbered 50 men in January, 1943; the unit commanded by Shmuel Jegier, composed of Jewish POWs who had escaped from the Lublin camp; the unit commanded by Avraham Amsterdam, which numbered 47 men and succeeded in breaking through the front and meeting up with Soviet forces, with heavy losses; the unit commanded by Shmuel Gruber, containing 30 men; and the unit named after Mordecai Anielewicz, which fought in the Warsaw area and was made up partly of fighters who had survived the Warsaw ghetto rebellion.

Nine Jewish units eventually joined the Polish AL forces. According to Shmuel Krakowski, "Most of the Jewish partisan units spilled all their blood in combat operations over the course of a year and a half. The few men who remained alive from these units joined Polish groups." It may be assumed that hundreds of Jews fought in the AK, disguised as Poles. There were also Jews who did not hide their Jewish origins and some who achieved high ranks in their units. Many Jews fought in both the Polish and the international units of the AL. Most of the Jewish units operated in the Lublin, Kielce, and Radom areas. About 1,000 Jews, among them survivors of the Warsaw ghetto, took part in the Polish uprising in Warsaw in August 1944.

GERMANY

German Jewry was the first Jewish community to suffer after the Nazis gained power. Yet until the outbreak of the war, there was no combat against the regime at all on the part of Jews.

German Jews dealt with the anti-Jewish decrees and attacks of the regime and the German public by increasing their internal unity and communal ties, while searching for collective responses to the challenges they faced. As their position became increasingly intolerable during the mid-1930's, the Jewish community became more closely knit, especially in smaller towns. Professional retraining was organized for Jews who had been laid off from their jobs. Emigration and aid organizations were established. The underground itself, the pale, hesitant underground which began forming in Germany, included Jews, but they were not there as Jews nor as the representatives of Jewish groups or organizations, but rather as individuals associated with opposition political groups, mostly of the left. The motives for their opposition were ideological and not necessarily Jewish. Most of the Jews imprisoned in concentration camps during this early period were arrested for their political views, not because of their Jewish origins.

Within the Jewish community, the feelings of Jewish identity grew. At this time, there was little interference with Jewish educational and propaganda activities, as long as they remained within the Jewish community. Paradoxically, the Jews enjoyed more freedom of thought and self-government than the Germans did. Of course, the discussions and debates were under observation and were allowed only if meant for Jews and not for Germans, and not if intended to create ideological or political links between Jews and non-Jews. In fact, similar phenomena appeared later on in the occupied countries such as Poland and Holland.

The young people who organized themselves in Zionist groups took an uncompromising stand with regard to their identity and to organized German anti-Nazi activity. The scholar Shaul Esh wrote that

> Jewish youth, while loathing even the non-anti-Semitic aspects of the Nazi regime, became apathetic to events in Germany and among the German people. Its sole interest was in Israel. Any act of rebellion against the Nazis was a matter for the Germans. For this reason, any Jew who engaged in underground activity outside the specifically Jewish context as much as declared his identification with the German people.

There were many Jews who could not accept their exclusion from participation in the German nation. The denial of their German identity and their right to be considered and called Germans was, for them, a personal tragedy, an unhealable wound. There were many suicides against this background, a kind of plague. There were others who insisted on carrying the burden of the attacks on their honor and the insults, and put on a front of cultured, restrained behavior. These attitudes were different from those of the Jews of Eastern Europe. During the first stage of the invasion there were almost no suicides among them, although many Jews took their lives during the period of the transports, when there was no longer any chance of surviving. The Jews in the East did not feel insulted, and felt no need to remain on good behavior with the Germans. They simply did not see the Germans as people with whom they had anything in common. Janusz Korczak, whose heart and mind were open to every man, wrote in his diary on August 4, 1942, the day before he was taken with the children from his orphanage to *Umschlagplatz*: "What would [the German policeman] do if I greeted him with a nod? If I greeted him with a friendly wave of my hand?" Korczak wondered whether the man before him was a human being from whom one could expect a human response.

During the war, and with the beginning of the mass deportations from Germany in 1942, members of the Jewish youth groups debated whether it was their duty to go together with the deportees to the East, in order to help the old and weak there, or to avoid deportation, assume a different identify, and disappear from the Nazis' sight. As long as it was possible, groups of young people left Germany for neighboring countries like Denmark and Holland under the auspices of Zionist training camps for agricultural work. Agricultural work units were established in Germany itself, and these later granted protection from deportation. The young people tried, to the very end, to preserve the communal framework, not only in being together but also with ceremonies, parties, Sabbath meals, and other activities, as in the past. Two groups were especially important; the religious group *Brit Halutzim Dati'im* and the pioneer labor movements. Annalise-Ora Borinska who was active in such a youth group, wrote in her memoirs:

> At that time [the period of deportations in 1942] we had to decide a matter of principle: "the parents question." More and more members learned that their parents had received orders to prepare, within a short time, for evacuation. Almost all the parents expected their children to come with them. . . . The work camps were still safe, to a certain degree. In group, every individual was important as a support of the whole — even if it came to evacuation. A group with a unified will was a better guarantee that we could succeed in our own way. The individual, with his concern for his parents pressing down on him, was liable to be lost. These, more or less, were the

considerations which brought us to this decision of principle. . .
And those members who went with their parents with the agreement of the group were given an early morning goodbye, before we
left for work. There were unforgettable moments, horribly moving
us each time anew, for all those who were at any time part of our circle. Everyone in work clothes, with coats and jackets, stood with
their arms on the shoulders of their neighbors — a few words, then
we sang *Beshalom* — someone else tore a piece off the flag, which
the friend leaving us took with him. . . . Then the last *hazak*, last
handshakes with everyone in the circle — and then we had to hurry
to get to work on time. . .

These agricultural training groups in Germany became the nuclei of
resistance and the initiators of daring and adventurous rescue operations in different European countries. Notable were Shosho-Joachim
Simon, who became leader of the young resistance fighters in Holland, and Kurt Reinlinger, who was active in France in helping Jews
cross the borders and in revenge operations against the Nazis. A resistance action which won much publicity was the burning of an anti-
Soviet exhibition presented in Berlin in May, 1943. The "Baum
Group" was at the center of the operation, led by Herbert Baum; the
members were almost all Jews, including young people who had previously been members of Zionist youth movements. The operation
was a symbolic act — the Baum Group was part of the Communist
underground. Dozens of Jews were arrested and executed in the
wake of the operation, and the persecution of the Jews became even
more severe. The operation raises the difficult question of whether
Jews organized in a non-Jewish framework should be seen as part of
the Jewish resistance movement. But in the Baum incident, the instance is not of an individual Jew in non-Jewish company, but of an
entirely Jewish group which performed the major part of the operation. There can be no doubt that among the motives of their organization and activity (the group had committed a series of operations
prior to this one) was the Jewish factor, the desire to avenge and help
Jews as Jews.

Eliahu Maoz, who was a member of a German youth movement, wrote:

It is doubtful whether the Jews of Germany could have organized a
mass revolt as was done in the East, or gone underground in an organized fashion in order to rescue and smuggle Jews over the border, as in the West. The few Jews left in Germany [in the period of

the transports] were under sentence of death. There were among them, however, young people who chose heroes' deaths. In their lives and in their deaths they served those same forces which would, in the end, wipe out the Nazis and save the remnant of the Jews and of humanity as a whole.

As a matter of fact, during the period which preceded the war, the exclusions, and the extermination, there was room for separate Jewish activity, both secret and public, which united the people and strengthened its image and its efforts to survive, and made it possible for people to get out of Germany. Political resistance in the underground did not serve Jewish ends and did not solve Jewish problems. It was the path chosen by Jews who considered themselves German. The situation was different during the war and the exclusions. In this stage, Jewish resistance activities, which were also aimed at helping Jews as much as possible, could receive assistance only from a pan-German resistance movement, and perhaps only from cells of the leftist underground.

SLOVAKIA

Slovakia was created in March, 1939, ostensibly as an independent state, but actually a puppet of the Nazi Third Reich. Slovakia was severed from Czechoslovakia, and was ruled by the Hlinka party, a Catholic party with a nationalist-fascist platform. During the first months of its existence it passed anti-Jewish laws, meant to force Jews out of the economic life of the country.

In the middle of 1940, the anti-Jewish policy became more severe. In 1940, Dieter Wisliceny arrived in Slovakia. He was attaché in charge of Jewish affairs to the Slovakian government. It was clear from this that the Third Reich wished to impose its anti-Jewish policy on Slovakia. In September, 1940, a Jewish institution called *Ustredna Zidov,* "the Jewish Center" and known as the UZ, was established. This was, for all intents and purposes, the *Judenrat* of Slovakia. In the fall of 1941, Slovakia approved the "Jewish Codex," a decree composed of 270 racist measures. These brought the Nuremburg laws to Slovakia — forced labor for Jews, removal of Jews from public and cultural life, the requirement that Jews wear yellow stars of David on their clothing, and transports of Jews to work camps in Sered, Novaki, and elsewhere.

It was the Slovakians themselves who, it seems, proposed to the Germans that a certain number of Jews be removed from the country. At the beginning of 1942, negotiations between Germany and Slovakia opened, with discussion of the organization of transports of Jews from the country and their delivery to the Germans. A shipment of 20,000 Jews was agreed upon. From March until October, 1942, some 58,000 Jews were expelled from Slovakia, most of them young, to Majdanek and Auschwitz. Some 22,000 Jews remained in Slovakia.

At the height of the period of transports, people from the "work groups" conducted intensive negotiations with the authorities. A small faction in the UZ and outside it took it upon themselves to help Jews in trouble, alert the world and prevent the continuation of the expulsion. The most prominent members of this group were Gisi Fleischmann, an active Zionist, and a young orthodox rabbi, Michael Ber Weismandel. The negotiations were carried out on two levels. There was an effort to persuade Slovakian politicians to stop the transports and make them understand the seriousness of expulsion, and there were contacts with Dieter Wisliceny. These contacts are well-known, and can be seen as the first attempt to prevent the transport of Jews to the camps in exchange for money and other goods. Wisliceny agreed to stop the transports in exchange for payment in dollars. There are those who believe that the exclusions ceased thanks to this agreement with Wisliceny, although this has not been proven.

Furthermore, the members of the "work group," and Rabbi Weismandel in particular, kept up their contacts with Wisliceny, who agreed — according to him, in coordination with the SS — to halt the execution of the "final solution" for a sum of $2-$3 million. Weismandel and his friends tried to raise this money from outside sources but were not successful. Weismandel believed, and he voiced this belief sharply in the memoirs he wrote after the war, that the proposal was an honest one, and that it failed because of the Jews' inability to obtain the money. It is difficult to determine the reality of the plan, called the "Europa Plan." It is impossible to know whether it was a Nazi-style trick or a real offer. It is strange that a sum of $2-3 million, a sum which was only a small percentage of the property the Nazis confiscated and stole from the expelled and murdered Jews, could decide the fate of most of the Jews of Europe. Wisliceny actually argued this before he was executed after the war, but he was then trying to save his life. We have no reliable German testimonies which can verify his claim.

Gisi Fleischmann.

Slovakian Jewry made an important contribution to the creation of a bridgehead in Zelina, which took in refugees from Poland and helped them get to Hungary — thought until the spring of 1944 to be a safe haven. Many of the members of the youth movement underground who feared the renewal of the exclusions from Slovakia crossed the border into Hungary for a "visit." In the middle of 1944, when the expulsions from Hungary began, they began to make "return visits" to Slovakia. In the Sered and Novaki work camps there were still relatively tolerable conditions. An underground was organized there, including a regiment made up of members of the Zionist and leftist youth groups. These young people trained, collected weapons, and prepared themselves for what was to come. The moment to act came with the outbreak of the Slovakian military rebellion in August, 1944.

In the face of the approach of the Red Army, the Slovakian authorities retreated from the northeastern part of the country. This step led to the declaration of a free Slovakia and the opening of a military struggle involving rebels from the ranks of the Slovakian army and prisoners from Allied armies, in particular, Soviet prisoners. Jews from Bratislava in the south, and the young people in the Sered and Novaki camps, as well as Jewish underground groups, penetrated the liberated area around Banska Bistrica and joined the rebel army. Akiva Nir, who fought with the rebels, related:

> Army units were on all the roads, and in Bistrica there was a tense atmosphere of headiness and freedom. Our fellows were organized into three army units; the Novaki camp partisan unit; Captain Bielov's unit, which was stationed in the small village of Bukowitz east of Banska Bistrica; and in the partisan unit which operated in the Liptov Mountains. The largest of the [Jewish] units was that of Captain Bielov. All the members of the Bratislava chapter were there, old and young. Egon Rot organized the work.

Another youth group member among the rebels, David Goldstein, said: "When we came to the rebel headquarters, we presented ourselves to the partisan command and asked to join the combat units. This was an express order from the movement, to integrate ourselves into the partisan fighting forces."

In September, 1944, at the height of the rebellion, four Jewish paratroopers from Palestine arrived in Slovakia: Havivah Reik, Rafael Weiss, Zvi Ben-Ya'akov, and Chaim Chermesh. The paratroopers went to work helping the Jews in the liberated territory, about 5,000 in number, who had come as exiles, many of them without means of survival. Once the Germans sent forces to Slovakia, the rebel force was quickly subdued, and in October, 1944, they surrendered. Most of the Jewish rebels, including paratroopers Havivah Reik and Zvi Ben-Ya'akov (Weiss and Chermesh had been sent to Hungary) led an organized retreat into the mountains. Along the way, the unit was surrounded and captured, and its members executed. The remainder of the Jewish force went to the Tatra Mountains and continued the struggle there until the liberation.

With the failure of the revolt, Slovakian Jewry became easy prey for retaliation operations. Some 10,000 Jews were captured, 2,257 murdered on the spot, and the rest sent to concentration camps.

Havivah Reik, paratrooper.

Zvi Ben-Ya'akov, paratrooper.

YUGOSLAVIA

There were about 80,000 Jews in Yugoslavia before the war, some Ashkenazic, but the majority Sephardic. The Yugoslavian community was noted for its internal unity and national organization. Yugoslavia, which refused to surrender to the Germans and fought for its independence, was divided into several occupation areas. Serbia (which included Belgrade) fell under German control, and in this area there was a constant and stubborn resistance movement. The Communists, led by Yosef Broz Tito, were the nucleus of the partisan forces there. Although at the start there were not many Jews in the partisan movement, many Jews were executed as hostages and as being responsible for the partisan movement. After a time, the remnant of Serbian Jewry was sent to concentration and extermination camps.

Croatia was a puppet state sponsored by the Nazis and run by the Fascist *Ustashe* movement. Croatia had a long history of enmity with Serbia, based on religious and national differences, and they took advantage of their new status to pay back the Serbs, using unrestrained cruelty. Tens of thousands of Serbs were murdered. The Croatian Catholics used the same methods against the Jews. About 20,000 of Croatia's 40,000 Jews were murdered in the Jasenovac Camp. In accordance with the Nuremburg laws, adopted by Croatia, Jews wore yellow stars on their clothing and were shut out of the economic life of the country, their leadership was arrested, and the great majority of the community was imprisoned in camps.

Western Yugoslavia, along the Adriatic Sea, was under the control of the Italian army, and the Jews' status was different. The Italians not only protected the Jews and refused to turn them over to the Germans, but also allowed Jewish refugees from other areas, especially Croatia, to enter its area of control, and refused to return them to the Croatians and Germans.

In time, a relatively large number of Jews joined the partisan ranks, and later, Tito's army. Among them were members of Zionist youth groups. The Yugoslavian Communist Party had many Jewish members. The party was without anti-Jewish feelings and did not restrict or discriminate in accepting Jews into the partisan ranks. Nevertheless, in the wider partisan movement there was some anti-Semitic feeling, and many of the Jews who joined preferred, it seems, to keep their origins to themselves.

The Yugoslavian partisan movement did not include separate Jewish movements. Thousands of Jews fought in its ranks, with some putting their number at 4,000. One of Tito's closest associates was the Jewish Communist Moshe Piade. Jews reached positions of high command. Robert Domiano was the commander of a partisan regiment and William Dreksel was the political commissar of a corps. Jews also stood out in Tito's medical corps. Eleven Jews received the "National Hero" medal for their outstanding service in the partisan forces. Among Tito's soldiers were also Jewish paratroopers from Palestine, including Reuven Dafni.

Yugoslavian partisans.

In September, 1943, in the wake of the fall of Mussolini and the revolution in Italy, the Raab camp on the Adriatic shore was liberated. Jews were gathered in this camp under the protection of the Italian government. It was very different from the camps controlled by the Germans and Croatians. Some 240 young people (including 40 women) from the camp joined the partisans and founded the Jewish Raab Battalion. They fought as a unit alongside the other partisan units until the fall of 1944, when it disbanded and its members were absorbed by the other units.

GREECE

On the eve of the Second World War there were about 76,000 Sephardic Jews in Greece. Greece fell to the Germans after bitter battles, in which a British expeditionary force, including Jewish volunteers from Palestine, took part in the fighting alongside the Greeks. More than 1,000 of them had fallen prisoner to the Germans by the end of the heavy fighting in Greece and Crete. Occupied Greece was divided into two areas. Historical Greece, including Athens, fell under Italian control, while the capital of Macedonia, Salonika and its environs, as well as the Aegean islands and the area bordering Turkey, came under German rule. This division was a great disaster for the Jews. Salonika was home to an ancient Jewish community which had a special character of its own, and comprised two-thirds of Greek Jewry. The Jews of Greece were disconnected, to a large measure, from the events in occupied Europe with its millions of Jews. During the first year of occupation, the regime in Salonika was relatively tolerable. In the summer of 1942, forced labor and ransom payments were imposed on the Jews. In January, 1943, the preparations for the "final solution" began, under the supervision of Dieter Wisliceny, infamous after his activity in Slovakia. (He later arrived in Hungary with Eichmann during the German invasion in March, 1944.) Within a few short weeks, he had imposed harsh restrictions on the Jews of Salonika, packing them into ghettos, forcing them to put a special insignia on their clothing and businesses, and performing an inventory of their property.

On March 15, 1943, the Germans began taking transports of Jews to Auschwitz. The Jews of Greece had not the slightest idea of what awaited them. Of the more than 50,000 Jews in Salonika, nearly all were sent to Auschwitz where they perished. Seventy-seven percent of them were murdered in the gas chambers immediately upon arriving at Birkenau.

A Greek guerrilla force began forming fairly early on. The Greek underground was composed of two organizations. The first, called the National Organization, carried out combat operations, whereas the second, called the National Liberation Front, concentrated on urban guerrilla warfare. Jews who found it difficult to move freely to distant places mostly joined the National Liberation Front. Hundreds of Jews took part in its operations. Public figures in the Jewish community of Salonika, and to a lesser extent of the Athens community, took part in the wide-ranging intelligence-gathering activity of the organization.

The military activity of the guerrilla forces in Greece increased in 1942. There was information that Greece was being used as a conduit for supplies to Rommel's army in Africa, using the railroad which crossed the Gorgopratamos Bridge. The bridge was blown up in an operation in which 40 Jews took part. Jews took part in many operations, such as "sabotage of army centers, destruction of factories, sabotage of German ships carrying ammunition and, most important, cutting off supply routes. Jews excelled in these actions in an exceptional way."

HOLLAND

The Jewish underground in Holland concentrated, for the most part, on rescue activities. A Zionist group, most of them refugees from Germany, formed the nucleus of these operations. The group was aided by Dutch Jews and non-Jews. Among the latter was Jup Westerweel, later executed for his activities. The central figure in the Jewish group was Joachim Simon. The group helped smuggle Jews to Switzerland, France, and Spain, helped Jews escape from the Westerbork collection camp, and helped hide Jews in Holland.

Members of the Dutch underground, among them Joachim Simon (Shosho).

The rest of the Jewish underground groups in Holland, among whose ranks were members of Zionist and leftist parties, also concentrated their efforts on rescue operations. The members of these groups were in conflict with the *Judenrat*. They succeeded in destroying some of the Jewish census cards, according to which orders to report for transports were sent, and according to which the search for

Jews was organized. In their operations, the Jewish groups were aided by the Dutch underground and by church institutions.

BELGIUM

The rescue operations in Belgium reached large dimensions, and the lives of 3,000 Jewish children can be credited to them. The crowning achievement of these operations was the blocking of a transport train containing 1,500 Jews, from which hundreds were able to escape. In 1942, urban guerrilla operations began, with the participation of dozens of Jews.

FRANCE

The Jews of France were not a homogeneous community. They were divided in many ways. Some 300,000 Jews lived in France on the eve of the war, among whom close to two-thirds were "foreign Jews" who had immigrated to France from Eastern Europe just before the First World War and during the period between the two wars. The great majority of them were not French citizens; many among them spoke French with difficulty and preferred to speak and read in Yiddish. Most of them were artisans, and were part of the lower middle class. They tended to live in closely-knit communities, to frequent their own clubs, to publish Yiddish newspapers, and to operate their own welfare projects. In addition to this, they were loyal to the political views they had brought with them from the old country. Most of these "foreigners" favored the political left — they were Communists, Bundists, or members of one of the left-wing Zionist groups.

Beginning in 1933, tens of thousands of German Jews arrived in France. At that time, France did not live up to its traditional image of a land which welcomes political refugees. The German refugees — both Jewish and non-Jewish — who fled to France found they could not receive work permits or residence permits, and the French were apathetic, and sometimes unfriendly, to them. The organizations set up to assist the refugees were weak and without means. The hatred of foreigners which characterized France then was the result, in part, of the economic crisis from which the whole Western world suffered. It would be more precise to say that the trauma of that time was still felt, and created bitterness towards foreigners who competed with the French for jobs. In addition to this, the French were frightened of undesirable political complications. The right-fascist movements, small but noisy, often conducted public propaganda campaigns against the refugees.

France's native Jews were also not of a kind. There were differences between the Alsatian Jews in eastern France and the Parisian Jews. The native Jews were rooted in and proud of French culture, and thankful to France for granting them equal rights and opportunities in all areas of life. The representative Jewish organization, the *Consistoire*, was a sort of religious association which avoided all political involvement, and was headed by members of wealthy and noble families. The Jewish consciousness and identity of the native community had become restricted to religion, while the Eastern European Jews, including those of the left, saw themselves as Jews in an ethnic or national sense, and continued to foster Yiddish culture and language, as well as traditional ways of life. The native community feared that the boldly Jewish character of the "foreigners" and their political views would increase anti-Semitism, and this led to tension and disputes. There were even those of the old community who did not hesitate to maintain contact with French movements of the extreme right, movements which did not hide their anti-Semitic leanings.

After the Nazi invasion in the middle of 1940, France was divided into two parts. One was ruled by the *Wehrmacht* and the German police, and the second, the Vichy area, was called "Free France." There was also an Italian enclave in the south. While Vichy France was free in many ways, it was in no way a continuation of pre-war France. The people who signed the surrender and led the Vichy government for the entire period — most importantly, the aged Marshal Petain and, for a long time, Pierre Laval — drew their support from the right and the reactionary factions with fascist leanings. They worked to establish a new France free of liberalism, republicanism, and separation of church and state, based on the worship of the family and the state, conservatism, and isolationist patriotism, rejecting foreigners.

Jews and refugee fighters from Republican Spain, who did not have residence permits, were imprisoned in camps. In the fall of 1940, anti-Jewish laws were legislated in France. This legislation, which closed a list of professions to Jews, was not instituted at the insistence of the Germans, but rather at the initiative of the leaders of

"Free France." Soon afterwards, an Office for Jewish Affairs was set up, and the Jews were forced, though now under German pressure, to form a sort of *Judenrat* (the *Union Générale des Israélites de France*, known as the UGIF). The anti-Jewish laws were later made more stringent, and Jewish property was confiscated. The French acted to assume control of Jewish property, both for material gain and from fear that if it was not put into the hands of French guardians, it would fall into the hands of the Germans.

The first French Jews to become active in the underground were those from leftist groups — Communists from Eastern Europe and members of the left. This activity was not always in tune with the Communist party line, which, during the period of the Ribbentrop-Molotov agreement, functioned in a state of confusion and evasiveness. The first underground group to go into action was *Rue Amelot*, named after the street where headquarters were located, headed by David Rappaport.

French partisans.

During the summer and fall of 1942, when the Germans invaded southern France and the entire Jewish community faced destruction, the Jewish underground gained momentum. There was debate among French Jews over whether to go underground immediately or to first exhaust all legal means. Then another problem arose: whether to concentrate on rescue operations or to join the ranks of the fighting underground, the *Maqui*. Many of those who wished to give underground activity a clearly Jewish character preferred rescue operations, despite the fact that the two areas of activity were, in the end, interdependent. The position of the Jews and the concern for their safety in the face of the exclusions which began in the summer of 1942 made it necessary to concentrate on rescue operations which involved obtaining false papers, concealing people, helping thousands cross the border, and organizing children's houses. The underground forged documents and identify cards on a large scale. Many who held these papers, however, did not know French well, and the forgeries did not easily solve their problems.

There were two roads over the border and out of France — the English Channel and the road to Switzerland and Spain. Many children were sent to Switzerland, in operations in which members of the youth movements played a large part. About 600 people, including 100 children crossed the Pyrenees into Spain. Between 7,000-9,000 Jews had been saved by the end of the war. The Jews were aided in different parts of the rescue operation by members of the underground, political organizations, and by senior clergy. Despite the fact that the Petain regime was the to the clergy's liking, and most of them supported it, when the expulsions began, there were many among them who took part in saving Jews. Both Protestants and Catholics in Lyon and Toulouse, the cities which led to Switzerland and Spain, were prominent in this effort. The senior clergy condemned racism. Cardinal Saliége, Archbishop of Toulouse, and Cardinal Gerlier of Lyon both gave their blessings to the rescue effort. One of the outstanding figures in this effort was Alexander Glasberg, a priest of Jewish origins, who worked from the early states of the war to save Jews. This work required close contact with the underground.

Many of the Jews active in the Jewish resistance organizations worked simultaneously with the general resistance. There is no doubt that the experience of Vichy and the rescue effort sharpened the Jewish identities of many members of the Jewish underground in France.

The Drancy camp, from which transports of Jews were sent to the East, was liberated by a combat unit of the *Organisation Juive de Combat* (OJC), a Paris group commanded by Charcot Naville. The unit also took part in the liberation of France. Jewish fighters also participated in the liberation of the city of Castres. The Jewish Association for Resistance and Mutual Aid, the members of which included many Communists from different factions, was active in the liberation battles of the final months of the war. Jewish *Maqui* units concentrated on areas in which there were large-scale rescue operations.

During the later period of the underground, the *Conseil Représentatif des Israélites de France* (CRIF), was established, uniting all Jewish factions, with their widely-varying ideologies. While this closing of ranks did not survive the end of the war, it contributed much toward moderating the conflicts among them after liberation.

Some 76,000 Jews were expelled from France, and the question remains as to whether the Jewish resistance can be said to have accomplished much.

Among the six founders of the French organization *Liberation*, three were Jews. In the national committee, which was formed later and was the highest authority in the French resistance movement, there were three Jewish members among a total of 16. Jews also stood out in the group surrounding Charles de Gaulle and in other resistance groups. The most prominent of them were Pierre Mendes-France, later to become Prime Minister, and the French historian Marc Bloch.

Other Jews who were prominent in the French resistance include Jean-Pierre Levy who founded one of the most important French resistance movements. The commander of a section of a strong Communist organization in the Paris area was Jewish, "Colonel Juliet" (his real name was Josef Epstein and he was from Warsaw). Marcel Diamant, a 19-year old Jew who was the moving force behind some daring guerrilla operations in Paris, was caught by the Germans early on in the struggle and executed, entering the pantheon of the French resistance. Jacques Bingen left France in 1940 and joined De Gaulle's forces. He returned secretly in 1943 and headed the Free French forces in the north of the country; France has issued a stamp in his memory.

The Jewish Scouts, who had Zionist and traditional leanings, carried out an important role in establishing a system of aid to escapees, especially Jewish children, in obtaining forged papers, in finding hideouts, and in transferring Jews from dangerous places to less dangerous ones. A group which entered France secretly from Holland operated, for the most part, in organizing escapes and helping Jews cross the mountains into Spain.

The united Jewish forces created a Jewish Army (*L'Armee Juive*) in which Robert Garnzon was one of the leading activists who established the Jewish *Maquis*. This force took part in many operations, including overcoming German trains, attacking traitors, sabotaging factories producing German war material, and attacking German airplanes and transport vehicles of the occupying army.

In Algeria, young Jews organized in a defense group, disguised as a sport club. Jews played a decisive part in aiding the American forces which penetrated Algeria in November 1942. Most of the fighters who helped the attackers by taking hold of key positions in the city were Jews.

Chapter 8

Jews in the Allied Armies

The Jewish soldiers in the Allied armies during the Second World War fought for different reasons than those who fought in previous European wars. From the time the Jews achieved equal rights in various European countries, they were required, like all other citizens, to perform military service and fight under patriotism, out of loyalty to their countries. This was apparently the motivation for the great majority of Jews who fought in the German Kaiser's armies during the First World War, beginning in 1914. Jewish soldiers could not, however, free themselves from the uneasiness they felt in fighting Jewish soldiers from the other countries. For example, Jews who served in the Russian and French armies fought against Jews who served in the German and Austrian armies. This was a problem for those Jews who had relatives in other countries, and who knew that members of their own families were fighting in the enemy army.

From this point of view, World War II was different. Jews were not accepted into the *Wehrmacht* after March 1935, when Hitler rebuilt it unilaterally and in violation of the Treaty of Versailles, and reinstituted compulsory military service in Germany. And in the wake of the racial laws legislated in 1938 in Italy, Jews were dismissed from the Italian army. The result was that Jews did not serve in the Axis forces. Jewish fighting forces could be found on only one political front — the one opposing Nazism and Fascism.

245

In previous wars, Jews fought the battles of their countries, and their struggles did not express any specifically Jewish interest.

It is true that World War II did not break out in response to Jewish misery, or in opposition to the racism and anti-Semitic policies of the Nazis. These were not factors in the political conflict and crisis which led to war. Hitler, of course, declared throughout the war that it was a Jewish war, that the Jews were responsible for it and that only the Jews had an interest in it. The disproof of this was that the European democracies, which were supposedly ruled by Jews who had led them into war, completely ignored the fate of the Jews in the Third Reich, or, in any case, did not see the persecution of the Jews and their horrible fate as something which required formal involvement. Most of the democratic countries, however, did take a clear anti-Nazi position because of their abhorrence of racism, anti-Semitism, and the Nazi treatment of the Jews. During the course of the war, Western leaders made many declarations to the effect that this war was not a war of power and interest as were previous wars, but a struggle to uphold the basic values of Western culture and human equality. The fate of the Jews, however, took second place in the explanation of the reasons for the war and its ideological righteousness. Documents from the period show that the allies did not use the Jewish aspect of the war in their propaganda for fear that emphasizing this point would justify Germany's argument that the war was being fought "for the Jews and under Jewish direction."

The disregard for the problems of the Jews is even more notable in the position taken by the Soviet Union. From August, 1939, to June, 1941, the German Reich and the Soviet Union were linked by a treaty which required, among other things, that they not conduct propaganda campaigns against one other. The Soviet Union kept this obligation, and, as a result, the Soviet press did not report either the persecution of the Jews in the Third Reich or in the occupied countries. Therefore, the people of the Soviet Union and the areas annexed to it at the beginning of the war did not know anything of the situation of the Jews under the Nazi regime. During the war, the Soviets maintained that the war was being conducted to preserve the peoples of the Soviet Union under the leadership of the Russian people. The suffering of the Jews and the threat to their existence was rarely mentioned. When the Soviets spoke publicly about the fate of the Jews and the Jewish interest in the war, they did so outside the Soviet Union. For instance, the representatives of the Jewish Anti-Fascist

Committee, established in April, 1942, were sent in May, 1943, to the United State and other countries to enlist support and aid for the Soviet Union from the Jewish public, emphasizing the special interest the Jews had in the war. When the war ended, this committee was disbanded and its newspaper *Einikeit* was closed. Most of its central figures were murdered during the Stalinist terror campaign.

Despite this, the significance of the war for the Jewish people was known to every Jew who enlisted in an army which fought against the Nazis. The Jewish soldiers knew that in this war, in addition to fulfilling their duty to their country, they were struggling for the Jewish people's right to survive.

JEWS IN COMBAT FORCES DURING THE FIRST STAGES OF THE WAR

This special Jewish motivation was notable at the beginning of the war and throughout it. The Jewish soldiers knew that they were contributing to wiping out the greatest, most dangerous enemy that had ever risen against the Jewish people and Judaism. Wherever they were, they searched out Jews, aided them, and returned them to life and the outside world. This role was filled first and foremost by the "Brigade" of Jewish soldiers and volunteers from Palestine who served as the pathbreakers for the *yishuv* and the Zionist ideal when they met with the survivors during the first months after the war. A similar role was played by American rabbi-chaplains, Jews in the British army, and a few Jewish soldiers and officers in the Red Army.

Close to the outbreak of the war in 1939, the extreme anti-Semitic campaign of the second half of the 1930's in Poland ceased. Polish Jewry enthusiastically harnessed itself to a public undertaking   collecting money for emergency funds, contributing money to buy armaments, and digging defense fortifications. They also participated in the military effort against the Nazis in September, 1939, in the ranks of the Polish army. Records indicate that ten percent, or 130,000 of the enlisted men in the Polish army in September, 1939, were Jews. Some 32,000 of them were killed or wounded in battle against the Nazi enemy, with between 34,000 and 64,000 Jews taken prisoner by the Germans.

In 1940, Italy attacked Greece and the Greek people united in the defense effort. The Jews of Greece took part in this struggle wholeheartedly — 13,000 Jews served in the Greek army, among them 343 officers. Of these soldiers, 631 fell in battle and 3,743 were wounded. The Jewish losses in the Greek army were higher than average. This is an indication of the motivation and spirit of sacrifice Greek Jewry displayed in the war. After Greece was forced to sign a cease fire, part of the Greek army, including many Jews, regrouped in the southern districts of the country, hoping to continue the struggle against the invaders. This hope was not fulfilled, but many of these escapees went on to form the nucleus of the Greek partisan movement.

On September 3, 1939, France and Great Britain declared war on Germany, thus keeping their commitment to Poland and joining it in the anti-Nazi campaign. Much time passed, however, between the declaration of war and the beginning of actual combat. This period was called the "strange war" or the "do-nothing war." During this period it was Germany, and not the Western democracies, which took the initiative. In April, 1940, Germany attacked Denmark and Norway, and in May, Holland, Belgium, and France. We do not know how many Jews served in France's large army — France did not keep records of the religious affiliations or ethnic origins of its enlisted men. We do know that 40,000 Jews who were not French citizens (and were thus not drafted) volunteered for military service. Among them were Jews from the "International Brigades" of the Spanish Civil War who had retreated to France, and refugees who had arrived in France from Germany at the beginning of the war. The special Jewish interest in the war was an important factor in the decision to volunteer. Many of the volunteers lacked military training and combat experience. The Jewish volunteers were made part of foreign companies 21, 22, 23, and the Foreign Legion.

French officers were not always happy to receive Jewish volunteers. The Jewish fighting units were sometimes called the "tailors' companies." The western campaign ended, as is known, with the crushing defeat of the Allies. This was the height of the success of the German *blitzkrieg* tactic and an impressive display of the military power of the Third Reich. This campaign was not a stubborn struggle over each inch of territory, trench opposite trench, as it had been in World War I. France had surrendered by the third week of June, and its army found itself in a hopeless situation. The British forces retreated, and escaped across the English Channel. This retreat of the great British army from the European theater turned defeat into an important gain, because the British were thus able to save their main forces and continue to prepare them for the battles ahead.

Paradoxically, the position of the Jewish POWs in German hands was better than the fate of those Jews who remained in France, both in the area under German control and in Vichy France. The Germans tried to isolate the Jewish prisoners from the French, but the Vichy government, which had passed anti-Jewish and racist laws and collaborated with the Nazi authorities in turning over and expelling Jews, rejected the "separation of Jewish prisoners from their comrades-in-arms." On the other hand, those Jews who were freed in accordance with agreements between Vichy and the Germans resumed their former status, which meant that after being freed from German POW camps, they were sent in transports to camps in the East.

Jews made a major contribution in the ranks of the British army. Among these were also many Jewish volunteers who were not required by law to serve. We may assume that the number of such volunteers would have been even larger, if the British had not dealt with refugees from enemy countries with great suspicion, including Jewish refugees from Nazi Germany. It is estimated that some 62,000 Jews served in the British army (including 14,000 in the RAF), and about 25,000 Jews served in the units which took part in the war in other parts of the Empire. Some 1,500 Jews fell in battle in the ranks of the British army.

Many Jews stood out as exceptional soldiers, and 570 of them were decorated at the end of the war. Among the best known was the Jewish pilot from South Africa, Lionel Cohen, who was the commander of a wing in the RAF, and who was still in active service at the age of 68. Cohen took part in 45 combat flights and received the highest honors. Many Jewish pilots served with great heroism, sacrifice, and devotion, and were examples to others. The first RAF pilot to fall in the Second World War was H. Rosopsky, a Jew from Rhodesia.

The volunteer spirit was especially marked in the South African community, which had many family connections in Lithuania and Poland. Among those enlisting from South Africa were the seven sons of the Gordon family of Johannesburg. Soldiers and officers who had passed their sixtieth birthday, young men not yet of draft age, and thirty-five of the 60 young men in the Jewish orphanage in Johannesburg volunteered for military service in the first days of the enlistment campaign.

From the small Australian Jewish community came some 3,000 soldiers. Immigrants and refugees from Germany and other European countries asked not to be passed over, and were allowed to serve in support units. Among the Australian Jews, General John Monash stood out as an exemplary soldier who had excelled as a field commander during World War I. Many of Australia's Jews served with excellence in the Second World War. Of them, 846 served in the Australian air force.

JEWS IN THE RED ARMY AND IN THE ARMIES OF EASTERN EUROPE

We have no reliable record of the number of Jews who served in the Red Army, which played a decisive role in defeating Germany. Estimates are that there were about half a million. About 200,000 of them fell in action. More than 160,000 were decorated, many with the highest award, "Hero of the Soviet Union." Thousands of Jews served as officers, according to estimates. More than 100 of them achieved the rank of General, and some of these won great glory.

Most of the Jews were drafted into the Red Army like other Soviet citizens, but there were many volunteers, despite the fact that the Soviet press did not highlight the anti-Jewish character of National Socialism and the Third Reich. As mentioned previously, in the period between the end of August, 1939, and the German offensive against the Soviet Union (the "Barbarossa" operation) in June, 1941, the Soviet press abstained from publishing material offensive to Germany. For this reason, the citizens of the Soviet Union, and the Jews among them, did not have a clear picture of what was happening in Germany and the occupied countries, and did not know the dimensions of the persecution of the Jews during the war. It must be noted that, during the 1930's the Soviet Union had undertaken a methodical campaign to eliminate Jewish institutions, cultural projects, education, and publications, and the link of its Jews with their origins, people, and culture was much weakened. There was much assimilation, especially among the younger generation, and Jewish consciousness was almost completely wiped out.

Among the Red Army volunteers were many "western" Jews — that is, Jews from Poland, the Ukraine, and Byelorussia who had managed to escape the German invaders and find shelter in Russia.

Many of these "western" Jews were arrested or exiled to camps as part of the Soviet policy directed against Jews considered to be capitalists and/or those whose loyalty might be to their countries of origin rather than to the Soviet Union. A large portion of the "western" volunteers were removed from active duty and included in "work companies" — forced labor units — in the rear. The policy of discharging the "westerners" was not directed only at Jews, however; it resulted from suspicion of the Ukrainians and other nationals from the western border areas of Russia, many of whom collaborated with the Nazis in the expectation that the Nazi regime would aid them in achieving national independence. The Soviets did not trust them, and placed special restrictions on them. The Jews were especially angry that this suspicion fell on them and that it led to their discharge from combat units and transfer to the rear. After all, it was the "western" Jews who were most aware of the character of the Nazi regime and the essential Jewish interest in the war against the Third Reich.

Jews fought in all the units of the Red Army. Among them were not only young men doing mandatory service, but also many scientists and writers who believed that, as Jews, they were obligated to do their part in the battle against the Nazi enemy. There were also enlisted women. They served not only in support units, but in combat units as well. Among the 119 soldiers who received the highest military honor, "Hero of the Soviet Union," was a Jewish woman pilot.

The Jews in the Red Army stood out in the commanding ranks, in the large and important battles, and in heroism and personal sacrifice. We know of the deeds of many Jews thanks to the Jewish newspaper *Einikeit*, which began appearing in 1942 under the sponsorship of the Soviet Anti-Fascist Committee, established by the Soviet authorities in order to win favor among Jews and non-Jews in the United States and free world. It is important to remember that the Soviet Union, in the face of the danger, moderated its national policy, and its leaders showed interest in reviving patriotism. The Russian national tradition was celebrated, with its symbols and heroes. But raising the national consciousness of other peoples was also allowed and even encouraged. This campaign had some influence on the renewal of Jewish national life as well. This renewal was strengthened through contacts with the "western" Jews who arrived in the Soviet Union and because of the special interest the Jews had in the war against the Nazis. In fact, there was a notable resurgence of Jewish literature during the war, including the publication of Yiddish newspapers and the revival of Yiddish theater and Jewish art. As is known, these were only temporary, and disappeared completely when peace came. Furthermore, Jewish writers and activists paid a heavy price for their enthusiasm and naivete during the war. Their activities and ideas were later considered sins and a "nationalist deviation," and they perished in Stalin's murder campaign.

Nevertheless, we owe our knowledge of Jewish achievements in the war to these Jewish publications. The detailed and comprehensive article by Y. Guri, which appears in the book *Jewish Soldiers in the War Against the Nazis*, quotes newspaper articles and other material demonstrating the part Jews played in the Soviet Army. Berl Mark, who worked as a correspondent for *Einikeit*, was quoted in the Israeli newspaper *Davar* on August 16, 1943:

> A number of Jewish soldiers distinguished themselves in the battle of Orel and in the fighting in the streets of the city. Moshe Mittelman removed 150 mines in a single day, opening a path for the army to the gates of Orel. Sniper Moshe Belegolov was noted in the day's order as the outstanding soldier of the unit. Sergeant Shlomo Karelitzky of Kiev received an order to stretch a bridge over the Oka River. He carried out the order under massive enemy fire and was killed. Hirsch Rodinitzky succeeded in capturing a German corporal who had in his possession documents and important information for the Soviet command. Artilleryman Shmuel Siegelman of Minsk shot down four enemy planes in one day.

Guri published short biographical sketches of some of the Jewish officers who distinguished themselves in decisive battles:

> Many Jews distinguished themselves in the defense of Stalingrad, both officers and soldiers. Among them was General Ya'akov Kreizer, second-in-command of the Second Guard Army. A Lieutenant-General in the artillery forces, Yisrael Baskin, commanded large artillery units ... and the tank corps of the 62nd Army under the command of Podpolkovnik M.G. Weinraub displayed original ability in the most effective exploitation of tanks in urban street warfare. .... Because of the small number of tanks, the tank forces took advantage of dispersion and put one or two tanks in each important defense position. In coordination with the riflemen and the artillery, the tanks made sorties in the direction of the enemy or pushed back its attacks. In the battle over Stalingrad, Mathew Weinraub was only 33 years old. He was born in Byelorussia and volunteered for the army at the age of 19. He grad-

uated from tank corps military school and, after that, from the Prozna Military Academy in Moscow. His brother Yosei finished the academy on the same day and also became an officer in the tank corps. In 1944, Mathew had already reached the rank of Major-General. On April 6, 1945, the rank of Major-General was granted to Mathew Weinraub, and to his brother, Podpolkovnik Yosei Weinraub, the title "Hero of the Soviet Union."

The powerful Red Army attack on Berlin began on April 16, 1945. On April 21 the Soviet forces battled their way into the city's suburbs. On April 22, at 10 in the morning, the first three Soviet tanks broke into Berlin. The tanks were from the armored corps commanded by Lieutenant-General Shimon Ben-Moshe Kariboshein, who was born in 1899 in the city of Veronez. Kariboshein filled important positions in the Tank Corps from the first day of the war. In the heavy fighting around Bilgorad on July 6-15, his armored division destroyed 500 enemy tanks, among them 100 heavy tanks, and 1,905 cannon of various types. He shot down 27 planes and killed more than 11,000 Nazi officers and soldiers. He was awarded the high Soborov medal for this operation and promoted to Lieutenant-General. His corps also took an active part in the liberation of Warsaw. After the war, he was awarded the title "Hero of the Soviet Union," for the superior leadership ability he evidenced in different tank units during the war, and in particular for his victories in the battle of Berlin.

Guri also relates the stories of heroic women in the Red Army, the most outstanding of which is the Jewish woman pilot Lili Litbach:

Pilot in a combat aircraft, Lieutenant Lili Litbach from Moscow succeeded in destroying six German planes by the middle of 1943. She won her fifth victory over the enemy in the battle over Rostov. She was wounded in a duel with a German plane, but did not retreat until she shot her opponent to the ground. . . . On August 19, 1943, after Lili fell in a dogfight, the Political Office of the southern front published a leaflet displaying her picture. Among other things, the leaflet states: "She won fame as a brave warplane pilot in the cruel battles near Stalingrad. Lili died a hero's death in an unequal battle."

The only woman among the 119 Jewish "Heroes of the Soviet Union" was Galman Mahumel from Poland. After finishing high school, she was accepted by the history department of Moscow University. At the beginning of the war, she participated for half a year in a pilot training course, and graduated as a navigator for the light U-2 plane. She fought in the Caucasus, Crimea, and other fronts. She shelled the Germans at the front 860 times. She received 14 medals for distinguished service in addition to the title "Hero of the Soviet Union." After the war, she returned to her studies at Moscow University at the College for Foreign Languages.

Jews also served with distinction in support positions in the rear. Guri quotes a feature which appeared in *Einikeit* and was copied in *Davar* on June 28, 1943:

Shimon Laubchenk from Roslavl (Smolensk District) received the high honor "Hero of the Socialist Labor" for his inventions in the design of a new type of warplane which proved its superiority in battle to the German Messerschmidt. Laubchenk's warplane, LA-5, had outstanding characteristics for those years; it achieved a speed of 650 km per hour, and an altitude of 6 km. This plane made a surprise appearance in the skies of Stalingrad, and began terrorizing the enemy planes.

The author Ilya Erenburg was not noted for his Jewish sentiments and did not always emphasize his origins, and he at one stage even wrote against Soviet Jewry. During the war, however, Erenburg filled a post of a special character. He wrote a regular column in the Red Army newspapers. There articles dripped with intense hatred for Nazism and the German invaders. There can be no doubt that Erenburg's writing in those days was infused with the emotions of sorrow and terror felt by a Jewish writer, and their effect encouraged and excited the soldiers. Ilya Erenburg and another Soviet author of Jewish origins, Vassily Grossman, also recorded testimony and stories of Jewish martyrdom in the Soviet Union. This material was collected in a work called *The Black Book*. It was not published in the U.S.S.R., because it emphasizes the suffering of the Jews. The book was published in Israel (in Russian), and in the United States and England.

It should be noted that Jewish feelings were often awakened in soldiers during the war when as they liberated Nazi-occupied cities, they met the remnants of the Jewish communities and the Jewish partisans who had emerged from the forests. Doctors and medical corps personnel in the Red Army, many of them Jews, devotedly cared for the former inmates of the liberated concentration camps and during the period of the "flight," Jewish activists who had fallen into the hands of the Red Army would often encounter officers who, as fellow Jews, sympathized with their circumstances and set them free, with blessings for success.

The Baltic armies (the Lithuanian and Latvian Divisions) were organized by the Soviet Union and became part of the Red Army. There were also other national armies affiliated with the Red Army — i.e., the Polish and Czechoslovakian armies. At the beginning, the Polish Army was headed by the Polish General Anders and was called "the Anders Army." It was established on the basis of an agreement made between the Polish government-in-exile and the Soviet Union, and was composed mostly of Polish citizens who were liberated from camps and prisons in the Soviet Union. Relations between the Poles and the Soviets were very tense because of the role the U.S.S.R. had played in the division of Poland at the beginning of the war, and because of the Poles' fear that the Soviets intended to expand westwards at their expense yet again.

During the first stage of the organization of the "Anders Army," many Jews joined its ranks, making up about 40 percent of the enlisted men. With them, the anti-Semitic tone common to Polish officers gained strength, and Jews who wished to enlist began being rejected. At the same time, many Jews who had already been accepted were expelled, partly because of Soviet instructions that the army should not take in people not considered Polish citizens. Members of the Revisionist Zionist Movement in the Soviet Union tried to establish a Jewish legion within the Anders Army, which would eventually serve Jewish national interests, but this attempt was not successful.

With time, the friction between the Anders Army command and the Soviet authorities increased. The Soviets apparently thought they could rid themselves of the national Polish force on its land and agreed that the Anders Army should leave the U.S.S.R. During the course of this evacuation, Jews were treated unequally. More than once the Poles prevented the evacuation of Jews who were rightfully permitted to leave in accordance with the spirit of the agreement with the Soviets. In total, some 3,500-4,000 Jewish soldiers left the U.S.S.R. in 1942 as part of the Anders Army. The Army traveled southward across the Soviet border into Iran and went from there to Palestine. There, in the Land of Israel, there was mass desertion by the Jews who remained in the ranks of the Polish army. According to General Anders himself, 3,000 of his 4,000 soldiers deserted. It should be noted that most of the deserters later enlisted in units of the Jewish army in Palestine.

Menachem Begin, who later became Prime Minister of Israel, was among those who arrived with the Anders Army.

There were also a number of Jewish non-combatants and a group of "Teheran children" among the arrivals, who were later absorbed by settlements and *kibbutzim* in Palestine.

After the Anders Army left the Soviet Union, the Soviets began organizing a Polish Communist army. Many of the Poles who had not left with the Anders Army were enlisted into this new unit, including the remnants of the Polish Communists in the Soviet Union and many Jews. Some 13,000 Jews served in this army. This number would have been larger, but the proportion of Jews in this army was monitored and controlled. Close to 1,300 Jewish soldiers fell in action with the Polish Army, and thousands were cited and decorated with distinguished service medals. The Jews played a special part in the organizational stages of the unit, when its character was established. They adjusted easily to army conditions, and quickly rose in the ranks, with more than 3,000 of them becoming officers. During the time when the Polish Army was on Soviet land, every other Polish officer was Jewish. The distinction of the Jews in the Polish army and the important positions they filled were not a result of favoritism by the authorities, but of the fact that Jews excelled during training and showed high motivation on the battlefield.

The Polish forces passed a series of tests and bitter battles before reaching the gates of Berlin. Along the way, the Jewish soldiers encountered the remnants of Polish Jewry. This painful encounter revived pride among the survivors and encouraged them. For many of the soldiers, it underlined their decision to be discharged as quickly as possible at the end of the war in order to take part in the effort to rehabilitate Jewish life in Poland.

Close to 25,000 Jews succeeded in fleeing Lithuania at the beginning of the Russo-German war, evading the border guards and making their way under a hail of shells into the Soviet Union. At the end of 1941, two Lithuanian leaders who had escaped to the Soviet Union took up the task of establishing a Lithuanian national division. The 16th Division was meant to be not just a military force, in the framework of the Red Army, but also to emphasize the establishment of a Lithuanian national force, participating in the anti-German military struggle alongside the Soviet Union. The Lithuanian division numbered 12,000-15,000 men and took part in the fierce battles in the central regions, in Byelorussia, and in Lithuania, and liberated hundreds of towns. At times, Jews comprised 80 percent of the force of the Lithuanian division.

After the Jews paid a bloody and heavy price in the battles in the Orel area, the Lithuanian division was still 50 percent Jewish. Dov Levin, who wrote the history of the Lithuanian division, noted that Jewish soldiers in the division were fond of saying that the unit was "Lithuanian in name but Jewish in character." Levin said that "the Jews felt at home in the Lithuanian division, and despite the fact that the way was not strewn with roses, the vast majority of them preferred this unit when they were given the choice (after being wounded) of being sent to another unit. . . ." The soldiers of the Jewish division wrote an honorable page of history in exhibiting exceptional heroism on the many battlefields where the division fought, from the Orel area to the shore of the Baltic Sea. This heroism derived, without a doubt, from the desire of the Jewish fighter to avenge the horrors that the enemy wrought on their families and relatives in Lithuania. In battle, alongside the routine Russian cry to charge: "Comrades for the motherland, for Stalin, forward!" one often heard the Yiddish cry *"Brider, far unzerer tates un mames."* (Brothers, for our fathers and mothers!) Five of the 13 members of the division who won the title of "Hero of the Soviet Union" were Jews.

JEWS IN THE UNITED STATES ARMY

We do not have comprehensive material on the role Jews played in the United States Army, because religious affiliation is not tabulated in this army, either at the time of enlistment or during service. It is clear that Jews served in all the branches of the U.S. armed forces: their total number has been estimated at 55,000. About 10,500 fell in action and 24,000 were wounded. Estimates are that 36,000 Jewish soldiers and officers were decorated. Twenty-three Jews reached the ranks of general and admiral.

Among those who volunteered for the American army were Jewish refugees from Germany and other European countries who came to the United States after Hitler's ascension to power. These Jews were to fill a special role in the struggle because of their knowledge of German and of the character of the enemy the United States faced. Later, when the U.S. forces ruled occupied Germany, these refugees served as translators and guides through the tangle of problems involving identifying prisoners, establishing a system of justice, and preparing for the Nazi war-crimes trials.

Jews were not only soldiers in active service, but also made an extremely important contribution to scientific development and the increase of industrial power in the U.S. during the war years. Jews were among the central figures who established the scientific and research foundations for the atom bomb.

The rabbis who served in the army had a special mission. These 310 men accompanied the army along its entire course, through all its engagements. In addition to being religious and spiritual guides for the Jewish soldiers, they worked for the welfare and rehabilitation of the remnants of European Jewry after the liberation of the concentration camps. Many Jewish soldiers also took part in this work, as well as non-Jewish soldiers who gave first aid to the survivors — not just material aid like food, clothing, and shelter, but also moral and spiritual help and understanding. A special role was filled by the advisers on Jewish affairs to the Commander of the U.S. Forces. Through their contacts with the army command they were able to organize and initiate activities and projects involving large groups of refugees. Rabbi Abraham Klausner and others won much appreciation for their dedicated work among the survivors, seeing to their immediate needs and health care, initiating the establishment of separate Jewish refugee camps, making contact with the Jewish world at large, and putting survivors in contact with their relatives and friends in the free world.

JEWS FROM THE YISHUV

The communal institutions of the *yishuv*, the Jewish community in Palestine, demanded, from the beginning of the war, the establishment of a Jewish military force to fight alongside the allies. They wished to enlist young volunteers from the land of Israel into this force, as well as refugees and Jewish volunteers from neutral countries. There were two major factors behind the demand by Zionist groups for a Jewish military force: (1) Nazi Germany was the sworn enemy of the Jewish people, and it was only natural that the Jews of Israel and the members of the Zionist movements saw themselves as a party to the war against Nazism; and (2) The leadership of the *yishuv* and of the Zionist movement assumed that, at the end of the war, these Jewish soldiers would be able to help the Jewish people in the struggle for Jewish immigration and political independence in the Land of Israel.

Although there was no doubt about their determination to fight against Nazism, for many Jews from Palestine supporting Britain in the war was a difficult decision. Shortly before the war, the British government had published a white paper restricting Jewish immigration to Palestine and the purchase of land by Jews in Palestine, its aim being to ensure that the Jews would remain a minority in the Mandate area.

Despite this, the *yishuv* resolved to harness itself to the war effort on the assumption that the war and its results would, in any case, bring about changes in British policy towards the *yishuv*. The National Committee and the Zionist Executive decided to register volunteers for service in Israel and overseas, should this be required, and tens of thousands expressed their readiness to volunteer. The heads of the *yishuv* and leaders of the Zionist Executive, especially Chaim Weizmann, applied to the British government and British army headquarters, as well as conducting a public campaign. All this was met with rejection and evasion. The British authorities feared that the establishment of a Jewish Israeli force would anger the Arabs, and appeasement of the Arab states and the quiet the British wished to achieve in the area were more important to them than the military potential of the *yishuv*. Pro-Arab elements in the British government opposed the establishment of a Jewish military force, something which could only add to the political weight of the anti-British sentiments within the Zionist movement and increase the determination of the *yishuv* to build its armed force for the future.

The British insisted on the establishment of "Palestinian" rather than national Jewish units. These were to exhibit numerical equality between Jews and Arabs. This equality did not actually come about because Arabs were not eager to enlist and those who did did not remain in the service for very long.

The Zionist Executive and the Political Department of the Jewish Agency continued to demand from the British the establishment of a large Jewish military force. These institutions soon decided to open a public campaign in support of this demand.

In December 1941, there was public activity in this spirit in the United States as well, which gained momentum with the help of a delegation from the *Irgun*, the underground Revisionist force in Palestine. The delegation succeeded in enlisting the help of influential public figures in support of the Jewish effort. Pressure was applied in London, and the campaign gained much attention as a result of the real danger which threatened Palestine in 1942. In the wake of these pressures, the British agreed to take another step forward, and announced the establishment of a Palestinian regiment composed of separate Jewish and Arab divisions. But it soon became clear that this plan would not be carried out. The roles of these units were restricted to "guarding vulnerable positions," and the Jewish units were forbidden to fly a Jewish flag or wear a Jewish insignia.

It was only in August, 1944, that the British cabinet decided to establish a Jewish brigade and send it to Italy. It became difficult for the British to stand firm on their anti-Zionist political position when the reality of the war required making use of the ready and waiting Jewish forces. It was for this reason also that the British were forced to accept Jews into the air force in the Middle East in opposition to the principal of Jewish-Arab parity, when Jews were qualified and willing to volunteer and Arabs were not. Some 2,650 Jewish men and women from the *yishuv* enlisted in the British air force between 1940 and 1945. Similar phenomena occurred in other professional units created in Palestine. In the summer of 1940, more than 3,000 Jews of the *yishuv* volunteered for transport and fortification units. By the beginning of 1941, the total number of enlisted men from Palestine was 9,000 men, of which 6,534 were Jews.

In the battle of Greece in the spring of 1941, more than a thousand Jewish soldiers from the British army were taken prisoner. Many elements in the *yishuv* argued that the Jews had been employed in support roles in the engagement and were abandoned when the British evacuated Greece — hence the high number of Jewish prisoners. This fact heightened the demand to use the Jewish force to defend the Land of Israel, especially since Axis forces were advancing through the desert and had become a real danger to the Jewish community in Palestine.

In May, 1942, the Jewish national institutions in Palestine issued a compulsory service order, followed by the issue of draft notices. This operation met with difficulties and internal debate, however, since the *yishuv* was not a government and could not enforce its orders. Hence, enlistment remained voluntary.

Over the course of the Second World War, 26,620 Jews from the *yishuv* enlisted in the British army — 22,682 men and 3,938 women. If we add to this number the guard units, which in 1942 became an official military force, the number exceeds 30,000. Of these, 250 fell in battle.

CONCLUSION

It became accepted theory in the wake of the war and the Holocaust that the Jews did not defend themselves or fight for their lives, and that their docile obedience was indicative of the weakness of the Jewish people in general and of Diaspora Jews in particular. Many, among them the Jewish-American scholar Raul Hilberg, argued that the Jews of the Diaspora had become accustomed to obedience as a behavioral pattern. They lowered their head and surrendered to the evils which befell them, and while pleading for the mercy of heaven and humanity, waited for it all to end. The evils which were the lot of the Jews before the Holocaust ended in expulsion, forced conversion, and homelessness, but did not endanger the existence of the Jewish people. During the Holocaust, the Jews were faced with the Nazi effort to physically exterminate them.

The opinion that this trait of obedience was part of the Jews' traditional behavior was voiced frequently, both during the war and thereafter. According to this theory, other nations do not pay attention to the cries of the troubled nor of those who plead for mercy. They take note only of people who were willing to fight for their survival. Similar arguments have been made at times by non-Jewish underground organizations. Certain Polish groups argued, for example, that they could not help the Jews because the Jews were not ready to help themselves, and even rejected offers to help them fight.

It is interesting that the feelings of regret and shame for not having resisted and fought the enemy were common among the survivors of the Holocaust. They felt acutely their failure to convince the Jewish masses in the ghettos of the need to resist and fight.

The concept of the Jews "going like lambs to the slaughter" became accepted in Israel and in Jewish society in general, as well as among non-Jews. This harmful stereotype has its origins in a superficial knowledge of the facts — not only among the general public, but among public figures and scholars as well.

The idea that the Jews have been characterized by obedience and acceptance of fate throughout the Exile has no basis in fact. It is true that during periods of great persecution and slaughter, such as the Crusades, the Spanish Exile, and the disturbances of 1648-49, the Jews as a group chose the tactic of "not by might and not by power." But Jewish heroism found its highest expression during the Crusades in large-scale martydom. During the pogroms at the end of the 19th century and in the 20th century in Russia and Poland, there were independent Jewish defense organizations and active centers of resistance.

The changes which evolved in the social structure and the intellectual world of the Jews in Europe from the "Enlightenment" of the 18th century through the Holocaust led many to abandon traditional models and adopt methods of struggle and resistance no different from those among non-Jews. Jews played a relatively large part in armed movements between the two world wars, such as in the international brigades which fought with the Republican forces in the Spanish Civil War.

If the Jews were incapable of resistance, how could we explain the pioneer groups who left Europe to establish defense organizations and a military infrastructure in Israel, who defeated the armies of the Arab countries in the War of Independence, and trained armies with modern weaponry? Can there be any doubt that the hundreds of thousands of young Jews organized in Zionist and non-Zionist organizations in the Diaspora had, both ideologically and physically, the potential for military organization and armed struggle?

For this reason, it is impossible to assume that the lack of Jewish resistance during World War II was something that had been imprinted on Jews over the generations. It is true that there is an expectation that innocent people sentenced to a cruel death will resort to any measures to resist, without taking into account the chances of success. History has proven, however, that such resistance is not inevitable. It has already been made clear that of all the most persecuted and oppressed groups of people during the period of Nazi rule *none* resisted and *none* rebelled against the Nazis' overwhelming strength. Among these groups were concentration camp prisoners, Soviet POWs, and slave laborers taken from their homes and employed in the camps in humiliating and inhuman conditions. We know that millions of Soviet prisoners of war who died or were killed did not rebel and did not fight for their lives. The concentration camps saw only a handful of rebellions, most of them in extermination camps such as Treblinka, Sobibor, and Auschwitz-Birkenau, and these were planned and undertaken by *Jewish* prisoners. It is clear that for a human being to rebel, it is not enough that his life be seriously threatened; there must also be room for freedom, hope, and a chance of escape for the fighters.

None of these factors existed for many Jews in World War II. It is interesting that few people have considered the question of whether Jewish fighters had any chance of succeeding. When the fighters called on the public to fight, there was a stage in which they seemed to feel an obligation to rise up and fight, without considering the results, since a cruel death awaited all in any case. But at a later stage, the leaflets and other writings of the fighters indicate that they had second thoughts. From this we learn of the development of two directions taken by the Jews. On the one hand, the fighters understood that most Jews were not persuaded by their pronouncements that it was better to choose one's death in honor than to let the Nazis carry out their plans. On the other hand, the leaders of the resistance could not ignore the fact that even the fighters themselves were looking for possible ways of being saved. Death by throwing oneself at the enemy, as an act of revenge for and identity with the Jews in the ghettos was not accepted by the masses. When partisan bands began appearing in the areas around the ghettos and the opportunity to join this movement became a real one, it was necessary to revise the concept of rebellion within the ghettos. In Warsaw, where the ghetto uprising was the method chosen, the leaders of the resistance groups had to invest much organizational and propaganda effort to keep the nucleus of fighters constantly motivated to fight until death.

It is understandable and natural that the idea of resisting arose among Jews only when the meaning of the "final solution" was truly realized. Until then, the struggle had been concentrated on preserving life and soul.

After the Nazi plan to exterminate the Jews became widely known, the idea of revolt in the ghettos became acceptable. It was proclaimed by the members of the youth movements, especially by those in the Zionist groups. The ghetto uprisings should not be measured by their accomplishments or the extent of the fighting. It is important to emphasize that, in organizing and carrying out uprising, these young people personified their loyalty to Jewish national and human values at a time when their public and national motives for action had been almost completely uprooted.

Partisan fighting, which was a mixture of battle and struggle to survive, was organized in those places topographically appropriate for it. The partisan groups in most of Eastern Europe absorbed Jews, but in central Poland, the Jews had almost no shelter in the forests or opportunity to join the partisans. Jews who searched for hiding places among the Poles or other nationals, or who tried to live among them under an assumed identity, could expect to be turned in, and lived in constant danger. It should be noted, however, that there were Poles who acted with untiring devotion to save Jews, and thanks to them, tens of thousands of Jews were saved.

In Western Europe — France, Belgium, and Italy — Jews encountered no barriers when they joined the resistance. Dedication to Jewish interests, however, posed a dilemma for potential Jewish fighters: should they undertake military activity shoulder-to-shoulder with the local underground movement, or should they direct their efforts towards rescuing Jews, especially refugees who were not fluent in the local language and culture? In France, there was some attempt to integrate the two missions. Echoes of these divisions and debates can be seen in the evaluations and descriptions of events written by people who took part in them and by historians of the period. The same question arose in certain areas of Eastern Europe, as was noted in the description of the events in Polish Silesia. Under the conditions which prevailed in Hungary, the youth groups saw rescue operations as their most important function. The resistance groups of various countries had different attitudes with regard to the fate of the Jews. These attitudes were a direct reflection of the tradition of anti-Semitism of each country. The Polish underground was, in general, apathetic to the plight of the Jews, at least until the later stages of the war and occupation. Neither did the Jewish issue interest the various parts of the German underground. In France and Holland, the rescue of the Jews was not always a clear and defined mission. But many resistance fighters in these countries went to the aid of the Jews. In two countries — first and foremost Denmark, and to a large extent Italy — the rescue of the Jews was not only a matter for the underground, but had the character of a human and national obligation, in which many took part.

The question remains: was Jewish resistance of large or small dimensions? What answer can be given to this question? If we wish to measure the influence and achievements of the Jewish resistance in terms of the number of survivors, then it was small. We have seen, however, that partisan fighting was not a mechanism for saving the masses, especially in Eastern Europe, where there was a huge Jewish population. Jewish underground fighters could not save lives on a large scale. Only a combination of good will and initiative on the part of the local population, together with Jewish planning, could have saved large numbers. Unfortunately, Russia and Poland, home to millions of Jews, were totally under Nazi control, and the local population showed no great love for the Jews during their great crisis. Some national groups, like the Ukrainians and Lithuanians, took a part in the killing itself, collaborating with the Nazis, and supporting their anti-Jewish policy.

In order to complete the picture, we must examine the positions and actions — or more exactly, the failure to act — of the free neutral states and of countries which fought the Nazis. British obstruction of the way to Palestine remained in force during the war, at the same time that the United States carefully observed its immigration laws and quotas. These are outstanding examples of great power policy with regard to the Jews suffering under Nazi domination. The great powers based their actions on the principle that there should be no diversion from the goal of victory at the front, and that this focus on victory was for the good of all those suffering in the occupied countries, including the Jews. This was no consolation to the Jews. Ghetto diarists wrote, on numerous occasions, that the rescue would come too late, that there would be none left alive to hear the bells of liberty.

This discussion has not dealt with Jews in the free world, in particular in the United States, who also faced the choice between loyalty to their country's policies and the need to break the law for the sake of their fellow Jews' survival. It focused mainly on fighting of the Jews in the ghettos, camps, and forests, a chapter in the chronicle of the Jewish people of which little is known. These accounts of the many individuals and groups who stood and fought represent only a small part of the story of this period in which cruelty and unrestrained murder were countered with devotion to the highest human values as expressed in acts of sacrifice and heroism. The author expects that his readers will not be satisfied with what he has related here, and that the introduction this book has given them to the annals of Jewish resistance in the occupied countries will inspire them to broaden and deepen their knowledge of this chapter in Jewish history.

Co-sponsors—International Quiz on Jewish Heroism During World War II

Yad-Vashem
Lohamei-Haghetaot
Moreshet
Museum of the Combatants & Partisans
Massua
World Federation of Jewish Fighters,
Partisans & Camp Inmates
National Youth Movement of the
National Labor Federation in Israel